Three Great Econor

D. D. Raphael is Emeritus Pro
the University of London. His
Problems of Political Philosoph, ,   ,
1990) and *Moral Philosophy* (OUP, 1981, second
edition 1994).

Donald Winch is Professor of the History of Economics
at the University of Sussex. His previous publications
include studies of classical political economy, the relationship of economics and policy during the twentieth
century, *Adam Smith's Politics* (1978), and (with
Stefan Collini and John Burrow) *That Noble Science of
Politics* (1983).

Lord Skidelsky is Professor of Political Economy at
Warwick University. He is the author of the widely
acclaimed biography, *John Maynard Keynes*.

Past Masters

Forthcoming

Three Great Economists

Smith
D. D. Raphael

Malthus
Donald Winch

Keynes
Robert Skidelsky

Oxford New York
OXFORD UNIVERSITY PRESS
1997

Oxford University Press, Great Clarendon Street, Oxford OX2 6DP

Oxford New York
Athens Auckland Bangkok Bogota Bombay
Buenos Aires Calcutta Cape Town Dar es Salaam Delhi
Florence Hong Kong Istanbul Karachi
Kuala Lumpur Madras Madrid Melbourne
Mexico City Nairobi Paris Singapore
Taipei Tokyo Toronto

and associated companies in
Berlin Ibadan

Oxford is a trade mark of Oxford University Press

Smith © D. D. Raphael 1985
Malthus © Donald Winch 1987
Keynes © Robert Skidelsky 1996
This composite volume © Oxford University Press 1997
Foreword © Keith Thomas 1997
First published as an Oxford University Press paperback 1997

British Library Cataloguing in Publication Data
Data available

Library of Congress Cataloging in Publication Data
Data available

10 9 8 7 6 5 4 3 2 1

Typeset by Best-set Typesetter Ltd., Hong Kong
Printed in Great Britain by
Mackays of Chatham,
Chatham, Kent

Foreword

What is economics? The dictionary tells us that it is the science relating to the production and distribution of material wealth. But that science requires the study of human behaviour in all its aspects. In a famous passage, John Maynard Keynes wrote that:

the master economist must possess a rare combination of gifts ... He must be mathematician, historian, statesman, philosopher —in some degree. He must understand symbols and speak in words. He must contemplate the particular in terms of the general, and touch abstract and concrete in the same flight of thought. He must study the present in the light of the past for the purposes of the future. No part of man's nature or his institutions must lie entirely outside his regard.

The first of the three thinkers to whom this book is devoted certainly conformed to this description. For Adam Smith was a man of the widest intellectual interests. Author of *The Wealth of Nations* (1776), undoubtedly the most influential book on economics ever written, he was also a moral philosopher and psychologist, a historian and philosopher of science, an authority on rhetoric and belles-lettres, a student of law and government, and a comparative sociologist. It is not surprising that previous commentators have attempted to show inconsistencies between different parts of his work. In particular, it has long been urged that there is a conflict between Smith's assumption in *The Wealth of Nations* that self-interest is the most constant human motive and his emphasis in his *Theory of Moral Sentiments* (1759) on the social importance of the binding force of sympathy. In his study, D. D. Raphael shows how this so-called 'Adam-Smith problem' was mistakenly formulated. He also brings out the extraordinary range and clarity of Smith's analysis of economic life. The fundamental principle of the division of labour makes the inhabitants of a developed society dependent upon each other through the working of a free market. 'It is not from the benevolence of the butcher, the brewer, or the baker, that we expect our dinner, but from their regard to their own interest.'

Thomas Robert Malthus's interests were not as wide as those of Adam Smith. But as Donald Winch points out, they were much wider than those of most modern social scientists. For Malthus believed that the science of political economy bore 'a nearer resemblance to the science of morals and politics than to that of mathematics'; and his ultimate objective was a science of morals. He was the author of the principle which has done most to give economics its label of 'the dismal science'. Population growth, he maintained, has an innate tendency to outpace food supply. Without voluntary restraint, by which he meant celibacy or late marriage (for he regarded contraception as immoral), the only checks on demographic growth were disease and mortality. Donald Winch identifies the historical context of these ideas. Not only did Malthus reject the belief of his predecessors that a rising population was a sign of economic health; he also challenged the faith in human perfectibility which had been generated by the French Revolution. His first *Essay on the Principle of Population* (1798) was a counter-revolutionary tract. His later economic writings are important because of their stress on the need for an expansion in effective demand to expand to match the economy's capacity to produce. His contemporary opponent David Ricardo, by contrast, had attributed the depression after the Napoleonic Wars to the need for more capital accumulation. As Keynes would later lament: 'If only Malthus, instead of Ricardo, had been the parent stem from which nineteenth-century economics had proceeded, what a much wiser and richer place the world would be today!'

Keynes himself was a man of universal curiosity, who, as

Robert Skidelsky observes, was able to use economics as the vehicle for all his obsessions. For him economics was a branch of statesmanship rather than a self-enclosed academic discipline. He was an aesthete and a bibliophile, as well as a profoundly influential man of action. He was also one of the very few economists in history who have been any good at making money for themselves. His profound insight, and the foundation of the Keynesian revolution in economics, was his perception that a modern economic system has no automatic mechanism to adjust demand to supply and that, when demand falls short of supply, government intervention is required if 'involuntary unemployment' is to be avoided. His *General Theory of Employment, Interest and Money* (1936) set out principles which influenced public policy in Britain, the USA, and elsewhere until the monetarist reaction of the 1980s. He invented macroeconomics and he made the maintenance of full employment a government priority. Robert Skidelsky shows how Keynes's economic thought was a response to two great developments of his time: the Great Depression of the 1930s and the effect on the British economy of the USA's unbalanced creditor position. Nowadays, Keynesian remedies are out of favour because they are believed to generate inflation and make countries 'ungovernable'. But modern monetarism has no solution for persisting unemployment.

The three studies contained in this book originally appeared as individual volumes in the Past Masters series, whose object is to convey to modern readers the ideas of great thinkers of the past in a lucid and authoritative way. Smith, Malthus, and Keynes are Past Masters because they are writers of enduring relevance. Adam Smith has (not altogether correctly) become the patron saint of believers in an unfettered free market. Malthus is regularly invoked by those who are worried about the current growth in the world's population. Keynes's ideas remain the stuff of contemporary political argument. The three essays which follow bring out the enduring importance of these thinkers, while countering any anachronistic misapplication of their ideas by placing them in their proper historical context and explaining just what it was that each of them was trying to do. No one can afford to neglect Smith, Malthus, and Keynes, for they sought to understand, and to improve, the conditions in which human beings live their lives. As Keynes rightly observed, economists are the trustees of the possibilities of civilization.

Corpus Christi College
Oxford

KEITH THOMAS
General Editor
Past Masters

Contents

Smith

D. D. Raphael

Acknowledgements

I wish to thank the Leverhulme Trust for awarding me an Emeritus Fellowship to cover expenses incurred in writing this (and another) book.

I also wish to thank three people for their help. My wife, Sylvia Raphael, read the typescript and suggested a number of improvements in the presentation. My friend and former colleague at Glasgow University, Professor Andrew Skinner, to whose published work I was already indebted, kindly agreed to read Chapter 4 and gave me valuable advice on some particular points in my exposition of Adam Smith's economics. Ainslee Rutledge typed the text with great efficiency.

Some paragraphs of Chapter 6 repeat, in a revised form, part of a lecture on Adam Smith which I gave to the Royal Institute of Philosophy in a series called 'Philosophers of the Enlightenment' and subsequently published as a book with that title.

D. D. R.

Contents

Abbreviations

All page references in the text are to The Glasgow Edition of the Works and Correspondence of Adam Smith, published by the Clarendon Press, Oxford. Abbreviations are as follows:

M   *The Theory of Moral Sentiments*, ed. D. D. Raphael and A. L. Macfie (1976)

W   *An Inquiry into the Nature and Causes of the Wealth of Nations*, general editors R. H. Campbell and A. S. Skinner, textual editor W. B. Todd (1976)

P   *Essays on Philosophical Subjects*, ed. W. P. D. Wightman, J. C. Bryce, and I. S. Ross, general editors D. D. Raphael and A. S. Skinner (1980)

R   *Lectures on Rhetoric and Belles Lettres*, ed. J. C. Bryce, general editor A. S. Skinner (1983)

J   *Lectures on Jurisprudence*, ed. R. L. Meek, D. D. Raphael, and P. G. Stein (1978)

C   *The Correspondence of Adam Smith*, ed. E. C. Mossner and I. S. Ross (1977, second edition 1987)

1 A master for many schools

Adam Smith is a past master for all manner of persons, for Conservatives and for Marxists, for liberals and for anti-radicals, for economists, philosophers, and sociologists. Different groups admire different things in his work and one may sometimes doubt whether all the different things can be held together consistently. Still, each of them is persuasive enough to have made its mark as a truth of some profundity.

An Inquiry into the Nature and Causes of the Wealth of Nations is best known for its advocacy of free trade. Nineteenth-century liberals believed, like Adam Smith himself, that freedom of trade goes hand in hand with other kinds of freedom and adopted it as a cardinal principle of policy. More recently their clothes have been stolen by the Conservatives, and in Britain at least, since the end of the Second World War, the most fervent disciples of a free-market economy have been leading lights of the Conservative party. When in May 1979 Sir Keith Joseph took office as Secretary of State for Industry in Mrs Thatcher's first government, he sent round to his senior civil servants a 'reading list' which included both the *Wealth of Nations* and Adam Smith's earlier book, *The Theory of Moral Sentiments*.

It is not surprising that right-wing politicians should praise a work which finds in capitalism the root of all economic good. It is surprising, at first sight, that Karl Marx should be indebted to the *Wealth of Nations*; but the reasons are clear enough. Marx's materialist interpretation of history is a theory of stages of society, each having a distinctive social structure in terms of property and depending on a distinctive system of production. The essence of such a theory underlies the *Wealth of Nations*, which is as much a sociological as an economic treatise. Smith writes of four stages of society, beginning with an age of hunters, followed by one of shepherds, and then proceeding through an age of agriculture to an age of commerce. The analysis of economic activity, which forms the main subject of the book, belongs to the fourth stage of the process. The historical picture is intended to explain the development of law and government, which, according to this account, are first needed in the age of shepherds, when the concept of property arises. Hunters consume at once what they catch; shepherds tend flocks for future as well as present use. Property has to be protected, and this, in Smith's view, is the primary aim of government. 'Civil government, so far as it is instituted for the security of property, is in reality instituted for the defence of the rich against the poor, or of those who have some property against those who have none at all' (W 715). Adam Smith is not the only writer in whom Marx will have read of stages in the history of human society, but none struck a more radical note than this.

Yet Adam Smith can also be quoted by opponents of radicalism, at any rate of political radicalism. 'The man of system', Smith wrote, 'is apt to be very wise in his own conceit; and is often so enamoured with the supposed beauty of his own ideal plan of government, that he cannot suffer the smallest deviation from any part of it' (M 233–4). He thinks he can arrange society like the pieces on a chess-board and forgets that 'in the great chess-board of human society, every single piece has a principle of motion of its own, altogether different from that which the legislature might chuse to impress upon it.' We are back to arguments for freedom, this time political freedom, but a conception of political freedom that goes against the reforming radicalism of constitution makers.

James Boswell was once a student of Adam Smith at the University of Glasgow. In later years Smith told Boswell that his great fault was acting upon system and Boswell thought this was strange criticism to come from a philosopher. As a philosopher, and indeed as an economist, Smith certainly sought system but he kept it in its proper place. Systematic theory was one thing, essential for satisfactory explanation. Acting upon system, a necessarily simplified system, without regarding the practicalities of the individual case, was quite another thing.

Adam Smith did not found the study, even the scientific study, of economics. Ancient and medieval thinkers had glimpses of some economic truths in their reflections on the workings of human society. In the seventeenth century, and in the eighteenth before the publication of the *Wealth of Nations*, there were significant advances in constructing theories of value, of money, and of international trade. Mercantilism, the doctrine which advocated governmental control of foreign trade, developed a systematic theory, notably in the treatises of Thomas Mun in the seventeenth century and of Smith's fellow-Scotsman Sir James Steuart a few years (1767) before the publication of the *Wealth of Nations* (1776). In France the physiocrats had worked out a very different account of economic activity, favouring a policy of free trade. While the origins of their doctrine depended on philosophical ideas of natural law, it was turned into a scientific system by François Quesnay with his *Tableau économique* (1758). This was a quasi-physiological model of the annual flow of payments from one class of citizens to another, in the form of rent, prices, wages, profits. It was probably conceived on the analogy of the circulation of the blood (Quesnay was trained and practised as a doctor) and was a landmark in the history of economics as a systematic enquiry. Quesnay had been influenced by an earlier work (1755) of Richard Cantillon, which some scholars regard as the first scientific treatment of the principles of economics.

The *Wealth of Nations* is much more comprehensive in scope and more detailed in its factual data than these French models. Despite that, it is remarkably systematic in connecting together different features of what we would now call the economic life of society. The book is impressive, as Darwin's *On the Origin of Species* is impressive, for combining a systematic theory with a wealth of illustrative empirical data. But the systematic character of the theory is a matter of showing connections rather than focusing upon a single explanatory principle, as Darwin does. Smith's appeal to the 'obvious and simple system of natural liberty' (W 687), criticizing mercantilism, expresses a deep-seated ideological conviction, but he does not use it as a universal principle to explain all economic activity. The *Wealth of Nations* put all earlier treatises of political economy in the shade because it was so comprehensively systematic, not because it blew the trumpet of free trade. It became the standard model to be studied, tested, revised, and improved.

More recent economists have looked at the work from a different angle. Their attention to economic growth has led them to see that Smith's *Inquiry into the Nature and Causes of the Wealth of Nations* is, as the full title implies, an examination of economic growth or development and so continues to be in the mainstream of economic thought as envisaged today. The book begins with the division of labour in order to bring out sharply from the start the enormous difference in productivity between the manufacture of a pin by one man and the sharing of the process by ten men. Smith then goes on to relate the division of labour to the accumulation of capital, the increase of employment, and a self-regulating mechanism for preventing wages from rising too high to inhibit further growth. In this perspective of economic growth, Smith's sociological excursus on the history of society, with its four stages of development, falls into place as the essential background of his picture.

The sociological interest of Smith's work is not, however, confined to his theory of social history. In the *Wealth of Nations* there are striking disquisitions on education, on the clergy, on the character of different classes in society, on the psychological effects of specialization. If the reader of the *Wealth of Nations* also reads *The Theory of Moral Sentiments*, he will see that the whole of Smith's thought on human behaviour is permeated by a sociological approach. The *Moral Sentiments*, primarily a book of moral philosophy, deals with morality as a social phenomenon. In Smith's account of ethics the central place is given to sympathy, the cement of society. The resulting approval or disapproval of other people for what a man does is the mirror in which he sees his own character. While Smith's economics follow up the social effects of self-interested behaviour conditioned by the market, his ethics point to the equally firm structure of social solidarity built up by sympathy and our desire for esteem.

The *Moral Sentiments* remains a work of philosophy for all that. It stands out as a peak in the history of one type of ethical theory, basing moral values on human feelings. Adam Smith's book is less widely read nowadays than the slightly earlier work of his friend David Hume. If one thinks of their respective contributions to philosophy generally, Smith comes nowhere near the eminence of Hume (of which Smith himself had a warm appreciation). If, however, one thinks of moral philosophy in particular, the honours are shared more evenly. Smith followed up and improved upon Hume's highlighting of the role of sympathy in ethics; and then he added his own, more distinctive, concept of an imagined 'impartial spectator' to explain conscience, the moral judgements that a person makes about his own actions. The theory resembles that which Freud was to produce, in the twentieth century, of the super-ego, but with the difference that Smith begins with social approval and disapproval while Freud begins with parental.

Among scholars of the history and philosophy of science, those who also go into the history of their own subject know that Adam Smith is one of the pioneers in that field with his essay 'The History of Astronomy'. It is philosophical as well as historical. In both respects the essay is outstanding for its time. The historical treatment is now outdated but the accompanying philosophical theory, which takes scientific systems to be products of the imagination, still arouses admiration as a remarkably bold feat of Smith's own rational imagination.

Both in his ethical theory and in his philosophy of science Smith's strength lies in philosophical psychology. This will be apparent from his emphasis on sympathy and imagination and from my comparison with Freud. The theories of philosophical psychology, whether they come from professed philosophers or from would-be scientists like Freud, contain a speculative element and are not easily confirmed or refuted by hard empirical data. Adam Smith, however, impresses his readers as an empirical psychologist too. Both in the *Moral Sentiments* and in the *Wealth of Nations* he shows himself an acute observer of behaviour.

The mob, when they are gazing at a dancer on the slack rope, naturally writhe and twist and balance their own bodies, as they see him do, and as they feel that they themselves must do if in his situation. (M 10)

A bully tells many stories of his own insolence, which are not true, and imagines that he thereby renders himself, if not more amiable and respectable, at least more formidable to his audience. (M 240)

Two greyhounds, in running down the same hare, have sometimes the appearance of acting in some sort of concert. Each turns her towards his companion, or endeavours to intercept her when his companion turns her towards himself. (W 25)

The social anthropologist Edward Westermarck described the *Moral Sentiments* as 'the most important contribution to moral psychology made by any British thinker'. The historian H. T. Buckle said of the *Wealth of Nations*: 'looking at its ultimate results, [it] is probably the most important book that has ever been written, and is certainly the most valuable contribution ever made by a single man towards establishing the principles on which government should be based.' The first opinion is no more than just; the second is rather wild, though by no means ridiculous. The two together illustrate the enthusiasm that Adam Smith has kindled in different quarters as a past master.

2 Life

Adam Smith was born in Kirkcaldy on the Fife coast. The precise date of his birth is uncertain but he was baptized on 5 June 1723. He was a posthumous child, his father having died in January of that year. The father, also named Adam, was a lawyer and civil servant. He was twice married and had one son from each marriage. His first wife, Lilias Drummond, died in 1717, when her son Hugh was about eight years old. His second wife, mother of the famous Adam, was Margaret Douglas. Their marriage took place in 1720, when she was in her twenties and he was about forty. She was widowed after less than three years. In such circumstances an only child, born after the death of her husband, must have been doubly precious, and the ties between mother and son remained exceptionally close for the rest of her long life. Adam Smith himself never married and Freudians will no doubt say that this was the consequence of the bond with his mother. However, filial affection did not stop him from falling in love at least twice and his susceptibility is plain enough in passages of the *Moral Sentiments*.

There is a tale that at the age of three Adam Smith was stolen by a band of gypsies when he was visiting his uncle. His biographer, John Rae, writes 'He would have made, I fear, a poor gipsy', no doubt thinking of Smith's notorious absent-mindedness as well as his bent for speculative thought. I am not sure that Adam Smith himself would have agreed. He thought that abilities owed more to nurture than to nature. 'The difference between the most dissimilar characters, between a philosopher and a common street porter, for example, seems to arise not so much from nature, as from habit, custom, and education' (W 28–9). In any event, Smith is not the only absent-minded professor to be eminently successful at practical administration and I dare say he could have been a very useful member of a gypsy band. However, his enforced sojourn with them lasted only a few hours.

After attending the burgh school in Kirkcaldy, Smith entered the University of Glasgow in 1737 at the age of fourteen, a little older than was usual in those days to begin university studies. Why he was sent to Glasgow rather than to one of the nearer universities at Edinburgh or St Andrews is not known. It may have been because he had an aunt living in Glasgow or it may have been because the University of Glasgow offered the opportunity of going on to Balliol College, Oxford, with the Snell Exhibition, as Smith in fact did. One of his fellow-students recalled in later years that Smith's favourite subjects at Glasgow University were mathematics and natural philosophy (physics). His competence in those subjects is shown in his essay on the history of astronomy but his works generally do not suggest a particular bent in that direction. The strongest influence on Smith as a student was that of Francis Hutcheson, the Professor of Moral Philosophy, whose lectures on ethics, jurisprudence, and economics laid the foundations of Smith's own ideas in those areas.

From Glasgow Smith proceeded to Oxford in 1740 with a Snell Exhibition, an award originally intended to support the training of Scottish students for the ministry of 'the Church in Scotland', meaning the Episcopal Church. That requirement of the benefaction was nullified when the Church of Scotland became Presbyterian in 1690, and in Adam Smith's time, as today, the Snell Exhibition was available for talented students of Glasgow University to go to Oxford and study whatever they wished. Smith was at Oxford for six years and his studies seem to have been largely self-directed. Like Edward Gibbon, he found the teachers at Oxford University scandalously idle and incompetent. He wrote in the *Wealth of Nations* (761): 'In the university of Oxford, the greater part of the publick professors have, for these many years, given up altogether even the pretence of teaching.' There could hardly be a greater contrast with

Glasgow, where teaching had the first priority and where Hutcheson in particular was a brilliant lecturer.

However, at Balliol College Smith had the run of a good library and he read widely in Greek and Latin classics and in French literature (passages from which he enjoyed translating into English). He also read a certain amount of modern philosophy, including the recently published *Treatise of Human Nature* by his fellow-Scotsman, Hume. Smith told his friends in later years that he was reprimanded when found reading this book at Oxford and that the work itself was confiscated. The *Treatise* was generally regarded as atheistic and subversive of morality. Smith himself seems to have had a shrewder understanding of some of its more original features. His references to Hume's ethics in *The Theory of Moral Sentiments* show a perceptive, if not altogether accurate, recollection of parts of the *Treatise*, and his essay on the history of astronomy depends on a grasp of Hume's subtle theory of the imagination which eluded most professional philosophers for a couple of centuries.

From Oxford Smith returned to his mother's house in Kirkcaldy and no doubt explored the possibilities of earning his living. Two years later, arrangements were made by a group of well-wishers in Edinburgh, including a leading member of the Scottish Bar, Henry Home (later a judge with the title Lord Kames), for Smith to give a series of public lectures on rhetoric and *belles-lettres*. The lectures were not part of any university course in Edinburgh, but were well attended, mostly by students of law and theology, and were continued in the following two years, bringing Smith an annual income of over £100. In at least the last of the three years, Smith added to the lectures on rhetoric and *belles-lettres* a further series on civil law for the benefit of his law students. The lectures were attended also by a number of older people prominent in the cultural life of the city.

They made a great impression and when the Chair of Logic at the University of Glasgow became vacant at the end of 1750, Smith was at once offered the appointment and took it up in

1751, supplementing the customary account of logic and metaphysics with a treatment of rhetoric and *belles-lettres* such as he had given in Edinburgh. He thought this subject would be 'more interesting and useful' to his students (P 273). There was, however, another good reason for making use of his Edinburgh lectures. In the summer of 1751, before Smith began his teaching duties, the Professor of Moral Philosophy was taken ill and was advised to go abroad to a warmer climate for the winter. Smith was asked to take over part of the Moral Philosophy course in addition to his work with the Logic class. The people at Glasgow knew that Smith's successful lectures in Edinburgh had included a discussion of law and government, and so it was suggested that his contribution to the lectures of the Moral Philosophy class should be the parts on 'natural jurisprudence and politics' (C 5). Since he had to take on this additional commitment in his first year of teaching, it was obviously convenient to ease the burden by using the material of his Edinburgh lectures for part of his Logic course too.

Smith's tenure in the Chair of Logic was short-lived. The ailing Professor of Moral Philosophy, Thomas Craigie, died in November 1751 and in the following April Smith was appointed to succeed him. The subjects covered in the Moral Philosophy class (theology, ethics, general principles of law and government, economics) were more to his taste than logic and metaphysics, although he continued, in his new post, to give his course on rhetoric and literature as an addition to the regular course of moral philosophy. A student report of the rhetoric lectures in the 1762–3 session came to light in 1958, together with a similar report of the second half of the moral philosophy course. A summarized report of the lectures on 'jurisprudence' (law, government, and economics), as delivered in 1763–4, had previously been made known in 1895.

Adam Smith held the Chair of Moral Philosophy at Glasgow for twelve years. He was an admirable professor. Although he could not match the eloquence of Hutcheson, his own teacher and Craigie's predecessor, Smith had a gift for clear exposition and happy illustration, and his actual theories showed more

originality, greater coherence, and a sharper awareness of difficulties than did the theories of Hutcheson. Like Hutcheson,
Smith took his responsibilities to his students very seriously
indeed. He gave his regular or 'public' course of lectures at an
early hour on each weekday, followed it up with an informal
discussion or 'examination' later in the morning, and then
delivered his additional or 'private' course on rhetoric at mid-
day. He gave individual tutorials to selected pupils and showed
meticulous concern for the health and personal development of
students who were private boarders in his house. Smith was
outstanding also in university administration. He undertook far
more of such work than the average professor and was judged to
be especially capable at it. He was College Quaestor (Treasurer)
for six years, a much longer period than usual, and towards the
end of his time at Glasgow he acted as Dean of Faculty, Vice-
Rector, and chairman of a special committee set up to try to
resolve a long-standing wrangle about the respective powers of
the Principal and the Rector. Whenever the university had to
undertake ticklish negotiations with outside bodies such as the
town council in Glasgow or the Treasury in London, more often
than not it asked Smith to act as its spokesman. Despite his
reputation for absent-mindedness, he was clearly hard-headed
and efficient in matters of practical business.

Smith's lectures on moral philosophy were divided into three
sections, natural theology, ethics, and jurisprudence. This followed the practice of his predecessors and indeed the general
tradition of Scottish moral philosophy of the period.

Of the content of his lectures on natural theology we know
virtually nothing. A report by John Millar, originally a pupil and
then a colleague and friend, says simply that in this part of his
course Smith 'considered the proofs of the being and attributes
of God, and those principles of the human mind upon which
religion is founded' (P 274). Some inkling of his approach to the
latter topic is given in one chapter of the *Moral Sentiments*,
where he talks of divinities as originally the object of religious
fear and as conceived to resemble human beings in their sentiments and passions. The suggestion here that man creates gods

in his own image may explain a complaint that was made by some people to the effect that Smith's lectures on natural theology 'were too flattering to human pride'.

The second part of his lectures, on ethics, was eventually turned into *The Theory of Moral Sentiments*. Smith's inclination in the study of any subject was to approach it historically in the first instance and then to form his own ideas from reflections on past history. There is reason to think that his lectures on ethics in their earliest form began with a historical survey of moral philosophy from Plato to Hume. In his own ethical theory he starts from the same base as Hutcheson, his teacher, and Hume, by now his friend, but moving in a new direction to accommodate weaknesses in their positions. There is also clear evidence that Smith's ethical theory developed significantly in the course of his twelve years as Professor of Moral Philosophy, both before and after the publication of the first edition of *The Theory of Moral Sentiments* in 1759.

The third part of his lectures, on jurisprudence, is described by John Millar as a third and fourth part, the third dealing with 'justice' in the form of a history of law and government, and the fourth dealing with 'expediency', the subject-matter of the *Wealth of Nations*. It seems, however, that at first Smith did not think of economics as something separate from the history of law and society. He included both in his lectures on 'jurisprudence', as can be seen from the two reports that we have of those lectures, a full but incomplete recital of the lectures of 1762–3, and a more summary but complete account of the lectures of 1763–4. Economics is a central feature of the workings of society and Smith believed that evidence of its development could often best be found in the history of changes in the law. The basic attitude, historical and sociological with liberty as the leading value, owed much to Montesquieu, and the detailed account of legal and economic structure was built upon a foundation inherited again from Hutcheson; but Smith's own advance upon them, in working out a firm, complex, and coherent theory of social change and economic process, is far more marked than his originality in ethical theory and is plain for all to see. As with his lectures on ethics, there is evidence that Smith was actively developing both his economic theory and his history of law in the annual delivery of his lectures.

One of Smith's own remarks about his lecturing procedure has been recorded. In order to gauge the interest of his audience, he used to keep his eye on one student whom he judged to have a specially expressive face. 'If he leant forward to listen all was right, and I knew that I had the ear of my class; but if he leant back in an attitude of listlessness I felt at once that all was wrong, and that I must change either the subject or the style of my address.'

There is some conflict of evidence about another of Smith's habits concerning his lectures. When he died in 1790, an anonymous obituary notice in the *Gentleman's Magazine* mentioned that during his professorship at Glasgow he was afraid of plagiarism and would say, when he saw students taking notes, 'I hate scribblers.' On the other hand John Millar, who was undoubtedly in a position to know, wrote of 'the permission given to students of taking notes', in consequence of which many of Smith's observations in his rhetoric lectures had become known through the works of others (P 274). The reports which we now have of very full notes taken by a student (or two students) of Smith's courses of lectures in the 1762–3 session make it difficult to believe the story in the obituary notice. A different interpretation of that tale appears in an anonymous biography of Smith, prefixed to a Glasgow edition of the *Moral Sentiments* in 1809 and probably written by one of Smith's former colleagues. The author says that Smith was 'uneasy when he observed notes of [his lectures] taken down in his class' because 'to be sufficiently full, they must be written with a haste which precludes any thing like accuracy, and, if shewn about in this state, the errors are as likely to be imputed to the original as to the copy'.

The students themselves had no complaints to make about Smith's practices in his lectures. Quite the contrary. When he left the university in 1764, it was in the middle of the academic session, and although he arranged for a substitute to read the rest of his lectures on his behalf, he nevertheless thought it proper to return to his students the fees they had paid for the year. (Fees were paid directly to the professor of each class and formed the major part of his salary.) The students protested vigorously. The first one called up to be given back his money 'peremptorily refused to accept it, declaring that the instruction and pleasure he had already received was much more than he either had repaid or ever could compensate, and a general cry was heard from every one in the room to the same effect'. Smith, however, insisted that his conscience demanded that the fees be returned and thrust the money into the young man's pocket.

By this time Smith had acquired a considerable reputation, both in Britain and on the continent of Europe, through the publication in 1759 of *The Theory of Moral Sentiments*. The immediate success of the book in London is described by David Hume in one of the most delightful of his letters. After tantalizing Smith with tales of interruptions, he prefaces his account of the book's reception with the warning that philosophy can be properly appreciated only by a select few and that 'the approbation of the multitude' is more likely to attend falsehood than truth.

Supposing, therefore, that you have duely prepard yourself for the worst by all these Reflections; I proceed to tell you the melancholy News, that your Book has been very unfortunate: For the Public seem disposd to applaud it extremely. It was lookd for by the foolish People with some Impatience; and the Mob of Literati are beginning already to be very loud in its Praises. Three Bishops calld yesterday at Millar's Shop in order to buy Copies, and to ask Questions about the Author: The Bishop of Peterborough said he had passd the Evening in a Company, where he heard it extolld above all Books in the World. You may conclude what Opinion true Philosophers will entertain of it, when these Retainers to Superstition praise it so highly. . . . Millar exults and brags that two thirds of the Edition are already sold, and that he is now sure of Success. You see what a Son of the Earth that is, to value Books only by the Profit they bring him. In that View, I believe it may prove a very good Book. (C 35)

Despite the implied hint, made not altogether with tongue in cheek, that from a strictly philosophical point of view Hume might not regard it as 'a very good book', he was genuinely pleased that his friend should enjoy a literary success which his own first book had never had. He went on to say that one of the leading lights impressed by the work was Charles Townshend, who talked of placing his stepson, the young Duke of Buccleuch, under the tutelage of Adam Smith when going abroad on the customary grand tour for his education. Four years later Townshend made Smith a formal offer to that effect and as a result Smith gave up his Glasgow Chair. The terms of Townshend's proposal were a salary of £500 per annum, to be followed, after the grand tour was over, by a pension for life of £300 per annum (probably more than Smith earned at Glasgow).

The fame of the *Moral Sentiments* quickly spread beyond Britain. It was read and admired in the literary circles of Paris and was quite soon translated into French. It was sufficiently known in Geneva for Dr Théodore Tronchin, a distinguished physician in that city, to decide in 1761 to send his son to Glasgow University to be taught by Adam Smith. In the same year two students, S. E. Desnitsky and I. A. Tret'yakov, came from Moscow for the same purpose. Both of them must have taken back a full report of Smith's lectures on jurisprudence, since their own lectures as professors of law in the University of Moscow include a repetition of Smith's views very close to the wording of the manuscript reports of Smith's jurisprudence lectures in 1762–3 and in 1763–4.

Smith's residence in Glasgow gave him ample opportunity to meet the merchants of the town, engaged especially in the thriving tobacco trade. He was a regular attender at three clubs, the most important of which was the Political Economy Club, founded by Andrew Cochrane, a leading merchant and banker, 'to inquire into the nature and principles of trade in all its branches'. In later years, when Smith was collecting detailed information for the *Wealth of Nations*, he acknowledged a debt to Cochrane for some of it. Discussions with Cochrane and other prominent Glasgow merchants such as William Cunninghame, Alexander Spiers, John Glassford, and James Ritchie must have given Smith a feel for the real world of commerce. It is worth noting, however, that his belief in the virtues of free trade owed nothing to them. Their own experience led them to support mercantilism. The striking growth of trade at Glasgow in the middle of the eighteenth century was greatly assisted by the protection of the Navigation Acts. Yet it seems, according to the testimony of one of these merchants, James Ritchie, that Smith converted many of them to the doctrine of free trade.

Adam Smith left Glasgow in January 1764 to take up his new post of tutor to the Duke of Buccleuch. The two left for France in February and after spending a few days in Paris proceeded to Toulouse, where they remained for eighteen months. Introductions to local people went slowly at first and life was dull, so much so, said Smith in a letter, that 'I have begun to write a book in order to pass away the time' (C 102). This does not mean that the project of writing the *Wealth of Nations* originated in Toulouse. At the end of the *Moral Sentiments* Smith had announced an intention of producing 'another discourse' on 'the general principles of law and government' (M 342), which would doubtless have included economics as a part of government, following the pattern of his lectures on jurisprudence. Some time later he must have decided to write about economics separately, since there is a manuscript draft of an early version of the first part of the *Wealth of Nations*, written before Smith's last session at Glasgow. A letter from the Glasgow merchant John Glassford, sent to Smith in France towards the end of 1764, expresses the hope that he is getting on with 'the usefull work that was so well advanced here' (C 104).

After a few months Smith began to find his feet in getting to know people in France and in speaking the language. The Duke of Buccleuch's younger brother, Hew Scott, joined them in the autumn. They visited several places in the South of France and then, in October 1765, they moved to Geneva, where they stayed for two months. At Geneva Dr Tronchin would have introduced Smith to everyone who counted, including Voltaire, whom Smith met on five or six occasions. Smith had an enormous respect for Voltaire, not only as the scourge of fanatics but also as a writer. His admiration of Voltaire's tragedies is excessive but he had good reason to appreciate Voltaire's services as a publicist in the cause of justice. In the last edition of the *Moral Sentiments* Smith writes movingly of the trial of the Protestant, Jean Calas, who was mistakenly convicted and executed at Toulouse in 1762 on a charge of having murdered his son. The protest of Voltaire was mainly responsible for the eventual decision to conduct a judicial re-examination of the case in March 1765, when the earlier verdict was overturned. The result was not well received by the local townspeople, and Smith must have heard much acrimonious discussion of the matter during his stay in Toulouse.

From Geneva Smith and his young charges went to Paris, where they arrived at the beginning of 1766 and remained until the end of October. In Paris their social life was as hectic as it had been dull in Toulouse. High society among the British community in Paris was of course completely open to a Duke and stepson of the politician Charles Townshend. Smith himself had his own lines of entry to British and French notables through his friendship with Hume, who had just left Paris after having been in charge of the British embassy. Like Hume, Smith was popular with the literary ladies of the Paris salons. One of them, Madame Riccoboni, an actress and successful novelist, wrote of him in letters to David Garrick: 'j'aime Mr Smith, je l'aime beaucoup. Je voudrais que le diable emportât tous nos gens de lettres, tous nos philosophes, et qu'il me rapportât Mr Smith.' 'Vous verrez un philosophe moral et pratique; gay, riant, à cent lieues de la pédanterie des nôtres.' And again, referring to Smith's forgetfulness: 'c'est la plus distraite créature! mais c'est une des plus aimables.'

In addition to the salons Smith enjoyed regular attendance at the theatre in Paris. But he found time for more serious pursuits too. He was frequently at gatherings of the group of French economists known as physiocrats. Their leader Quesnay was physician to the King and they used to meet at Quesnay's apartments in Paris or Versailles. The physiocrats held that agriculture was the only source of national wealth because it alone yielded a genuine surplus over the costs of production; other forms of production made use of the products of agriculture and turned them into consumable goods. Government policy should therefore give priority to agriculture instead of to manufacture and trade, as the mercantilists believed. One of the younger members of the group, Dupont de Nemours, later edited the works of Turgot and in one of his notes he referred to Adam Smith as having been a 'fellow-disciple' of Quesnay in Paris. Smith was not a disciple of Quesnay. The principles of his thought on economics had been worked out long before he came to France. These principles included freedom of trade and the view that the real wealth of a country does not consist in money but in commodities, doctrines which he shared with the physiocrats in opposition to mercantilism, but if he owed them to anyone it was to Hutcheson and Hume, not Quesnay. He was of course prepared to learn from the French economists, as they were from him. He did not agree with their basic tenet about the overriding importance of agriculture but he thought well enough of them to say in the *Wealth of Nations* (678) that their system 'is, perhaps, the nearest approximation to the truth that has yet been published upon the subject of political oeconomy'. He had a great personal respect for Quesnay and originally intended to dedicate the *Wealth of Nations* to him, but by the time it appeared Quesnay was dead.

The warmth of Smith's feeling for Quesnay depended on more than their mutual interest in economics. When the Duke of Buccleuch and later his brother Hew fell ill, Quesnay agreed to Smith's requests that he should attend them personally. The Duke recovered from his fever in the summer but Hew Scott's illness in October proved fatal. Smith himself scarcely ever left the young man's bedside. In addition to Quesnay and the doctor at the British embassy, Smith summoned the aid of his old friend Tronchin of Geneva, but their efforts were vain. Smith's letters to Lady Frances Scott, sister of his two pupils, are deeply moving expressions of his concern and care, as is the mere fact that he wrote to her rather than her stepfather, so that she might break the news to her mother in the way she thought best. The death of Hew put an end to the sojourn in France. Smith and the Duke of Buccleuch returned to London with Hew's body on 1 November 1766.

A few months later Smith went back to his mother's house in Kirkcaldy. He remained there until 1773, working with little interruption on his book. He had hoped to complete it well before that time. A letter from Hume in February 1770 implies that Smith is about to set off for London to look after the publication. In fact Smith did not go to London until April 1773, and even then revision occupied him for almost three more years. However, these London years were not so entirely taken up with working on the book. He consorted with fellow Scots at the British Coffee House and with a distinguished circle of English worthies at the Literary Club: Sir Joshua Reynolds, Edward Gibbon, Edmund Burke, Samuel Johnson and his shadow James Boswell, Oliver Goldsmith, Sir William Jones the orientalist, and David Garrick. It seems that his companions at the Club found his conversation instructive rather than lively, a very different picture from that conveyed by the literary ladies of Paris. Perhaps he had become a dull dog in the intervening years, weighed down by the mass of material facts with which he was dealing in his book; or perhaps the picture is distorted because most of the evidence comes from Boswell, who by this time had lost his affection for his old professor, now 'a professed infidel' and a man whose relations with Johnson were marked with coolness on both sides. A more agreeable vignette of Adam Smith in London was given by Benjamin Franklin, who said that Smith read each chapter of the *Wealth of Nations* to him, Richard Price (moral philosopher and writer on public finance), and others, listening patiently to their criticisms and then bringing back to them revised versions of what he had written. Smith will certainly have obtained much valuable information about America from Franklin, just as he had obtained information about France from his observations in that country and from his friendship with Quesnay, Turgot, and other physiocrats. However, in a letter he once dismissed Richard Price, quite unfairly, as 'a factious citizen, a most superficial Philosopher and by no means an able calculator' (C 290).

The *Wealth of Nations* eventually appeared on 9 March 1776. It met with immediate and resounding success. Smith's friends were all loud in their praises of its merits but thought that such a learned and complex work could not possibly be popular. They were wrong. The original edition was sold out in six months. The first volume of Gibbon's *Decline and Fall of the Roman Empire* had been produced by the same publisher a few weeks earlier. Hume said, both to Smith and to the publisher Strahan, that while both books were excellent, Smith's required 'too much thought' to be as popular as Gibbon's; but Gibbon himself hit upon the reason why the sale of the *Wealth of Nations* exceeded expectations: 'the most profound ideas expressed in the most perspicuous language'. The book sets out a highly complicated skein of thought but almost always expressed in remarkably simple terms, with homely illustrations and a great number of memorably vivid maxims. Would that economists today could recover the art!

Hume's initial reaction to the *Wealth of Nations*, though less amusing than his letter about the *Moral Sentiments*, deserves quotation for the warmth and sincerity of its first words. While Hume did not write a book on economics, his own contributions to the subject showed the same penetrating intelligence that is familiar to students of his philosophical work. The first two words of his letter express unparalleled enthusiasm. The first is Greek, the second Latin, meaning 'Well done! Splendid!'

Euge! Belle! Dear Mr Smith: I am much pleas'd with your Performance, and the Perusal of it has taken me from a State of great Anxiety. It was a Work of so much Expectation, by yourself, by your Friends, and by the Public, that I trembled for its Appearance; but am now much relieved. Not but that the Reading of it necessarily requires so much Attention, and the Public is disposed to give so little, that I shall still doubt for some time of its being at first very popular: But it has Depth and Solidity and Acuteness, and is so much illustrated by curious Facts, that it must at last take the public Attention. (C 186)

Hume and Smith had long been the closest of friends. Smith admired Hume more than anyone else in the world. He had learned from Hume in philosophy, in economics, and perhaps above all in thought about religion, though he was not prepared to be as outspoken as Hume on the subject. He regarded Hume as the greatest philosopher of the age and, while he differed in some points of moral theory, he thought that Hume's personal character and conduct exemplified moral goodness to perfection.

Hume had only a few months more to live when the *Wealth of Nations* appeared in the spring of 1776. He had been steadily declining as the result of a disease in the stomach and he died on 25 August. He was particularly anxious that his *Dialogues on Natural Religion* should be published immediately after his death and he had great difficulty in trying to persuade Smith to accept responsibility for seeing the book through the press. Smith's reluctance arose, I think, not simply, or even not so much, from apprehension of unpleasant consequences for himself, but more from a genuine belief that the *odium theologicum* would tarnish Hume's own reputation. In the event Smith was assailed for something different. Hume had written a short autobiography to be published after he was gone. Smith was so impressed with Hume's courage and good humour in the face of death that he resolved to add to the autobiography a brief account of Hume's last days, including an irreverently witty tale, inspired by a reading of Lucian's *Dialogues of the Dead*, about a conversation that Hume might have had with Charon, the ferryman who, in classical mythology, rowed the souls of the dead over the river Styx. Smith ended his account with a sentence imitating Plato's estimate of Socrates at the close of *his* account of the death of his mentor. Smith wrote that he had always considered Hume 'as approaching as nearly to the idea of a perfectly wise and virtuous man, as perhaps the nature of human frailty will permit' (C 221). Conventional Christians were shocked. How could an atheist be perfectly virtuous? Smith himself, they said, was promoting atheism by suggesting, through the example of Hume, that it afforded a protection against the fear of death. Smith reflected ruefully in a letter:

A single, and as, I thought a very harmless Sheet of paper, which I happened to Write concerning the death of our late friend Mr Hume, brought upon me ten times more abuse than the very violent attack I had made upon the whole commercial system of Great Britain. (C 251)

In 1777 Smith applied for and was readily granted an appointment as Commissioner of Customs in Edinburgh. It brought him an income of £600 a year and he thought that he should now give up the annual pension of £300 from the Duke of Buccleuch. The Duke, however, insisted that the pension had been promised unconditionally and must continue. So Smith spent his last years in Edinburgh a comparatively rich man. (He in fact gave away a good deal of his wealth to charitable causes in secret.) He took a fine house in the Canongate and brought his mother and his cousin, Janet Douglas, over from Kirkcaldy to join him. A little later he also brought into his household a nephew of Janet's, David Douglas, whom he eventually made his heir. The Board of Commissioners of Customs met on four days a week for most of the year, and Smith attended its meetings with great regularity apart from a brief visit to London in 1782 and a more extended one in 1787. The company of his friends meant much to him. He kept open house for them at Sunday supper, and on Fridays he dined at the Oyster Club, founded by him and two distinguished scientists, Joseph Black and James Hutton, who were later to be appointed his literary executors. The name of their club seems to suggest that they were gourmets, but as it happens all three were more interested in conversation than in food and drink. Black was a vegetarian, Hutton a teetotaller, and Smith more fond of sugar lumps than anything else. At his Sunday supper parties Miss Douglas would place the sugar-bowl on her lap after a time in order to halt his raids upon it.

During Smith's visit to London in 1787 he saw a good deal of the younger Pitt, a warm admirer of the *Wealth of Nations* and a fervent advocate of Smith's free-trade principles. It is said that on the first occasion when they met, the company stood up at Smith's arrival, and upon his asking them to be seated, Pitt replied on their behalf: 'No, we will stand till you are first seated, for we are all your scholars.' Smith for his part came to reciprocate the admiration as he got to know Pitt better. There is another story that at a dinner party attended by both of them Smith said to a companion: 'What an extraordinary man Pitt is; he understands my ideas better than I do myself.'

Pitt may have appreciated the *Wealth of Nations* more than most, but it had exerted practical influence on others too, beginning with Lord North's introduction, in his Budgets of 1777 and 1778, of new forms of taxation recommended by Adam Smith, and continuing with consultation of Smith by members of the Government in 1778 on policy towards America and in 1779 on the proposal to grant free trade to Ireland. The book itself was republished in a second revised edition in 1778, considerably expanded in the third edition of 1784, and then reprinted in two further editions of 1786 and 1789. Meanwhile it had been translated into German, French (in three different versions), Danish, and Italian.

Towards the end of his life Smith spent many months on producing an enlarged version of his first book, *The Theory of Moral Sentiments*. He also talked of being engaged on two other works, one 'a sort of philosophical history' of literature and 'philosophy' (no doubt including the sciences within that term), the other 'a sort of theory and history of law and government' (C 287). He said that he already had most of the materials and had made some headway with the actual writing. However, he never finished these books, and a week before his death he asked Black and Hutton to burn all his manuscripts, sixteen volumes of them, except for the few pieces which were later published as *Essays on Philosophical Subjects*. These, taken together with the report of his lectures on rhetoric and *belles-lettres* in 1762–3, give some indication of what the first of the two projected books might have been, just as the reports of his lectures on jurisprudence afford some evidence for the second. But when one compares the latter part of the jurisprudence lectures with the *Wealth of Nations*, one can see that the actual books, if Smith had brought them to fruition, would have been far superior to the initial writings from which they were to grow.

Adam Smith died in 1790 at the age of sixty-seven. He is buried in the Canongate churchyard, not far from the house in Edinburgh where he had lived for twelve years. His grave is at the foot of a simple monument with the following inscription:

Here
are deposited
the remains of
ADAM SMITH,
author
of the
Theory of Moral Sentiments,
and
Wealth of Nations;
&cc &cc &cc
He was born, 5th June, 1723.
And he died, 17th July, 1790.

3 Ethics

The first chapter of the *Moral Sentiments* is entitled 'Of Sympathy'; the first chapter of the *Wealth of Nations* is entitled 'Of the Division of Labour'. In each case the title is a signal of what Smith thinks most fundamental. The main subject of the *Moral Sentiments* is the nature of moral judgement and Smith founds it on sympathy. The main subject of the *Wealth of Nations* is economic growth and Smith founds that on the division of labour.

Sympathy

It is a mistake to suppose, as a number of nineteenth-century commentators did, that Adam Smith's first book treats sympathy as the motive of moral action. The role of sympathy in his book is to explain the origin and the nature of moral judgement, of approval and disapproval. For this purpose he uses the word 'sympathy' in a somewhat unusual way to mean not just sharing the feelings of another, but being aware that one shares the feelings of another. As often happens when a philosopher takes a term of common usage and employs it in a special sense, he sometimes forgets his own prescription and slips back into the normal meaning, but in general Smith is clear enough about what he is doing.

He uses his notion of sympathy to explain two different kinds of moral judgement or approval. The first is a judgement about the 'propriety' of an action; in plain language, the judgement that an action is right or wrong. The second is a judgement about an action's merit or demerit, the judgement that it deserves praise or blame, reward or punishment. According to

Smith, the feeling of approval which is expressed in a judgement of right or wrong is the result of sympathy with the agent's motive. We can illustrate what he means with a simple example. If I see Alma Goodheart help a lame old lady across the road, I 'sympathize' with her kindness and as a result I approve of it as the appropriate response. I would have responded in the same way if I had been in her shoes and so I must think her response reasonable and proper. I say that her action was the right thing to do. A further judgement that the action is praiseworthy expresses a second form of approval, which arises from sympathy with the old lady's feeling of gratitude. On the other hand, if I see Ira Grumpy kicking a cat that has got in his way, I feel antipathy to Ira's annoyance and sympathy with the cat's resentment. The antipathy produces disapproval of the action as wrong, and the sympathy with resentment produces an additional and different disapproving judgement of the action as blameworthy.

When Smith says that an average spectator (he actually says 'every spectator' but that is rhetoric) would sympathize with the kindness of someone like my Alma Goodheart, he means that if the spectator imagines himself in Alma's shoes, he finds that he too would want to help the old lady; he observes a correspondence between the feeling, the prompting to action, which he would have and that which Alma evidently has. Likewise the spectator's 'sympathy' with the old lady's gratitude is a perception that, if he were in the old lady's situation and were helped, he would have the same feeling of gratitude that the old lady has. Antipathy towards an Ira Grumpy is an awareness, when you imagine yourself in his place, that you would not feel the same annoyance with the cat as he does. It will be seen that Smith's concept of sympathy is linked with the exercise of imagination. The sympathy that causes approval or disapproval is not necessarily awareness of an actual feeling which reproduces here and now the motives of those who act or the reactions of those whom the action affects. It is the thought of a feeling which you would have if you were in their shoes, an awareness that comes from imagining yourself in the situations of those who are actually involved.

The two judgements of approval that arise from sympathy are clearly rational, in Smith's view. A spectator who finds that the feelings of those involved correspond to what his own would be, must regard those feelings as appropriate to the situation.

The man who resents the injuries that have been done to me, and observes that I resent them precisely as he does, necessarily approves of my resentment. The man whose sympathy keeps time to my grief, cannot but admit the reasonableness of my sorrow. He who admires the same poem, or the same picture, and admires them exactly as I do, must surely allow the justness of my admiration. (M 16)

Sympathy creates a social bond. This is plainly true of sympathy in its most common meaning of compassion; when one feels compassion for the sorrow or the need of another, one is moved to give comfort or help. Sympathy of this kind, serving as a motive of action, promotes a sense of responsibility to share the burdens of others. Sympathy in Adam Smith's sense is a socializing agent in a different way. Everyone, or nearly everyone, is pleased with the approval of others and uncomfortable with disapproval. I learn from experience that spectators approve when my feelings and reactions correspond to the feelings and reactions which they would have in my situation. If my natural reactions differ from the common norm, I shall meet with disapproval. So I have an inducement to conform, in order to win approval. If, for example, my natural reaction to sorrow or to injury is more vigorous than that of the average spectator, I am taught by his lack of approval to try to tone it down in future.

Such differences in sentiment between the observer and the person observed may arise from differences in the natural constitution of particular individuals. They are, however, also inherent in the process of imaginative sympathy. For all that the imagination allows us, in a sense, to identify ourselves with other people, imagining is not the same as actually experiencing, and the reproduction of feeling cannot match up to the original.

The person principally concerned is sensible of this, and at the same time passionately desires a more complete sympathy.... But he can only hope to obtain this by lowering his passion to that pitch, in which the spectators are capable of going along with him.... What they feel, will, indeed, always be, in some respects, different from what he feels ... These two sentiments, however, may, it is evident, have such a correspondence with one another, as is sufficient for the harmony of society. Though they will never be unisons, they may be concords, and this is all that is wanted or required. (M 22)

The spectator for his part is also aware that his feelings must fall short of those experienced by 'the person principally concerned'. The spectator too is influenced by the socializing tendencies of sympathy; he too would like to see a more complete concordance of feelings. So he strives to heighten his reaction by a closer identification, trying to take into his imaginative leap all the little details that make an experience more poignant.

   These two efforts, on the one side to damp down the violence of experienced feeling, on the other to enliven the weakness of imagined reproduction, produce two different kinds of virtue, the virtue of self-command and the virtue of 'indulgent humanity' or sensibility. Smith's own ethical doctrine (as contrasted with his contribution to ethical theory) emphasized the value of self-command. It was at the forefront of Stoic ethics, which had impressed him deeply in his early years, especially from his reading of Epictetus. Epictetus was a Greek slave in the time of the Roman Empire, who became emancipated but whose earlier period of slavery had taught him to face the harsh burdens of life with fortitude, with what we would now call the 'stoic' virtue of resignation. One can see from the *Moral Sentiments* that Adam Smith was fascinated by Stoic ethics, although he came to see that certain features of the Stoic doctrine were unacceptable. Even so, his own code of ethics is more Stoic than Christian. He thought of himself as putting the two together. 'As to love our neighbour as we love ourselves is the great law of Christianity, so it is the great precept of nature to love ourselves only as we love our neighbour, or what comes to the same thing, as our neighbour is capable of loving us' (M 25).

The impartial spectator

So far I have been dealing with Smith's theory of the moral judgements which we make as spectators of the behaviour and character of other people. What of judgements about ourselves? Smith's answer to this question constitutes the most original and the subtlest part of his ethical theory. According to Smith, I approve or disapprove of my own actions by imagining myself in the shoes of a spectator. Let us go back to my earlier example of judging another person's action to be wrong. Suppose that I, like Ira Grumpy, were annoyed by a cat and were tempted to kick it, but said to myself 'No, that would be wrong.' Smith thinks that my moral disapproval is the result of the disapproval of spectators. I know that most people disapprove of such actions. Obviously they would disapprove of me just as much as they disapprove of Ira Grumpy. If I were somebody else and looked at myself kicking the cat, I should feel the same antipathy as I feel towards Ira. The judgements of conscience, moral judgements about one's own actions, are in the first instance a reflection of the judgements of society. Smith himself uses the image of a mirror.

Were it possible that a human creature could grow up to manhood in some solitary place, without any communication with his own species, he could no more think of his own character, of the propriety or demerit of his own sentiments and conduct, of the beauty or deformity of his own mind, than of the beauty or deformity of his own face. All these are objects which he cannot easily see . . . and with regard to which he is provided with no mirror which can present them to his view. Bring him into society, and he is immediately provided with the mirror which he wanted before. (M 110)

We suppose ourselves the spectators of our own behaviour, and endeavour to imagine what effect it would, in this light, produce upon us. This is the only looking-glass by which we can, in some measure, with the eyes of other people, scrutinize the propriety of our own conduct. (M 112)

If Smith had stopped there, his theory would be too simple. Spectators can make mistakes; they may be unaware of some of the facts or may misunderstand motives. A man's conscience sometimes tells him that he must go against popular sentiment. This, Smith thinks, is because he is in a better position than spectators to know the relevant facts. Of course, he too may misinterpret facts from partiality to his own interest, and this is why he should try to look at them in the guise of an impartial spectator. In order to avoid self-deceit we must try to see 'ourselves in the light in which others see us, or in which they would see us if they knew all' (M 158–9). It remains true, however, that we may think the judgement of actual spectators to be misguided through ignorance of some of the relevant facts. Even so, says Smith, we reach our moral judgement by imagining ourselves as an ideal impartial spectator, a spectator who knows all the relevant facts but is not personally involved. If we find that this imagined impartial spectator, 'the man within the breast', would sympathize with what we plan to do, or with what we have done, that causes us to approve. If the impartial spectator does not sympathize, we disapprove.

The late Professor A. L. Macfie observed that Robert Burns, who knew and valued *The Theory of Moral Sentiments*, probably had in mind Smith's phrase, 'if we saw ourselves as others see us', when he wrote

> O wad some Pow'r the giftie gie us
> To see oursels as others see us.

The touch of religious language in that couplet is also to be found in Smith's account of the impartial spectator. Smith most commonly writes of 'nature' as the source of our moral and other capacities but at times he is prepared to use theological language.

The all-wise Author of Nature has, in this manner, taught man to respect the sentiments and judgments of his brethren ... He has made man, if I may say so, the immediate judge of mankind; and has, in this respect, as in many others, created him after his own image, and appointed him his vicegerent upon earth, to superintend the behaviour of his brethren. (M 128–30)

The association with biblical ideas and phrases does not mean that Smith has abandoned explanation in terms of human nature, what we nowadays call empirical psychology. There is a fair amount of evidence, including some in the *Moral Sentiments* itself, that he had reservations about accepting Christianity, though he did not carry religious scepticism as far as Hume did. Smith was probably a deist. Like a number of other thinkers of the Enlightenment, he considered that observable nature afforded sufficient reason for believing in the existence of God. Smith's account of natural processes can be read as a would-be scientific enterprise, with no need for an underpinning from theology. In his ethics, as in his economics, scientific explanation was what he was after. However, both for Smith himself and for most of his readers an account of natural process was more persuasive, as well as more vivid, if nature were personified or treated as the work of a personal God. The metaphor of legal language, when he speaks of man as the judge of mankind, serves the same purpose. Sympathy and antipathy, with consequent approval and disapproval, take place as a matter of course. Spectators do not set themselves up to imitate earthly judges in courts of law, still less to imitate a heavenly judge. But the effect of their behaviour is analogous to that of intentional judges. Its significance is brought out by the comparison with judges and by the traditional language about God.

In the same spirit Smith is ready to say that the general rules of morality are 'justly' regarded as laws of God. They come to us from experience. Having found that our sympathy and consequent approbation tend to be directed upon the same sort of object on different occasions, we generalize our experience into rules or principles: for example, that it is right to help people in need, wrong to harm those who have intended no harm to us, right to reward the beneficent and to punish the evil-doer. It is equally natural for men to ascribe to their gods those feelings which matter most for the conduct of human life; since moral rules resemble laws, they are treated as divine laws attended by divine sanctions. The natural tendency is refined and confirmed by 'philosophical researches', which lead to monotheistic belief and which also observe 'badges of authority' in moral judgement; these badges or marks of authority are signs that moral judgement was intended by God to direct our lives. The last part of this argument (M 165) echoes an earlier moralist of the eighteenth century, Bishop Butler, who influenced the mature thought of Smith's teacher, Hutcheson.

Smith's moral psychology

Smith's theory is primarily an explanation of the origin of moral judgement, something that nowadays would be assigned to psychology rather than philosophy. The eighteenth century did not distinguish between the two disciplines, and for Adam Smith, as for Hume, psychological explanation was the most fruitful method of dealing with philosophical problems. In consequence Smith's theory about the psychology of moral judgement tended to determine his views on the philosophical problem of the standard of right action. The problem is to find a principle or set of principles for deciding what is the right thing to do. One answer that has immediate attractions is the view of utilitarianism: the proper standard is maximum promotion of the general happiness. Utilitarianism received its name from Jeremy Bentham but its substance was prominent enough earlier in the eighteenth century, and Adam Smith was well aware of its appeal. He was prepared to allow that moral actions do in fact tend, as a whole, to promote the general happiness, and that this is the end intended by God, but he opposed the view that utility is the one and only standard of right action. In practice, he argued, the thought of utility has a subordinate role in the formation of moral judgement. Our approval arises first from sympathy with the motive of the agent and secondly from sympathy with the gratitude of the beneficiary. Thirdly it receives added support from noting that the action conforms to the general rules of morality (which in fact, as he has explained, have their origin in the two kinds of sympathy). Then fourthly it may gain further confirmation from the pleasure which attends the thought of utility. According to Smith, the last consideration is also the least in its contribution to the final judgement of approval.

Smith's objection to utilitarianism is that we do not in practice decide what is right by reference to utility. Now if the problem of the standard of ethics were one of positive psychology, finding out how we do in fact reach our decisions, the objection would be conclusive. But the problem is a normative one; it is concerned with the question 'How *should* we decide?' Smith would still say, however, that the answer is to be gleaned from actual practice. Even if social utility is the ultimate end, nature achieves that end through the workings of sympathy. Defending his view that the concept of ill desert depends on sympathy with resentment, Smith writes:

... the present inquiry is not concerning a matter of right, if I may say so, but concerning a matter of fact. We are not at present examining upon what principles a perfect being would approve of the punishment of bad actions; but upon what principles so weak and imperfect a creature as man actually and in fact approves of it. ... Though man ... be naturally endowed with a desire of the welfare and preservation of society, yet the Author of nature has not entrusted it to his reason to find out that a certain application of punishments is the proper means of attaining this end; but has endowed him with an immediate and instinctive approbation of that very application which is most proper to attain it. The oeconomy of nature is in this respect exactly of a piece with what it is upon many other occasions. (M 77)

The trouble with Smith's method of distinguishing between right and fact is that it ignores the practical problems which often face imperfect men in reaching moral decisions. In a dilemma, with the need to choose between competing goods (or evils), 'immediate and instinctive approbation' fails us. It is then that we want to ask the normative question 'How *should* we decide?'

If you were to ask Smith what is the standard of moral judgement, the criterion whereby you can decide what you ought to do, Smith would say it is the approval of the impartial spectator. That, however, will only tell you whether or not the impartial spectator has the same attitude to a proposed action as you have yourself. If your attitude is hesitation between conflicting goods, each of them affording some valid ground for choice, it does not help to know that the impartial spectator sympathizes. The function of the impartial spectator is to enable you to be impartial; if your initial inclination is affected by partiality, by a concern for your own personal interest, the impartial spectator will help you to take a more objective view. If, however, you have rid yourself of partiality but are still unclear about the respective merits of competing alternatives, the impartial spectator cannot help.

Nevertheless, as a psychological account of the origin of conscience the theory of the impartial spectator is impressive, especially in linking the moral judgements of the individual with those of society. The first stage of Smith's theory, his account of the approval of actual spectators, has a weakness. He says that the approval of a spectator is the result of awareness that he would share the agent's feelings if he were in the same situation. This does not distinguish between moral and other kinds of approval. When introducing his theory that approval depends on sympathy (in the sense of observation of correspondence), Smith himself gives a variety of examples to show that a judgement of propriety need not be a moral judgement.

The man whose sympathy keeps time to my grief, cannot but admit the reasonableness of my sorrow. He who admires the same poem, or the same picture, and admires them exactly as I do, must surely allow the justness of my admiration. He who laughs at the same joke, and laughs along with me, cannot well deny the propriety of my laughter. . . . If the same arguments which convince you convince me likewise, I necessarily approve of your conviction. (M 16–17)

Sympathy, the recognition of a correspondence, either of feelings or of opinions, produces approval. But what determines whether the approval, the judgement of propriety, is moral as contrasted with aesthetic or intellectual? Smith would say that moral approbation expresses sympathy with motives, but this seems too wide. Suppose I go to a concert from a desire to hear the music on the programme. A spectator who shares my tastes will approve of my action and its motive. Yet it would be distinctly odd to call his approbation moral.

However, this weakness in Smith's explanation of the judgement of propriety does not affect the value of his most important contribution to ethical theory, his concept of the impartial spectator. The approval of the imagined impartial spectator does indeed depend on Smith's earlier account of approval by actual spectators, so that it could apply to non-moral as well as moral approval; but this does not matter. Anyone who was bothered that his aesthetic tastes or his ambitions were unduly subjective could consult the judgement of an imagined impartial spectator. In practice such worries are concentrated upon moral issues, when we speak of an exercise of conscience. Even though Smith's concept of the impartial spectator could cover more than conscience, it can still be valuable as a psychological explanation of the latter.

Smith's explanation of the origin of conscience is in principle similar to that of Freud. Straightforward moral judgements about our own actions, according to Smith, are built up in the mind as a reflection of the attitudes of society, mediated especially in childhood through the influence of parents, teachers, and schoolfellows. The built-up set of attitudes in the mind acts as a second self passing judgement on the plans or actions of the natural self.

When I endeavour to examine my own conduct, when I endeavour to pass sentence upon it, and either to approve or condemn it, it is evident that, in all such cases, I divide myself, as it were, into two persons . . . The first is the spectator, whose sentiments with regard to my own conduct I endeavour to enter into, by placing myself in his situation, and by considering how it would appear to me, when seen from that particular point of view. The second is the agent, the person whom I properly call myself, and of whose conduct, under the character of a spectator, I was endeavouring to form some opinion. (M 113)

Freud writes of a super-ego, a second self built up in the mind as a reflection, largely, of the attitude of parents, acquiring the function of a censor to pass judgement on the desires and actions of the natural self.

There are significant differences between the two theories. First, Freud places particular emphasis on the influence of parental attitudes, while Smith thinks more broadly of social norms and mentions teachers and schoolfellows as well as parents in inculcating these norms into the child. Secondly, Freud's super-ego seems to do much more in the way of disapproval than of positive approval. It includes an uplifting 'ego ideal' as well as a repressive 'conscience', but Freud emphasizes the latter element. The primary role of the super-ego is that of a censor, inhibiting the exuberance of sexual and associated impulses. Smith thinks of the impartial spectator as being there both to approve and to disapprove. There is no perceptible leaning to one side or the other. Thirdly, Smith adds the vital qualification that 'the man within the breast' can be a superior judge to 'the man without' in being better informed about facts and motives.

Psychoanalysts presumably find Freud's theory useful in their medical practice. One can well understand that certain types of neurosis are connected with an excessive sense of inhibition and that this is often the effect of an excessively censorious parent in childhood. If, however, Freud's theory is generalized and taken to be an explanation of the conscience of most normal people, then it seems less satisfactory than the explanation given by Adam Smith. Parents are no doubt the major influence in the moral education of children during their earliest years, but teachers and fellow-pupils, and then friends and fellow-workers, all have a part to play later on. A repressive family background can produce a rigid, censorious conscience, more inclined to 'don't' than 'do'; but an affectionate background at home and at school results in a more liberal conscience, encouraging both the development of self and a concern for others.

What of the third difference between Smith and Freud, Smith's readiness to make conscience a 'superior tribunal' to the judgement of actual spectators? Having had our eyes opened by Freud and others to the dark recesses of the unconscious, we may be inclined to treat Smith's view as a typical piece of eighteenth-century optimism, blind to the prevalence of self-deceit. That, however, is too simple-minded. Smith knew nothing of explicit theories of the unconscious but he was well aware of the strength of self-deceit.

This self-deceit, this fatal weakness of mankind, is the source of half the disorders of human life. If we saw ourselves in the light in which others see us, or in which they would see us if they knew all, a reformation would generally be unavoidable. We could not otherwise endure the sight. (M 158–9)

Hence the need for the impartial spectator, to see ourselves as others see us—or rather, as 'they would see us if they knew all'. We do sometimes think that our own conscience is a better judge than popular opinion, and because of this it is a generally approved maxim that in such circumstances a person ought to follow the dictate of his own conscience. Smith tries to accommodate in his theory the facts of real life.

I have confined this account of Smith's ethics to his theory of moral judgement because that is the main topic of his first book and by far his most important contribution to moral philosophy. *The Theory of Moral Sentiments* has a good deal to say also about cardinal virtues. The earlier version of the book gave some prominence to the distinction between justice and beneficence, treating justice as primarily a negative virtue of avoiding harm to others, and beneficence as the positive virtue of doing them good. It balanced the Christian virtue of love, as the motive of beneficence, with the Stoic virtue of self-command, and it regarded prudence or rational self-interest as a proper object of approval, though not of warm admiration. The enlarged version of the book, put together some years after the publication of the *Wealth of Nations*, gives more prominence to prudence and also adds a little to the emphasis on self-command. This aspect of the *Moral Sentiments* invites comparison with the psychology underlying the *Wealth of Nations* and I shall say something in Chapter 5 about the comparisons that have been made. The *Moral Sentiments* itself, however, has suffered from the preoccupation of scholars with these comparisons. It has been misunderstood, and its primary aim, as a work of moral philosophy, has been neglected.

4   Economics

The *Wealth of Nations* has two major features. The first is an
analysis or (as present-day economists might say) a model of the
workings of the economy. The second is a policy recommenda-
tion of free trade and *laissez-faire* generally. Both are connected
with the underlying theme of economic growth. Adam Smith's
analysis is not confined to showing the interrelation between
the different elements of a continually maintained system. It
also explains how the system can generate the continual accumulation of wealth. And since, according to Smith, this process
is most successful when left to the play of natural forces, his
analysis leads him to urge governments to let well alone.

The division of labour

Smith believes that the most significant aspect of economic life
is the division of labour and he therefore begins his book with
that topic. In Smith's view, the division of labour is the essential starting-point for economic growth, for the development of
'wealth' or 'opulence' in a society or in the wider world of
international trade. In order to take this view he has to extend
the idea of the division of labour to include technological advances, when new tools and new machines enable men to
develop new specialized skills. Smith's suggestion is that concentration upon a single job or function makes it easier to think
of improvements. He is well aware that many of the greatest
improvements are due to engineers and manufacturers, but that
comes later. Initially, he claims, it must have been the workers,
the users of tools, who thought of ways to make their work

easier; and this goes on all the time. Smith backs up the claim by a reference to experience.

A great part of the machines made use of in those manufactures in which labour is most subdivided, were originally the inventions of common workmen, who, being each of them employed in some very simple operation, naturally turned their thoughts towards finding out easier and readier methods of performing it. Whoever has been much accustomed to visit such manufactures, must frequently have been shewn very pretty machines, which were the inventions of such workmen, in order to facilitate and quicken their own particular part of the work. (W 20)

In his Glasgow lectures he was more specific, showing that he had either himself visited a number of modern factories or had talked to people who had done so.

The inventions of the mill or the plow are so old that no history gives any account of them. But if we go into the work house of any manufacturer in the new works at Sheffield, Manchester, or Birmingham, or even some towns in Scotland, and enquire concerning the machines, they will tell you that such or such an one was invented by some common workman. (J 351)

Smith introduces his discussion of the division of labour with a very simple example, the manufacture of pins. He takes a simple example because this makes it easy to see the essential point. Ten men working together in a small pin factory, sharing between them about eighteen simple operations, can make about 50,000 pins a day. If one man had to do all those operations by himself, and without the benefit of special machines, which are themselves the result of the division of labour, he could probably make little more than one pin a day.

Having illustrated the basic idea so clearly, Smith goes on to note the vast extent to which the division of labour affects the lives of all of us. Just look at the possessions of an ordinary working man, he says. The man's coat has been produced as a complex result of the work of a shepherd, a wool-sorter, a wool-comber, a dyer, a spinner, a weaver, and so on. Then merchants and sailors have been involved in transporting some of the materials used by certain of these workers. The same sort of long tale could be told about the production of the man's shoes, his food, his furniture, his household utensils. Then the chapter, the first chapter of the *Wealth of Nations*, ends like this:

if we examine, I say, all these things, and consider what a variety of labour is employed about each of them, we shall be sensible that without the assistance and co-operation of many thousands, the very meanest person in a civilized country could not be provided, even according to, what we very falsely imagine, the easy and simple manner in which he is commonly accommodated. Compared, indeed, with the more extravagant luxury of the great, his accommodation must no doubt appear extremely simple and easy; and yet it may be true, perhaps, that the accommodation of an European prince does not always so much exceed that of an industrious and frugal peasant, as the accommodation of the latter exceeds that of many an African king, the absolute master of the lives and liberties of ten thousand naked savages. (W 23–4)

It is a splendid flourish with which to end an illuminating discussion, typical of the gifts of style which Adam Smith could summon up when necessary to drive home a point. Consider now just what the point is. First and foremost, of course, it is to show us how far economic growth, using the division of labour, has gone in developed societies as contrasted with static tribal societies. But it also shows us how far the inhabitants of a developed society depend on each other. The European peasant, unlike the African chief, has political power over nobody; yet his standard of life depends on the co-operation of perhaps as many people as are ruled by the tribal chief. The co-operation is neither commanded by a sovereign nor planned by the participants. It is nevertheless a firm sociological fact. Mutual dependence is, almost as much as economic growth, an underlying theme of Smith's analysis.

The dependence owes little or nothing to altruistic attitudes. A sociological study of the family or of religious communities or even of political society would have to take some note of those; but not a study of the economy. The benefits of the division of labour, says Smith, stem from simple self-interest in the practice of exchange.

> But man has almost constant occasion for the help of his brethren, and it is in vain for him to expect it from their benevolence only. He will be more likely to prevail if he can interest their self-love in his favour, and shew them that it is for their own advantage to do for him what he requires of them. . . . It is not from the benevolence of the butcher, the brewer, or the baker, that we expect our dinner, but from their regard to their own interest. (W 26–7)

Of course, the social benefits do not come from self-interest alone but from the effects of self-interest in the practice of exchange and before long in the conditions of a market. Smith attributes the practice of exchange to a 'propensity to truck, barter, and exchange one thing for another', and he shows curiously little interest in connecting this trait with his basic psychological and sociological analysis. He says it might be 'one of those original principles in human nature, of which no further account can be given', or it might be, 'as seems more probable', an outcome of 'the faculties of reason and speech' (W 25). His lectures at Glasgow indicate that by the latter phrase Smith has in mind 'the natural inclination every one has to persuade'. Offering a shilling, he says there, 'is in reality offering an argument' to persuade someone that it is in his interest to do as you suggest (J 352). Smith must have realized that this itself is not exactly a persuasive argument and so left it out of the *Wealth of Nations*. However, for the purposes of the economic analysis what matters is the result, not the original cause, of the practice of exchange. Exchange leads to a market and it is the laws of the working of the market that Smith wants to discover.

One discovery which Smith believed he had made was that the division of labour is limited by the extent of the market. The stimulus for the division and subdivision of labour is the opportunity to exchange products or services. If other people are ready to exchange some of the corn and meat which they produce for the shoes which I make, I have an incentive to specialize in making shoes so as to sell most of them, instead of spending part of my time on making shoes (for myself and my family) and part on growing corn and grazing cattle. In a large town there is more opportunity for exchange, a larger market, than in a small village; and that is why you will find in the town but not in the village a high degree of specialization. In the town carpentry, joinery, cabinet-making, wood-carving are separate occupations of different skilled men; in the village one man will turn his hand to all of them as occasion arises.

The size of a market does not depend simply on the number of people who live in a particular area. It depends also on ease of communication with potential buyers and sellers elsewhere. Improvements in the transport of goods extend the market for them. Smith noted that (in his time) transport by water was much cheaper than transport by land. Economic historians tell us that he exaggerated the difference so far as the cost of transport within Britain was concerned, but the general point was perfectly valid, especially for international trade, and Smith rightly connected it with the way in which ancient civilizations and modern colonies developed first along sea coasts and river banks. In an earlier piece of writing on the topic he recalled an apt metaphor that could be applied more widely.

What James the sixth of Scotland said of the county of Fife, of which the inland parts were at that time very ill while the sea coast was extremely well cultivated, that it was like a coarse woollen coat edged with gold lace, might still be said of the greater part of our North American colonies. (J 585)

If economic growth depends on the division of labour and if the degree of division of labour depends on the extent of the market, it follows that the continuation of economic growth requires an ever-widening market. This is one of the main reasons why Smith favoured free trade. He recognized, however, that the results of the whole process were not all welcome. The division of labour expanded material advantages but it also stunted the personality of many workers. The man who has to spend all his time on repetitive work, confined to a small number of simple operations, 'has no occasion to exert his understanding . . . and generally becomes as stupid and ignorant as it is possible for a human creature to become' (W 782). The rot spreads to his moral capacities, both domestic and civil, including his readiness to defend his country. In the Glasgow lectures Smith added that in England, where the division of labour had gone further than in Scotland, boys could get a paid job at the age of six or seven, had virtually no education, and when they grew up spent their leisure time in 'drunkenness and riot'.

Accordingly we find that in the commercial parts of England, the tradesmen [i.e. the artisans] are for the most part in this despicable condition: their work thro' half the week is sufficient to maintain them, and thro' want of education they have no amusement for the other but riot and debauchery. So it may very justly be said that the people who cloath the whole world are in rags themselves. (J 540)

The remedy, Smith said in the *Wealth of Nations*, was for the public authority to provide elementary education in every parish. He even went so far as to suggest that it might be made compulsory. 'For a very small expence the publick can facilitate, can encourage, and can even impose upon almost the whole body of the people, the necessity of acquiring those most essential parts of education' (W 785). Adam Smith did not believe in *laissez-faire* for all aspects of social life.

The economic system

Exchange can be carried out by barter, with a valuation of goods relative to each other. But this soon gives way to the use of some form of money, a non-perishable material, divided into standard units, which can serve as a generally accepted medium of exchange. Once money has been introduced, goods are priced in terms of it. Adam Smith draws a distinction between the 'real' price, or the value, of a commodity and its 'nominal' price or price in money. His account of value has given rise to much dispute and tends to obscure one's view of his account of 'nominal' or money price. It is the latter which is directly relevant to the working of the economic system. So let us put aside for the time being his theory of value and concentrate on (nominal or money) price.

The price that people are prepared to pay for a commodity depends on how much they want it. But the price that they are asked to pay depends not only on the demand but also on certain cost factors. Smith distinguishes three factors that may enter into the cost of a commodity: the wages of workers who have helped to produce it; the profit of the owners of 'stock' (capital in the form of money or of material things that are used in production); and the rent charged by the owners of land.

Smith goes out of his way to show that the three factors are different from each other. The profit of the farmer or factory owner is not a wage for his work of managing the enterprise. If it were, the amount of profit would vary with the amount of time, hardship, or ingenuity that was required by the work of management in a particular business; but in fact the amount of profit looked for by the owner varies with the amount of capital he has invested. Profit is a return on the investment of capital, which the owner could have used for other purposes, and which he risks losing in the enterprise to which he commits it. Rent on the other hand is different from profit as well as from wages. The landowner who charges a rent runs no risk of loss and has done no work for what he receives: 'landlords, like all other men, love to reap where they never sowed' (W 67), but unlike other men they are able to do so. 'They are the only one of the three orders whose revenue costs them neither labour nor care, but comes to them, as it were, of its own accord, and independent of any plan or project of their own' (W 265).

A few commodities may have nothing to do with rent and derive their cost from labour and profit alone; Smith gives the example of sea-fish, as contrasted with river-fish such as salmon, the taking of which involves a rent. Still fewer commodities, in a developed society, may have had only a labour cost with no element of profit for a provider of capital; Smith gives the example of certain coloured pebbles which were gathered from the sea-shore and sold by the gatherer to a stone-cutter. However, the price of most commodities has to include all three elements of cost. Corresponding to the three factors of cost are three economic groups, workers, providers of capital, and landowners, each of whom receives a portion of the cost of a commodity. They do not always have to be different individuals. A farmer might own his land, invest capital into using it, and join in the work of cultivation. Generally, however, the three functions are carried out by different people and an understanding of the economic system requires that they be distinguished.

Having done so, Smith next draws a distinction between 'natural price' and 'market price'. In principle his distinction is the same as that drawn later by Alfred Marshall between long-period and short-period price. Smith uses the term 'natural' because the long-period price is, in his opinion, the key to understanding a scientific law, a law of nature, about the working of the market. He more than once compares the natural price with a centre of gravity. 'The natural price, therefore, is, as it were, the central price, to which the prices of all commodities are continually gravitating' (W 75). Of course, it is not the natural price as such which exerts a quasi-gravitational force. The force is that of self-interest in the tension between supply and demand. However, the effect is an equilibrium which, Smith felt, could properly be compared with the equilibrium that the force of gravity can produce for moving bodies.

Smith in fact pays insufficient attention to the part played by demand. He recognizes it when writing of market price but he writes as if the natural price were determined solely by the three factors of cost. There is, he says, an average rate of wages, profit, and rent, depending partly on the general circumstances of a society (whether it is rich or poor; developing, stationary, or declining) and partly on circumstances peculiar to different occupations, enterprises, or pieces of land. The natural price of a commodity, according to Smith, is that price which just covers, no more and no less, the cost of production at average or 'natural' rates of wages, profit, and rent. The market price at any particular time can be at, above, or below the natural price and depends on the relation between supply and demand. (The relevant demand is 'effectual' demand, the demand of those who are able and willing to pay something like the natural price, the cost of making the commodity available for sale. A poor man would no doubt like to have a private carriage, but since he cannot afford to pay what it costs to produce such a carriage, his longing is not an effectual demand.) If demand exceeds supply, some people are prepared to pay more and the market price rises. If demand falls below supply, some goods are left unsold and dealers lower their prices in order to increase the demand and dispose of their stocks. However, any rise or fall in the market price above or below the natural price is bound to be temporary. When the market price is higher than the natural price, the prospect of a higher than average profit will induce more people to produce the commodity. The expanded supply, and competition between sellers, will reduce the market price. On the other hand, when the market price is lower than the natural price, the previous cost of production is not recouped. One or more of the three factors, wages, profits, and rent, will have to be reduced. The result of that will be that some workers will withdraw their labour and go off to another job; or some employers will reduce their use of capital for the production of these particular articles; or some landowners will refuse to let their land be used for the purpose connected with this particular production. So supply will fall, will be inadequate to meet the demand, and market price will rise. The general consequence is that the fluctuating market price must in time return to the natural price.

Since the natural price is in effect a semi-stable market price, to which other market prices tend to return, it is as much subject as they are to the influence of demand in relation to supply. Smith's own analysis shows that the average or natural rates of the cost factors, wages, profit, and rent, which are said to determine the natural price, are themselves subject to the play of supply and demand. The demand for labour, capital, and land from an enterprise producing one kind of commodity is in competition with demand for the same facilities from other enterprises producing other commodities; and the 'price' offered for these facilities, i.e. the rate of wages, profit, and rent, will depend on supply in relation to the competing demands. This is not to say that everything can be explained in terms of supply and demand. It is true, however, that Adam Smith's analysis should have been more explicit about the role of demand.

Smith does go on to show that the determination of wages, profit, and rent in the real world is a complex business that cannot be reduced to any single process like the play of supply and demand. He deals with each of the three factors of cost and is especially interesting on wages. Economists call this part of the work his theory of distribution, that is, his theory of how the money received for commodities is distributed among the three factors that make up the cost of production.

On wages Smith notes a conflicting set of determinants. Employers combine to keep wages low; workers try to combine to keep wages high. In this contest (at the time when Smith was writing) the employers had far the stronger position. There is, however, a basic minimum which must be paid, the cost of subsistence for the worker and his family, taking into account enough children (allowing for the early death of some) to replace him in due course. This sounds like a cold-blooded, purely economic consideration—the employer must not kill the goose that lays golden eggs for him—but Smith also speaks of the subsistence wage as 'the lowest which is consistent with common humanity' (W 86). Adam Smith the economist does not leave at home Adam Smith the moral philosopher.

However, workers are not always at the mercy of niggardly employers who have the power to keep wages down to a bare minimum. In a developing economy there is a demand for more labour, and employers are obliged to abandon their combination and to compete against each other in the hiring of workers, raising wages in the process. Smith illustrates the point by comparing the developing economies of Britain and America with the static economy of China and the declining one of Bengal. This leads him to the observation that 'It is not the actual greatness of national wealth, but its continual increase, which occasions a rise in the wages of labour' (W 87). He also notes that higher wages lead to a growth in population and in the health and energy of workers. The moral philosopher intervenes again in Smith's judgement on these consequences.

Is this improvement in the circumstances of the lower ranks of the people to be regarded as an advantage or an inconveniency to the society? The answer seems at first sight abundantly plain. Servants, labourers and workmen of different kinds, make up the far greater part of every great political society. But what improves the circumstances of the greater part can never be regarded as an inconveniency to the whole. No society can surely be flourishing and happy, of which the far greater part of the members are poor and miserable. It is but equity, besides, that they who feed, cloath and lodge the whole body of the people, should have such a share of the produce of their own labour as to be themselves tolerably well fed, cloathed and lodged. (W 96)

In the absence of economic growth, wages would tend in the long run to decline to the subsistence level and that would be the 'natural' rate.

In addition to discussing the natural rate of wages, Smith tries to explain the difference in the rates of wages paid in different occupations. He gives five grounds of differentiation.

(1) Disagreeable work must command a higher wage than agreeable work if it is to attract enough workers to do it. One job can be more disagreeable than another because the work is harder or dirtier or more dangerous or carries less status.

(2) Work which requires long or arduous training must have higher pay to recompense the cost or difficulty of that training. Smith compares training a man in a skill or a profession with creating an expensive machine. The cost of constructing the machine has to be recouped as part of the profit gained by its products, and it has to be recouped before the machine is worn out and replaced by another. Similarly the cost and difficulty (disagreeableness) of being trained for a skilled occupation or

being educated for a profession is reflected in a higher wage or salary.

(3) Work which is irregular or insecure has to be paid more than that which is constant. For example, masons and brick-layers depend on the weather, coal-heavers depend on the arrival of ships bringing the coal to port.

(4) Occupations that carry a high degree of trust must carry a high wage. Smith gives two kinds of example. Goldsmiths and jewellers are entrusted with precious materials. Doctors and lawyers are entrusted with the health and the fortune or repu-tation of those who consult them. It is not clear, however, just what is common to these two kinds of trust so as to require higher pay in terms of Smith's account of the economic system. The higher pay for the goldsmith and jeweller is presumably a hedge against the temptation for them to steal the precious objects with which they are entrusted. The lawyer, entrusted with 'our fortune and sometimes our life and reputation' (W 122), is perhaps analogous in that he might manage to make off with our fortune; but why should he be tempted to risk our life or reputation? And why should the doctor be tempted to ne-glect our health? Smith says that the confidence we place in the doctor and lawyer 'could not safely be reposed in people of a very mean or low condition' (W 122) and so we must enable the doctor and lawyer to have a high social status. I suppose his thought is that the doctor and lawyer must act in their profes-sions with a high sense of responsibility to their clients, in short with a degree of altruism, unlike the butcher, the brewer, and the baker, who go about their business purely in a spirit of self-interest.

(5) Improbability of success, in the law for instance, has to be countered by the prospect of an especially rich reward if you are successful. This final ground for giving higher pay to some jobs than to others is substantially the same as the third, which postulated higher pay to compensate for insecurity (as well as irregularity).

In connection with his fifth ground Smith makes an interest-ing psychological observation. Men are prone, he says, to overrate their chances in the fortunes of life. They overrate the chances of gain and underrate the chances of loss. He cites the examples of lotteries and insurances. Since a lottery must bring some profit to those who run it, the overall chances of the punters must be less than the money they put in. Yet that does not deter people from having a fling in the hope of winning one of the glittering prizes. Many of them think that they will have a better chance if they buy several tickets, but on a strictly rational calculation they are simply increasing the probability of loss, since that probability advances towards the certainty of loss which comes from buying all the tickets, winning all the prizes, and losing the amount taken in profit by the organizers. Insurances illustrate the tendency of people to underrate the chances of loss. Many people neglect to take out insurance against fire, not because of a rational calculation of balancing the cost of the premium against the risk of loss, but simply because they imagine that the misfortune will not hit them.

This irrationality diminishes the effect of Smith's fifth ground for differentiating wages. As Smith himself observes, the psychological tendency to overrate one's chances of good fortune leads young men to disregard the risks of becoming a soldier or a sailor—or of entering professions such as the law. Smith notes that the pay for soldiers and sailors in his time was not greater than that for common labourers, although the risk element should have made it so. Likewise, in his opinion, while the fees of successful barristers seem high, the profession of law as a whole is underpaid in relation to the real chances of success or failure.

The general idea that comes out of Smith's account of wages is of an equilibrium between the unattractiveness of work and the attraction of monetary reward. Work has to be made worth while to those who undertake it. They will not accept a job if they can get the same pay for another job which is less unattractive or if they can get higher pay for another job which is no more unattractive. Smith is assuming that work in general is unattractive—'toil and trouble'. The unattractiveness can take different forms: arduousness of the work itself or of the training for it, dangerous or unpleasantly dirty conditions, risk of failure. Where one kind of occupation is more unattractive than another, the attraction of a higher level of pay produces a balance. The inequalities of pay are offset by the counter inequalities in the degree of unattractiveness of occupations. Taking the advantages of pay together with the disadvantages of the relevant work, the inequalities disappear; or rather, they would disappear if there were no restraints on the natural economic process and if there were no limitations on the spread of relevant knowledge.

Smith's account of wages should also lead to the idea of an equilibrium between supply of and demand for labour; but, as in his account of natural price, he does not draw attention to this. If the disadvantages of an occupation are not balanced by higher pay, the demand for workers in that occupation is not met and so employers have to increase the wage. On the other hand, if the monetary rewards of an occupation outweigh its disadvantages, it tends to be flooded with applicants for jobs and so the offered wages are reduced.

When he turns to average or natural rate of profit, Smith suggests that this can best be inferred from the average rate of interest, because interest and profit are alternative forms of return upon capital. Profit, like wages, is affected by economic growth or decline but in a reverse direction. A couple of the reasons for unequal wages also operate to produce unequal profits. A business which is disagreeable or has a low status, like keeping a tavern, brings a high rate of profit. So does an especially risky form of business, such as foreign trade—or smuggling! As with high wages for disagreeable or risky work, people are willing to take on the disadvantages of a disagreeable or risky business only if the disadvantages are balanced by especially high rewards.

The natural rate of rent, according to Smith, is the highest that a tenant can afford to pay, subject of course to the difference made by the fertility or situation of the land concerned. The price of products has to cover the ordinary cost of wages and the ordinary rate of profit. The surplus over and above these two elements is what the landowner demands as rent. Whether rent is high or low depends therefore on whether prices are high or low. Rent differs in this respect from wages and profits, the rate of which is a cause, not an effect, of the rate of prices.

Now that we have a picture of the relation of natural price to its three constituents, wages, profit, and rent, we can turn back to Smith's distinction between 'real' price or value and nominal or money price. Smith describes the first as the 'real measure' of exchangeable value.

The real price of every thing, what every thing really costs to the man who wants to acquire it, is the toil and trouble of acquiring it. What every thing is really worth to the man who has acquired it, and who wants to dispose of it or exchange it for something else, is the toil and trouble which it can save to himself, and which it can impose upon other people. (W 47)

As we have seen in discussing different rates of wages for different occupations, Smith assumes that work, labour, is disagreeable; it is 'toil and trouble'. We undertake it for the sake of the useful things, the means to enjoyment, that it can bring. If we obtain goods, means to enjoyment, that have been produced by the labour of other people instead of our own, we are saved toil and trouble, and are prepared to pay for it. In a primitive state of society, a society of hunters, the only cost of acquiring goods is labour. In later stages of society the cost of profit and rent will be added. It remains true, however, that if I buy what others have produced I save myself toil and trouble, and that the purchase price represents a command over the toil and trouble taken by others instead of myself.

The value of any commodity, therefore, to the person who possesses it, and who means not to use or consume it himself, but to exchange it for other commodities, is equal to the quantity of labour which it enables him to purchase or command. Labour, therefore, is the real measure of the exchangeable value of all commodities. (W 47)

However, it is often difficult to quantify labour in comparing the value of different things in relation to each other. One can quantify the amount of time spent on a piece of work, but time is not the only factor that counts in making work disagreeable. Work can be more or less arduous and can require more or less ingenuity (though it is not clear why Smith should assume that the exercise of ingenuity is disagreeable). In practice, values are settled 'by the higgling and bargaining of the market' (W 49), making allowance for hardship and ingenuity as well as time.

Smith prefaced his account of value and price with a plea for indulgence. The subject, he said, is 'in its own nature extremely abstracted' and might 'appear still in some degree obscure' after he had done his best to explain it (W 46). It has certainly left plenty of room for argument. Marx and others accused Smith of confusing the ' labour embodied' in a product with the 'labour commanded' by it, in trying to work out a labour theory of value. Modern economic theorists say that Smith's theory of value is concerned with quite a different matter, the problem of finding a measure or index of welfare, of the balance of 'utilities' (things that are wanted as being enjoyable or means to enjoyment) over 'disutilities'. Smith's prefatory remark shows that he was not clear about the relation between his account of value and that of money prices, but the charge of confusing 'labour embodied' with 'labour commanded' is certainly false. One can see why he tried to relate the 'disutility' (as modern economists call it) of toil and trouble to his theory of prices, but his account of the working of the economic system does not really need his theory of value.

Smith's analysis can apply to a static economy. The cost of producing goods is repaid by the distribution of the money earned to the three 'orders' of workers, employers, and landowners. Smith's main concern, however, is to explain economic progress, to show how a dynamic economy can generate a continual increase of wealth. Having learned from the physiocrats the general idea of representing the economy as the circulation of money and materials among the different groups,

Smith went into much greater detail than they did in describing the functions of capital and income, the difference between fixed and circulating capital, the role of money and banks, and above all the importance of saving.

Smith points out that a man who does everything for himself, before there is a division of labour, can consume as he produces and does not need to keep a stock of goods. But once there is a division of labour and an exchange of the products of labour, a producer must keep the larger part of his products in stock against the time when they will be wanted by others. When they are sold, he uses part of the proceeds for his own immediate needs and part for the purchase of things (materials and tools) necessary to continue his production in the future. We may therefore divide his 'stock' (both of goods produced and of money received) into two parts, one for immediate consumption, the other for providing future income. The second part is capital and this itself is divided into two portions, circulating capital and fixed capital. Circulating capital is used for producing, buying, and selling, so as to make a profit; the money and the things that money buys circulate among producers, buyers, and sellers. Fixed capital is used for machines and tools, buildings, and the improvement of land; all these are means of production and they stay put, as contrasted with the money and goods that circulate.

As with the individual, Smith continues, so with the whole society. Its stock may be divided into a part which is reserved for immediate consumption or use, a part which consists in fixed capital, and a part which consists in circulating capital. However, when Smith applies his analysis to the economy of a country taken as a whole, its explanatory power becomes greater. The distinction between the categories is not necessarily the same as for an individual. For instance, a dwelling-house may bring revenue to a proprietor in the form of rent and so be part of his capital; but since the tenant has to pay the rent out of *his* revenue, the dwelling-house does not bring any additional revenue to society as a whole and so cannot be counted as capital but must be assigned to the stock reserved for consumption or use. Again, fixed capital for society at large includes the skills of the inhabitants—human capital—as well as the material means of production. Finally, the function of circulating capital is more complex and indeed central to the model of the economy. Here Smith is elaborating the idea of a circular flow which he had learned from Quesnay. Circulating capital consists of money and of goods (produced or in process of production) which will in due course be sold. Both money and goods circulate among the different groups of society. Money, obtained as wages, profit, or rent, is exchanged for goods, which eventually are withdrawn from the category of circulating capital, being transferred either to the stock of commodities reserved for immediate consumption or to that of fixed capital. The withdrawals need to be replaced by new production of raw materials or finished goods. Thus consumption and fixed capital both depend on circulating capital. Consumption so depends because nearly all goods for consumption are bought, not produced by the consumers. Fixed capital too depends on circulating capital, both when it is bought in the first place and when it is used to produce further goods.

The replenishment of circulating capital must come from production, and we need to realize that only part of the labour force of society contributes to production. Many of the workers who provide services do not add to the value of production—servants, the armed forces, the public services, many of the professions, entertainers in the arts. Smith is not suggesting that these people are useless drones, like the idle rich. Their work is undoubtedly useful or (in the case of entertainers) pleasurable to society generally. Productive and unproductive labour both have value, but the value of productive labour is added to manufactured goods so as to be used later, while the value of unproductive labour is used up immediately.

But the labour of the manufacturer [i.e. the worker engaged in manufacture] fixes and realizes itself in some particular subject or vendible commodity, which lasts for some time at least after that labour is past. It is, as it were, a certain quantity of labour stocked and stored up to be employed, if necessary, upon some other occasion. That subject, or what is the same thing, the price of that subject, can afterwards, if necessary, put into motion a quantity of labour equal to that which had originally produced it. The labour of the menial servant, on the contrary, does not fix or realize itself in any particular subject or vendible commodity. His services generally perish in the very instant of their performance, and seldom leave any trace or value behind them, for which an equal quantity of service could afterwards be procured. (W 330)

The same thing goes for other unproductive labour, including as it does 'some both of the gravest and most important, and some of the most frivolous professions'.

The labour of the meanest of these . . . and that of the noblest and most useful, produces nothing which could afterwards purchase or procure an equal quantity of labour. Like the declamation of the actor, the harangue of the orator, or the tune of the musician, the work of all of them perishes in the very instant of its production. (W 331)

Production can be increased either by increasing the number of productive workers or by improving their productive power with more and better machines or with more subdivision of labour. All these methods require additional capital, to pay for wages or machinery. The accumulation of capital depends on saving, on spending less in immediate consumption and using what is saved to increase production, either directly as an employer oneself or indirectly by lending the capital, for interest (a form of profit), to those who do undertake production. Saving is not leaving capital to lie idle but allowing it to be used productively instead of unproductively.

What is annually saved is as regularly consumed as what is annually spent, and nearly in the same time too; but it is consumed by a different set of people. That portion of his revenue which a rich man annually spends, is in most cases consumed by idle guests, and menial servants, who leave nothing behind them in return for their consumption. That portion which he annually saves, as for the sake of the profit it is immediately employed as a capital, is consumed in the same manner, and nearly in the same time too, but by a different set of people, by labourers, manufacturers, and artificers, who re-produce with a profit the value of their annual consumption. (W 337–8)

What is more, the savings of one year do not simply provide additional employment for one year. Since the additional labour produces goods that can more than pay its own cost, it can keep going in future years, so that the one lot of savings 'establishes as it were a perpetual fund for the maintenance of an equal number in all times to come'. When the benefits of saving are seen, additional savings are made available and wealth increases progressively. The circular flow of a static economy becomes a widening spiral movement in a growing economy.

It can just as well become a narrowing spiral movement in a declining economy, if excessive spending on immediate consumption leaves insufficient capital for maintaining the existing numbers of productive labour. Fortunately for human nature, the motive for saving is more pervasive than that for spending.

the principle, which prompts to expence, is the passion for present enjoyment; which, though sometimes violent and very difficult to be restrained, is in general only momentary and occasional. But the principle which prompts to save, is the desire of bettering our condition, a desire which, though generally calm and dispassionate, comes with us from the womb, and never leaves us till we go into the grave. (W 341)

Natural liberty

It will be seen that the whole of this elaborate network of analysis depends on the motive force of self-interest, starting from entering into exchange, for easing toil and trouble, and ending with the accumulation of capital, for bettering our condition. The complex system, with its equilibria and its circular or spiral flows, owes nothing to deliberate planning. It exhibits a high and ever-increasing degree of mutual dependence, yet it all comes about naturally from the interplay of self-interest. In one section of the *Wealth of Nations* Smith uses a striking metaphor to reflect the paradox that a regard to self-interest can lead to the kind of universal benefit imagined by idealistic moralists and theologians.

As every individual . . . endeavours as much as he can both to employ his capital in the support of domestick industry, and so to direct that industry that its produce may be of the greatest value; every individual necessarily labours to render the annual revenue of the society as great as he can. He generally, indeed, neither intends to promote the publick interest, nor knows how much he is promoting it. . . . he intends only his own gain, and he is in this, as in many other cases, led by an invisible hand to promote an end which was no part of his intention. (W 456)

Smith had previously used the image of the invisible hand even more colourfully in the *Moral Sentiments*. He there described the effects of economic growth in terms of employment.

The earth by these labours of mankind has been obliged to redouble her natural fertility, and to maintain a greater multitude of inhabitants. It is to no purpose, that the proud and unfeeling landlord views his extensive fields, and without a thought for the wants of his brethren, in imagination consumes himself the whole harvest that grows upon them. The homely and vulgar proverb, that the eye is larger than the belly, never was more fully verified than with regard to him. The capacity of his stomach bears no proportion to the immensity of his desires, and will receive no more than that of the meanest peasant. The rest he is obliged to distribute among those, who prepare, in the nicest manner, that little which he himself makes use of, among those who fit up the palace in which this little is to be consumed, among those who provide and keep in order all the different baubles and trinkets, which are employed in the oeconomy of greatness; all of whom thus derive from his luxury and caprice, that share of the necessaries of life, which they would in vain have expected from his humanity or his justice. . . . The rich . . . consume little more than the poor, and in spite of their natural selfishness and rapacity, though they mean

only their own conveniency, though the sole end which they propose from the labours of all the thousands whom they employ, be
the gratification of their own vain and insatiable desires, they
divide with the poor the produce of all their improvements. They
are led by an invisible hand to make nearly the same distribution
of the necessaries of life, which would have been made, had the
earth been divided into equal portions among all its inhabitants,
and thus without intending it, without knowing it, advance the
interest of the society, and afford means to the multiplication of
the species. (M 184–5)

There is a significant difference between the two passages.
The one in the *Wealth of Nations* says that the self-interested
individual unintentionally helps to maximize the wealth of
society. The one in the *Moral Sentiments* adds that he unintentionally helps to distribute it more widely, so as to approach
equality. In writing this passage Smith had in mind Rousseau's
Discourse on the Origin of Inequality and was implicitly contesting Rousseau's claim that the acquisition of property causes
inequality. He probably had in mind also the opposed view of
Bernard Mandeville, in *The Fable of the Bees: or Private Vices,
Public Benefits*, that the so-called vices of luxury, pride, and
fickleness were public benefits in spreading employment and
increasing trade. Smith says that the poor obtain from the
'luxury and caprice' of the 'proud' landlord those necessities of
life which they could not expect from 'his humanity or his
justice'. Humanity or benevolence would seek to maximize the
happiness of others; justice would seek to distribute it more
equitably.

Adam Smith's image of the invisible hand is not a piece of
theology. No doubt Smith would say that the beneficial results
are ultimately due to nature or the divine author of nature, but
he does not mean that a providential God pulls the strings all
the time. He uses the phrase for vivid effect, to give us a picture
of an imaginary controlling device, but he knows very well that
the effect comes about automatically through the interplay of
individual interest and the system of exchange. His perception

of this truth is one of his great contributions to economic understanding.

Smith did not invent the phrase 'invisible hand'. It seems to have been an idiom of religious reflection. When the warship *Prince George* survived a great storm which wrecked several other ships of the Royal Navy in 1703, Flag Captain Martin wrote in the ship's log that 'the invisible hand of Providence relieved us'. In his early essay on the history of astronomy Smith wrote of pagan religion ascribing irregular events to 'the invisible hand of Jupiter'. He did not believe that the God of theism controlled the working of the economy any more than he believed that Jupiter controlled 'thunder and lightning, storms and sunshine' (P 49–50). He drew on the familiar heritage of religious language simply in order to make his readers appreciate the remarkable character of the phenomenon. I do not mean that he deliberately placed a false halo around it. He was led by an invisible hand to choose evocative words.

No doubt Smith was predisposed to see a beneficent order in the natural running of human affairs. He probably acquired the idea from the ethical theory of the Stoics, which had impressed him deeply in his youth. Among other things, the Stoics believed in a cosmic harmony, which they described by the Greek word *sympatheia*, from which the modern word 'sympathy' is derived. They did not mean that all the elements in a harmonious universe literally had a fellow-feeling with each other. They meant that the elements all fitted in together, worked with each other in harmony. Adam Smith's use of the concept of sympathy in his ethical theory was individual to himself, but he often illustrates it by speaking of harmony, and I have little doubt that the Stoic notion of a harmonious system is at the back of his mind when he describes the socializing effect of our feelings of sympathy. It is likely that the same Stoic idea of a harmonious system helped him to think of the market as a system tending to the general benefit of society.

He did not, however, simply assume that the facts would conform to a preconceived idea. Adam Smith never approached his enquiries in that sort of spirit. He was an empiricist, a thinker who began with experienced fact and then produced a hypothesis to explain the facts. In economics he was impressed by the way in which the market can be observed to work, producing automatically reactions to changes in cost, supply, and demand so as to set up an equilibrium. His talk of market prices 'gravitating' towards the natural price shows that he was reminded of the system of mechanics, and the unplanned beneficial effects could have reminded him of the Stoic idea of a natural harmony.

This Stoic idea went along with a prescription to live according to nature and was one of the sources of the tradition of natural law. Smith was familiar with that tradition in the work of seventeenth-century jurists and philosophers, notably Grotius, Pufendorf, and Locke. He made his own signal contribution to it by interpreting normative or prescriptive natural law as arising from scientific laws of nature. That is to say, Smith treated general principles telling us how we ought to behave as being the result of general truths about the way people do in fact behave. Sympathy and the desire to have the good opinion of others cause people generally to be helpful to each other and to avoid doing harm; such behaviour is approved as the way we ought to act. Common self-interest leads to enforcing the most vital of such practices with the sanctions of criminal law. A similar common self-interest among States leads them to agree upon limited principles of international law. Likewise the practices of economic life, initiated by self-interest, have become established practices precisely because they are generally beneficial, although no one has planned the result. Because they are beneficial, they should be treated as prescriptive, the way we ought to behave.

The tradition of natural law included a belief in 'natural' liberty and equality. In a state of nature (an ambiguous expression which could mean either an unspoiled primitive condition or a utopian ideal) all human beings are free and equal. Adam Smith frequently writes of natural liberty but almost as frequently of natural justice and natural equality. Towards the end of Book IV of the *Wealth of Nations* there is a commonly quoted reference to 'the obvious and simple system of natural liberty' (W 687). Smith's earlier references to natural liberty, however, usually couple it with natural justice or equality or both. Even the passage which I have just quoted goes on to explain that natural liberty is limited by justice. 'Every man, as long as he does not violate the laws of justice, is left perfectly free to pursue his own interest his own way.'

As with natural harmony, the idea of natural liberty is a background conception which adds a unifying framework and gives scope for some persuasive rhetoric; but it is not the primary source of Smith's arguments for *laissez-faire*. His arguments are directed mainly at two particular targets and are based on solid empirical evidence about those two particular things. The first is restriction on competition and the mobility of labour; the second is restriction on the freedom of international trade. It should be noted, incidentally, that Smith attacks the first for producing unnatural 'inequalities' in the labour market, another indication of his view that natural liberty goes together with natural equality.

Under the first heading Smith criticizes the exclusive privileges of corporations which enabled them to retain outmoded practices on apprenticeship. The number of apprentices was limited and the period of their training was much longer than it need be. Consequently the supply of labour for skilled occupations was restricted. On the other hand, the endowment of scholarships and similar awards for education in certain professions, notably the ministry, unduly enlarged the supply of people entering them beyond the level which natural competition would produce. Then again, there were laws which unnecessarily restrained the movement of workers; the Statute of Apprenticeship more or less restricted people to one skilled trade, and the English Poor Law made it difficult for a poor man to obtain a 'settlement' (eligibility for relief) in a different parish from that of his birth.

Smith observed in another connection (laws of hereditary succession) that 'Laws frequently continue in force long after the circumstances, which first gave occasion to them, and which could alone render them reasonable, are no more' (WN 383). Natural conservatism gets in the way of repealing obsolete laws which once were useful but which have come to be harmful. In this respect the natural tendencies of human behaviour are not beneficial and need the intervention of reforming legislation. So Smith's criticism of restrictive practices has its anti-libertarian aspect too.

When Smith turns, in Book IV of the *Wealth of Nations*, to freedom of international trade, he compares its advantages with those of exchange in a simple system of division of labour, and adds: 'What is prudence in the conduct of every private family, can scarce be folly in that of a great kingdom' (W 457). Free trade encourages countries to specialize in the kinds of production for which each has an advantage, and to benefit from exchange at cheap prices. This gives a country a greater total of desirable commodities than it would have if it produced everything for itself; for the latter policy would use up a larger proportion of the country's capital in producing the same amount of those goods that are imported cheaply under free trade. Smith's case is made, however, not with hazardous general statements of this kind, but with a detailed examination of the disadvantages of particular protectionist measures: bounties, duties, prohibitions of imports. He also adds reservations to the general case for free trade. First, he says, protectionist measures are justified in the interests of national defence, which is 'of much more importance than opulence' (W 465), and he gives as an example the introduction of the Navigation Act of 1651. Since the defence of Britain depended so much on ships and sailors, it was legitimate to give British shipping a preference in the carrying of goods. (Later in the book, however, when he came to discuss policy towards the American colonies, Smith was at pains to insist that in commercial terms the Navigation Acts were not beneficial.) Secondly, Smith approves of taxing imported goods if domestic goods of the same character are already taxed; otherwise there will not be fair competition. He also allows that there must often be a compromise with the principles of free trade in order to meet the circumstances of the real world: if a foreign country prohibits the importation of your goods, you may have to retaliate; when nearly every country limits freedom of trade in corn, it would be foolhardy for a small country to have no restrictions on the export of corn and so risk a famine. A general case for free trade must not blind us to realities. 'To expect, indeed, that the freedom of trade should ever be entirely restored in Great Britain, is as absurd as to expect that an Oceana or Utopia should ever be established in it' (W 471).

Laissez-faire in domestic policy is also subject to some limitation in Smith's proposals. He assigns three duties to the State: defence, the administration of justice, and the provision and maintenance of certain public works and institutions. He also has no objection to legal restriction on the rate of interest, although he does not prescribe this as a positive duty of the State. The first two of the three duties laid on the State would commonly be called political and not economic functions. Smith thinks of both in the traditional manner of libertarian thought; they are duties of protection. Defence is 'the duty of protecting the society from the violence and invasion of other independent societies'; the administration of justice is 'the duty of protecting, as far as possible, every member of the society from the injustice or oppression of every other member of it' (W 687). The third duty, however, goes beyond the traditional protective duties of what has been called the night-watchman State. This third duty requires the State to provide and maintain certain positive facilities for improving welfare. Smith's view is that the State should assume responsibility for those public works and institutions 'which it can never be for the interest of any individual, or small number of individuals, to erect and maintain; because the profit could never repay the expence' to them, though it may well do so to society as a whole (W 688). The public works which he has in mind are those necessary for commerce: roads, bridges, canals, harbours. When he turns to institutions, Smith thinks partly of commerce again and partly of education. Foreign trade requires

protective forts in some countries and ambassadors in all. As
for education, we have already seen that Smith believes the
State has a duty to remedy the evil effects of the division of
labour by encouraging or even 'imposing' elementary education
upon all who would not acquire it privately.

Public responsibility for such works and institutions should,
however, in Smith's view, be strictly limited to the areas where
there would not be sufficient inducement for private enterprise.
Moreover, even when facilities are publicly provided, the
maintenance and running of them should call on the normal
economic inducements for the sake of efficiency. Public
works—roads, bridges, canals, harbours—should be made to
pay for themselves, if this is possible, by means of tolls or port-
duties. This method of financing them ensures that they will be
constructed where they are needed and on the scale required by
use; otherwise they might be planned merely to suit the convenience or caprice of some powerful individual. In the actual
administration of tolls, sometimes private ownership is more
efficient, sometimes management by commissioners. For example, Smith says, there is a difference between canals and
roads. Canals will not be used unless kept in good order; a
private owner will therefore have an incentive to look after
them properly, while public commissioners might be slack. On
the other hand, roads which are not kept in good repair can still
be used, so private ownership of the tolls will not ensure proper
maintenance, while public management will. It is not easy to
see why public management cannot be equally zealous about
the maintenance of canals, so the example is not convincing,
but one can appreciate the general point that private ownership
sometimes has an adequate incentive and sometimes not.
When Smith turns to education, he warmly commends the
practice, in the Scottish universities and parish schools, of
making the income of teachers come partly from the fees of
their pupils. This gives the teacher a sense of dependency on
the pupils and induces him to put forth his best efforts. Where
the teacher has a fixed stipend, independent of the fees paid by
students, he has no such inducement; hence the slackness of
the university teachers at Oxford.

Adam Smith's faith in the virtues of natural liberty and natural equality is overdone. He looks at them through rose-tinted spectacles. The *Moral Sentiments* passage on the invisible hand is extravagant in its picture of natural equality. It says that the employment of the poor by the rich produces an almost equal distribution of the necessaries of life, and it then goes on to suggest that a near equality in 'real happiness' does not need employment anyway.

When Providence divided the earth among a few lordly masters, it neither forgot nor abandoned those who seemed to have been left out in the partition. These last too enjoy their share of all that it produces. In what constitutes the real happiness of human life, they are in no respect inferior to those who would seem so much above them. In ease of body and peace of mind, all the different ranks of life are nearly upon a level, and the beggar, who suns himself by the side of the highway, possesses that security which kings are fighting for. (M 185)

This piece of romanticism may be influenced by the egalitarianism of Rousseau, whom Smith seems to have had in mind when he wrote the whole paragraph. A trace of the same sort of optimism remains in the *Wealth of Nations* when Smith argues that all occupations, if different degrees of reward are balanced against different degrees of toil and trouble, yield an equal amount of welfare.

When he comes down to particular proposals, however, Smith does not rely on a general faith in the prowess of nature. Instead he calls on the evidence of history to show that a practice has been harmful or beneficial, and he makes detailed recommendations in the light of that evidence. The rhetoric of natural liberty and natural equality is used to add persuasive effect but not as the core of his arguments.

Smith's political economy

Smith begins Book IV of the *Wealth of Nations* with a definition of 'political economy'.

Political oeconomy, considered as a branch of the science of a statesman or legislator, proposes two distinct objects; first, to provide a plentiful revenue or subsistence for the people, or more properly to enable them to provide such a revenue or subsistence for themselves; and secondly, to supply the state or commonwealth with a revenue sufficient for the publick services. It proposes to enrich both the people and the sovereign. (W 428)

What he has written previously meets the first of the two aims of the subject. Book IV itself is a survey 'Of Systems of political Oeconomy' alternative to his own. It is comparable to the survey, in Part VII of the *Moral Sentiments*, 'Of Systems of Moral Philosophy' prior to Smith's own theory. Both surveys illustrate Adam Smith's method of making headway in a subject. He examines and criticizes earlier theories in order to advance to a sounder theory. The programme is designed to enable him to learn from the earlier theories. Smith is happy to adopt from them what he regards as sound, and in rejecting what is unsound he is led to suggest a more viable alternative.

In the *Wealth of Nations* he considers two systems of political economy, that of the mercantilists and that of the physiocrats. His criticism of the mercantilists is severe and leads to his arguments for free trade. The basic fallacy of mercantilism is set out in the first words of Chapter I, 'That wealth consists in money, or in gold and silver', instead of goods. Smith has a much warmer opinion of the physiocrats, from whom he had learned a good deal and whose basic ideas of liberty and trusting nature were close to those with which he himself began. Their 'capital error', he believed, was to regard agriculture alone as productive while manufacture and trade were unproductive (W 674). Nevertheless he was prepared to go along with them in thinking that agriculture was the most productive element in the economy. The great virtue of the French economists was that they, like Smith, had perceived the fallacies of mercantilism. His conclusion on the physiocrats was as follows.

This system, however, with all its imperfections is, perhaps, the nearest approximation to the truth that has yet been published upon the subject of political oeconomy . . . Though in representing the labour which is employed upon land as the only productive labour, the notions which it inculcates are perhaps too narrow and confined; yet in representing the wealth of nations as consisting, not in the unconsumable riches of money, but in the consumable goods annually reproduced by the labour of the society; and in representing perfect liberty as the only effectual expedient for rendering this annual reproduction the greatest possible, its doctrine seems to be in every respect as just as it is generous and liberal. (W 678)

The second of the two aims of political economy set out in Smith's definition of the subject requires a programme for taxation and other sources of public revenue. Book V of the *Wealth of Nations*, constituting well over a quarter of the whole work, is largely concerned with public finance, including proposals for raising revenue and a critical discussion of public debt. It also recognizes that the expenses required by the three duties of government raise special problems. The remuneration of members of the armed forces, of the people concerned with the administration of justice, and of those who maintain public works and public institutions (including teachers and the clergy) cannot be settled by the forces of the market. As is his wont, Smith faces these problems with a historical survey of different methods that have been tried.

When introducing the topic of taxation, Smith lays down four general maxims. First, taxes should be levied in accordance with the ability of people to pay. Second, taxes should be certain and not arbitrary. That is to say, the taxpayer should know clearly beforehand how much tax he is liable to pay and when; it should not be left to the arbitrary judgement of the tax-gatherer. Third, the time and manner of payment should aim to suit the convenience of the taxpayer. Fourth, the levying of taxes should be as economical as possible. It should avoid the waste of unnecessarily large administration; it should not kill the goose by being a disincentive to industry or by ruining evaders with stiff penalties. Smith describes these maxims as having 'evident justice and utility'. So they have, but the fact was insufficiently appreciated in his time. Not that Smith is particularly original in formulating the maxims. His teacher, Hutcheson, had said much the same thing in a summary form, and so had Smith's contemporary, Sir James Steuart, whose *Principles of Political Oeconomy* was published in 1767. As in so much else, however, Adam Smith set out with especial clarity the relation of the relevant points to his system of political economy as a whole.

This indeed is the cardinal virtue of the *Wealth of Nations*. Not all readers have shared in the general admiration of the book, and the comments of one important scholar are worth noting at this point. J. A. Schumpeter, in his monumental *History of Economic Analysis* (1954), made a number of deprecatory remarks about the *Wealth of Nations* as a contribution to economic science: 'But no matter what he actually learned or failed to learn from predecessors, the fact is that the *Wealth of Nations* does not contain a single *analytic* idea, principle, or method that was entirely new in 1776.' Yet Schumpeter felt bound to allow that the *Wealth of Nations* 'is a great performance all the same' because of its 'co-ordination'. This was intended to be rather faint praise. The task of co-ordination required 'a methodical professor' and Smith 'was fitted for it by nature'.

Schumpeter underrates the character of Smith's systematization. Methodical co-ordination of the ideas of other people could not have produced a comprehensive system of the whole economic process, all parts of which interact with each other so as to maintain a self-adjusting balance and steady growth. Smith derived much of his material from other people but it needed imaginative vision to use that material as constructively as he did. Even Schumpeter is virtually obliged to contradict himself when he describes the first leading feature of Smith's book: 'Though, as we know, there is nothing original about it, one feature must be mentioned that has not received the attention it deserves: nobody, either before or after A. Smith, ever thought of putting such a burden upon division of labour.' Whether Smith was right or wrong to do so, it was a new idea if nobody else had thought of doing it. In fact this feature of the *Wealth of Nations* is simply one aspect of the imaginative vision which Smith applied to his materials in order to build a comprehensive system. We shall see later how it links up with his own view of the imagination needed for scientific work. It is an example of the way in which Smith's philosophical interests colour his scientific work.

Schumpeter could not have seen this since he believed that philosophy has nothing to contribute to economics; it simply gets in the way. For all his great learning, Schumpeter had his blind spots. While appreciating the 'intellectual stature' of Smith's *Essays on Philosophical Subjects*, especially the essay on the history of astronomy, Schumpeter says of them: 'were it not for the undeniable fact, nobody would credit the author of the *Wealth of Nations* with the power to write them.' The words 'nobody would' mean 'Schumpeter would not'. Those who read the *Wealth of Nations* with more sympathy and imagination than Schumpeter did can see that the philosopher who began the essay on the history of astronomy with a theory of scientific systems is himself applying that theory in his construction of an economic system.

5 Comparisons

Although Adam Smith must have taken great care to find the best words for his many memorable aphorisms, he did not take enough to guard against apparent inconsistencies in his work. I said at the beginning of Chapter 3 that Smith uses the term 'sympathy' in a special sense but is liable to slip back into the common usage of the word. His special sense is the perception that an imagined feeling in oneself would correspond with an observed feeling in someone else. Smith uses this concept to explain moral *judgement*, the approval or disapproval of actions. The common usage of 'sympathy' refers to the actual experience of fellow-feeling, especially fellow-feeling with distress. This can and often does act as a *motive* of action, a motive to give aid and comfort. It is not surprising that Smith should slip back into this common usage, but it is unfortunate that he should have done so in the context of the main reference to economics in the *Moral Sentiments*. The 'invisible hand' passage in that book says that the poor obtain from the self-interested behaviour of the rich man the necessaries of life which they could not expect from his 'humanity' or his justice. Continuing the theme, Smith writes that a patriot who exerts himself for the public weal in not always motivated by 'pure sympathy with the happiness of those who are to reap the benefit', that a man who encourages the repair of roads does not usually act from 'a fellow-feeling with carriers and waggoners', and that a legislature which protects the manufacture of cloth 'seldom proceeds from pure sympathy' with the wearer, still less with the manufacturer (M 185). The word 'sympathy' is twice used as a synonym for 'humanity' and 'fellow-feeling', all these terms serving to denote a motive of action.

Scholars who have concerned themselves with the interpretation of the *Wealth of Nations* have, naturally and rightly, turned to the *Moral Sentiments* as a source of further information. Naturally, too, they have concentrated on those parts of the *Moral Sentiments* which are directly relevant to Smith's views on economics. More often than not, they have just skimmed over the rest of the book, with no particular interest in, and perhaps no particular capacity for, understanding Smith's primary aim in writing the work. They have seen that an emphasis on sympathy pervades the whole book and they have observed that the term appears, in the main passage relevant to economics, as an altruistic motive of action. The reference to an invisible hand at once recalls the same phrase in the *Wealth of Nations*, and the statement that publicly beneficial actions do not proceed from 'sympathy' recalls the aphorism of the later book that we do not expect our dinner from the 'benevolence' of the butcher, brewer, and baker. In this 'economic' passage of the *Moral Sentiments* Smith appears to go along with the doctrine of the *Wealth of Nations* about beneficial action motivated by self-interest (though in fact he is talking about the aesthetic love of order rather than simple self-interest), but using the words 'sympathy', 'fellow-feeling', and 'humanity' in place of 'benevolence'. So far, so good.

However, some of these scholars found a problem in the fact that the *Moral Sentiments* as a whole gives so much prominence to the effect of sympathy in human life. Apart from the 'economic' passage, Smith writes as if sympathy played the major part in binding society together. How, then, these scholars asked, can this be reconciled with the view of the *Wealth of Nations*, which is surely that self-interest is the mainspring of social activity and that benevolence (or sympathy) counts for nothing? This was 'the Adam Smith problem', over which much ink was spilled in the nineteenth century, mainly by German scholars, though the English historian H. T. Buckle must share in the responsibility for misunderstanding. Adam Smith's own carelessness in his use of the term 'sympathy' was a contributory factor, but if the problem-mongers had taken the trouble to read and follow the whole of the *Moral Sentiments* they would not have gone so wildly wrong.

Their assumption was that in the *Moral Sentiments* Smith took sympathy to be the most influential of human motives, while in the *Wealth of Nations* he gave that role to self-interest. Carl G. A. Knies suggested in 1853 that Smith changed his mind as the result of his visit to France between the writing of the two books. H. T. Buckle in 1861 had a different explanation. Smith did not change his mind; he was dealing with 'two divisions of a single subject', 'the sympathetic' and the 'selfish' parts of human nature, a classification which was, in Buckle's opinion, 'a primary and exhaustive division of our motives to action'.

In the *Moral Sentiments*, he ascribes our actions to sympathy; in his *Wealth of Nations*, he ascribes them to selfishness. A short view of these two works will prove the existence of this fundamental difference, and will enable us to perceive that each is supplementary to the other; so that, in order to understand either, it is necessary to study both.

Good advice, but Buckle had not taken it sufficiently to heart himself. He attached great importance to methodology and had some curious views about it. He had persuaded himself that all Scottish philosophers of the eighteenth century used deductive reasoning only and would have nothing to do with induction. Adam Smith, according to Buckle, went further still. He followed his own 'peculiar form of deduction', imitated from geometry, which required him to separate one set of premisses from another; and therefore he dealt with the two motives of sympathy and selfishness in two separate books. Buckle was presumably thinking of the fact that a theorem in geometry must confine its deductions to what follows strictly from its particular premisses. Adam Smith, in Buckle's view, began his first book with the premiss that a large class of human actions is motivated by sympathy and he was required by his method to confine himself to what is covered by that premiss; he began his second book with the premiss that the remaining class of human actions is motivated by selfishness and he had to confine himself in the second work to what is covered by that particular premiss.

This piece of fantasy was rejected by Witold von Skarżyński in 1878 on the ground that a device of logical method cannot remove inconsistency. Reverting to the view that Smith had changed his mind, Skarżyński then added his own fantasy that both of Smith's books were unoriginal anyway; the ethical theory was a botched repetition of Hume, and the economic was learned from the physiocrats. The report that Smith had included the substance of his economic doctrines in his Glasgow lectures on moral philosophy was dismissed by Skarżyński as incredible, all the more so since it included a story that these 'valuable lectures' (as Skarżyński ironically called them) were conveniently burned just before Smith's death.

The basic error lying behind all these interpretations is the supposition that Adam Smith in the *Moral Sentiments* gives sympathy a central role as a motive of action. In both books the influence of sympathy (or 'benevolence' or 'humanity') as a motive is very limited. In the *Moral Sentiments* the influence of sympathy as a binding social force of approbation is immense.

Although 'the Adam Smith problem' is a thing of the past, traces of it linger on. I do not think that anybody now says that the *Moral Sentiments* makes sympathy the predominant motive of human action in general, but one still finds able economists and historians of economic theory saying that Adam Smith regarded sympathy as the motive of morally virtuous action and self-interest as the motive of (non-moral, though not immoral) actions of economic life. In fact Smith explicitly criticizes his teacher Hutcheson for confining the motive of virtuous action to altruistic benevolence and for treating self-interest as a morally neutral motive. Smith himself thinks that rational self-interest (prudence) is a virtue from the moral as well as the economic point of view, though not one of the highest moral virtues except when it is infused with self-command, sacrificing immediate pleasure for long-term happiness. He certainly regards benevolence (or 'humanity', or 'sympathy' in the popular use of that word to denote a motive of action) as a more commendable moral virtue but he thinks that its effective occurrence is limited. He places rather more stress on other virtuous motives, self-command, the sense of duty (which he explains by his theory of the impartial spectator), and a regard to justice.

A different sort of contrast between the *Moral Sentiments* and the *Wealth of Nations* was made by the American scholar Jacob Viner in a widely praised article of 1927 called 'Adam Smith and Laissez Faire'. It is praised because it shows that Smith's support of *laissez-faire* is subject to substantial limitations and that his picture of the harmonious order of natural liberty includes a number of defects which 'would suffice to provide ammunition for several socialist orations'. Viner precedes these enlightening remarks by a review of the *Moral Sentiments* as containing a more idealized picture of the natural order which cannot be reconciled with the more mature and more realistic opinions expressed by an older Adam Smith in the *Wealth of Nations*.

He quotes at some length five passages from the *Moral Sentiments* as evidence for his view of that book. The first was in fact composed long after the *Wealth of Nations* for the enlarged version of the *Moral Sentiments*, published in 1790. It presents the idea of a benevolent God as one which has been held by many people and notably by the Stoic philosopher and Roman emperor, Marcus Aurelius. Smith says it is a helpful doctrine to those who believe it. He does not say it is true. The second passage would have been acceptable to virtually any pre-Darwinian scientist. It says that natural instincts tend to favour, more than anything else, self-preservation and the preservation of the species; it attributes these effects to an apparent intention in nature or the author of nature. The third passage is not at all idealistic. It says that the *economic* virtues of 'industry, prudence, and circumspection' commonly meet with 'success in every sort of business', with 'wealth and external honours' (M 166). This is hardly inconsistent with the *Wealth of Nations*. The passage is followed by a paragraph saying that our natural feelings would prefer to see moral virtues rewarded more than the economic virtue of industry, which can be possessed by a 'knave'. Viner detaches the subsequent passage and prints it as the last of his five quotations, presenting it as a 'concession' by Smith to the sad truth that nature can be unjust. The fact is that when the two passages are taken together, as they are given in Smith's book, they both show a fairly down-to-earth appraisal of the real world. Viner's remaining quotation, fourth on his list, is—inevitably—the invisible hand passage. This, as we have seen, does indeed end with a piece of romantic idealism about equality. It can be compared with the belief in the *Wealth of Nations* that the balance of toil and recompense is pretty well equal in all occupations, but the romanticism is more obvious in the sentence of the *Moral Sentiments* about the beggar who suns himself at the side of the road and has more security than kings who go to war.

Professor Donald Winch has drawn my attention to a later essay by Viner, in which he gave a sounder account of the *Moral Sentiments* and queried his earlier charge of inconsistency—but only on the general ground that Smith worked from systems or models and shifted from one 'partial model' to another. Viner's article of 1927 declared that in the *Moral Sentiments* Smith was 'a purely speculative philosopher', reasoning from allegedly self-evident axioms and 'failing to compare his conclusions with the facts'. One is tempted to say that nothing could be further from the truth—until one remembers Buckle and Skarżyński. Viner's original view is certainly the reverse of the truth. Smith took it for granted that Hutcheson and Hume had conclusively refuted the rationalist theories of moral philosophy which relied on reasoning from supposedly self-evident axioms. In all his work Smith followed the method of empiricism, of taking the facts of experience as the basic data and reaching general propositions by induction from them. To be sure, the *Wealth of Nations* contains a vast mass of empirical data, including much quantitative material, which the

Moral Sentiments cannot even begin to emulate. Nevertheless it is a feature of the ethics book that it relies, more than most of its genre, on examples from genuine experience, observed or gathered from works of history.

All this does not mean that the enterprise of comparing the two books is mistaken. The earlier commentators were right in thinking that the concept of sympathy is the pivot of *The Theory of Moral Sentiments*. There is indeed a need to compare the role of sympathy in that work with the role of self-interest in the *Wealth of Nations*. The comparison is best made in terms of sociology. Sympathy and imagination in the *Moral Sentiments* are the cement of human society in forming socializing attitudes. They produce approbation and disapprobation. Since pretty well all human beings enjoy esteem and dislike contempt, the effect of approbation and disapprobation is to induce conformity to social norms both in behaviour and in attitude. Even when the conscience of an individual differs from the prevalent attitude of those around him, it still, according to Smith, is a reflecting mirror of the attitude of spectators, but of spectators imagined to be as well informed as the person whom they are judging. Ethical feelings and ethical judgements reflect social solidarity and help to strengthen it.

A different kind of social bond, mutual dependence, is produced by the division of labour. We think of the author of the *Wealth of Nations* as emphasizing the role of economic man, everyone pursuing his own interest as a separate individual. We tend to forget, however, that Smith does this in the context of the need for co-operation. When Smith says that we expect the butcher, brewer, and baker to provide our dinner from self-interest, not from benevolence, he is talking about the importance of exchange. We all need the help of other people. To get it, we do not rely on their benevolence; we think of ways in which we can help them in return and we expect them to respond to that. Although Smith emphasizes the motive of self-interest, his purpose is to show us the character, and also the extent, of mutual dependence in society. The same thing comes out in his metaphor of the invisible hand. The workings of the market bring it about that the self-interested actions of individuals contribute to the benefit of all, or at any rate to the benefit of most. It is the social consequences that matter, not the individualistic cause.

The social bond created by sympathy and imagination, which plays so important a part in the *Moral Sentiments*, is quite different from the social bonds of mutual dependence described in the *Wealth of Nations* as resulting both from the division of labour and from the workings of the market. It is different but it is not inconsistent with them. The social bond of sympathy and imagination leads to our code of ethics and to a good part of our code of law. Economic behaviour, on the other hand, has to be explained in terms of self-interest. This does not imply that a person engaged in economic transactions has no regard to what other people will think of him. Apart from anything else, economic exchange depends on contract, and the legal notions about the duties and rights of contract are as much tied up with ethics as they are with economics. But in economic life the thought of social approval and disapproval takes second place to the idea of doing the best for oneself. Nevertheless, the economic motive of doing the best for oneself does in fact result in a different form of social solidarity, mutual dependence.

The sociological dimension of Smith's thought can be seen also in other parts of the *Wealth of Nations*; it is still more prominent in the *Lectures on Jurisprudence*, and can be seen to some extent even in the *Lectures on Rhetoric*. Parts of Book V of the *Wealth of Nations* are far more sociological than economic. The section about the State's duty to administer justice incorporates a summary version of Smith's theory of the four stages of society, a theory which explains that law and government proper arise in the second stage, the age of shepherds. This theory has a much larger place in the *Lectures on Jurisprudence* because Smith's main subject there is the history of law and government, economics being treated as one part of the conduct of government. Smith's emphasis upon the role of property undoubtedly foreshadows the economic interpretation of the history of society that is so prominent in Marxist thought. Recent scholarship has questioned the attribution to Smith of a 'materialist' or economic interpretation of history because Smith is not a strict determinist and also because he regards vanity as fundamentally a more influential motive than the desire for material goods. The fact remains, however, that in his account of the origin of law and government Smith highlights the causal role of property to a remarkable degree.

I should also say that the age of shepherds is that where government first commences. Property makes it absolutely necessary. . . . In the age of the hunters a few temporary exertions of the authority of the community will be sufficient for the few occasions of dispute which can occur. Property, the grand fund of all dispute, is not then known. . . . But here [i.e. in the age of shepherds] when . . . some have great wealth and others nothing, it is necessary that the arm of authority should be continually stretched forth, and permanent laws or regulations made which may ascertain [i.e. secure] the property of the rich from the inroads of the poor . . . Laws and government may be considered . . . as a combination of the rich to oppress the poor, and preserve to themselves the inequality of the goods which would otherwise be soon destroyed by the attacks of the poor. (J 208, session 1762–3)

The appropriation of herds and flocks, which introduced an inequality of fortune, was that which first gave rise to regular government. Till there be property there can be no government, the very end of which is to secure wealth, and to defend the rich from the poor. (J 404, session 1763–4)

The acquisition of valuable and extensive property . . . necessarily requires the establishment of civil government. Where there is no property, or at least none that exceeds the value of two or three days labour, civil government is not so necessary. (W 710)

It is in the age of shepherds, in the second period of society, that the inequality of fortune first begins to take place, and introduces among men a degree of authority and subordination which could not possibly exist before. It thereby introduces some degree of that civil government which is indispensably necessary for its own preservation . . . Civil government, so far as it is instituted for the security of property, is in reality instituted for the defence of the rich against the poor, or of those who have some property against those who have none at all. (W 715)

Later in the *Wealth of Nations* Smith foreshadows an economic interpretation of particular historical events in explaining why the sophists of ancient Greece were *itinerant* teachers, and why fixed academies grew up later.

The demand for philosophy and rhetorick was for a long time so small, that the first professed teachers of either could not find constant employment in any one city, but were obliged to travel about from place to place. In this manner lived Zeno of Elea, Protagoras, Gorgias, Hippias, and many others. As the demand increased, the schools both of philosophy and rhetorick became stationary; first in Athens, and afterwards in several other cities. (W 777)

Then again when he comes to discuss the role of the clergy, Smith sees an economic factor in the practices of the Roman Catholic priesthood.

In the church of Rome, the industry and zeal of the inferior clergy is kept more alive by the powerful motive of self-interest, than perhaps in any established protestant church. The parochial clergy derive, many of them, a very considerable part of their subsistence from the voluntary oblations of the people; a source of revenue which confession gives them many opportunities of improving. The mendicant orders derive their whole subsistence from such oblations. It is with them, as with the hussars and light infantry of some armies; no plunder, no pay. (W 789–90)

Smith shows a more broadly sociological outlook in his discussions of social class. In the *Moral Sentiments* he explains social status ('the distinction of ranks') as the result of sympathetic pleasure in the comforts of 'the rich and the great'. At the same time he notes that this form of approbation is apt to corrupt our properly moral approbation for wisdom and virtue. Admiration of the rich and the great leads them to care more for fashion and status ('the honour of exalted station') than for genuine virtue. In the *Wealth of Nations* Smith puts the last point in a slightly different way, relating two different codes of morality to two social classes. There is one moral code, 'the strict or austere', which is 'generally admired and revered by the common people', and there is another, 'the liberal, or, if you will, the loose system', which is 'commonly more esteemed and adopted by what are called people of fashion' (W 794).

The *Lectures on Jurisprudence* show a sociological bent throughout. Before they reach the final section on economics, they consist of a history, sociology, and philosophy of law and, to a lesser extent, of government. The three aspects go together. For Adam Smith, history and comparative sociology are the evidence from which to reach philosophical (or scientific) generalizations. However, the sociological aspect seems to come to the fore most frequently. For instance, when Smith discusses family law he shows a deep interest in the sociology of marriage and divorce, the status of women, and the historical changes in the social power of men as husbands, fathers, and heads of extended families. The most striking example, however, carried over into the *Wealth of Nations*, is his preoccupation with slavery—as a social, not just a legal, phenomenon. He is of course interested in the economics of slavery and believes that 'The experience of all ages and nations . . . demonstrates that the work done by slaves, though it appears to cost only their maintenance, is in the end the dearest of any' (W 387). But he is more profoundly moved by the persistently widespread practice of slavery.

We are apt to imagine that slavery is entirely abolished at this time, without considering that this is the case in only a small part of Europe; not remembering that all over Moscovy and all the eastern parts of Europe, and the whole of Asia, that is, from Bohemia to the Indian Ocean, all over Africa, and the greatest part of America, it is still in use. It is indeed allmost impossible that it should ever be totally or generally abolished. (J 181)

Smith's sociological interests can be seen even in his *Lectures on Rhetoric*. Professor W. S. Howell has shown that the most important feature of these lectures is their independence of tradition in widening the scope of the theory of rhetoric and adapting it to the needs of the time. This goes along with a sensitivity to the way in which different kinds of discourse are suited to the needs of different forms of society. 'The most barbarous and rude nations', such as those 'on the coast of Africa', Smith said, spend their leisure hours on dancing and singing together. For this they need to cultivate poetry but not prose. 'Tis the Introduction of Commerce or at least of opulence which is commonly the attendent of Commerce which first brings on the improvement of Prose' (R 137). Smith went on to suggest that differences in style between the speeches of Demosthenes and those of Cicero, or between the philosophical dialogues of Plato and those of Cicero, were related to the different social structures of Athens and Rome at the relevant times.

The Nobleman of Rome . . . would see . . . 1000 who were his inferiors for one who was even his equalls . . . As he spoke generally to his inferiors he would talk in a manner becoming one in that Station. . . . His discourse would be pompous and ornate and such as appeard to be the language of a superior sort of man.

At Athens on the other hand the Citizens were all on equall footing; the greatest and the meanest were considered as being noway distinguished, and lived and talkd together with the greatest familiarity. . . . It is observed that there is no Politeness or Compliments in the Dialogues of Plato; whereas those of Cicero abound with them. . . .

These considerations may serve to explain many of the differences in the manners and Stile of Demosthenes and Cicero.—The latter talks with the Dignity and authority of a superior and the former with the ease of an equall. (R 158–9)

In all his sociological discussions Smith draws his evidence from history and from such social anthropology as was available to him. That is to say, he used the comparative method. Like other thinkers of the Scottish Enlightenment, he learned the method from Montesquieu. He also took some of his evidence from Montesquieu, but he added a great deal more from other sources. The range of his evidence for comparative law, for example, is much wider than one would suppose. He had as a matter of course a fair stock of knowledge about Roman and Scots law. He acquired in addition a reasonable knowledge of English law and put it to good use for purposes of comparison.

One also finds, however, in his *Lectures on Jurisprudence*, references to particular laws or institutions in ancient Athens and Sparta, ancient Germany (as reported by Tacitus), among the Hebrews of the Old Testament, the 'Tartars', the tribes of the Guinea coast, and the American Indians, in modern France, Holland, Switzerland, Lombardy, Russia ('Moscovy'), Venice, the East Indies, Persia, Turkey, Egypt, China, and Japan. As any modern sociologist would agree, the comparative method is a thoroughly sound way of trying to reach scientific generalizations. This needs to be borne in mind when one considers Smith's attitude to nature and natural law. His evidence was often insufficient to give scientific backing to his hypotheses; but the errors to which he was led by his use of the comparative method are less gross than those of the commentators, discussed earlier in this chapter, who misunderstood the evidence in their comparisons of the *Moral Sentiments* with the *Wealth of Nations*.

6 *Philosophy, science, and history*

'Scratch a Scotsman and you will find a philosopher', says the old adage. Tom Stoppard gave it continued currency when, in his play *Jumpers*, he made the Scottish university porter as acute at philosophical criticism as the Professor of Moral Philosophy. Perhaps Adam Smith had such a porter in mind when he said that the native abilities of a philosopher and a porter were almost equal (J 348, 493). The Scottish university tradition of philosophy for all had in fact a marked impact in the eighteenth century and infected the thought of a wide variety of educated men. The lectures of a leading scientist like Joseph Black no less than the books of a leading lawyer like Lord Kames contain an undercurrent of genuine philosophical enquiry. Adam Smith himself began his professional career as a philosopher and remained a philosopher all his life. While it turned out that his finest gifts lay in the field of economics and social science, he never lost his philosophical interests. As late as 1785 he was still planning to complete 'a sort of philosophical history' of literature and philosophy, and in his last years he gave a great deal of effort to the revision and expansion of the *Moral Sentiments*. According to Sir Samuel Romilly, he 'always considered his *Theory of Moral Sentiments* a much superior work to his *Wealth of Nations*'. If he did, his judgement was at fault but the report confirms his abiding love for philosophical enquiry.

Smith would not have recognized any clear distinction between philosophy and the social sciences, or for that matter between philosophy and natural science. Generally speaking, he uses the two terms 'philosophy' and 'science' almost interchangeably. There is one place in the *Wealth of Nations* (796)

where he appears to imply a distinction between them, writing
of 'the study of science and philosophy'. He goes on in the same
paragraph to say that 'Science is the great antidote to the poison
of enthusiasm and superstition'. He has been talking about
religion and religious ethics; the phrase 'enthusiasm and superstition' means religion. Earlier in the chapter Smith has said
that much post-Christian moral philosophy has pandered to
absurd doctrines of religion. I think this is why he now implies
a distinction between philosophy and science. Some philosophy can be irrational, and so Smith, for the moment, thinks of
science as not quite the same; it is that kind of enquiry which
conforms to empirical fact. Generally, however, Smith would
call such enquiry a form of philosophy, reputable philosophy,
whether it was dealing with the material world or with human
behaviour.

For Smith, a 'philosopher' is a reflective observer, who can
think of connections that allow theoretical explanation or practical invention. He gives a virtual definition in the first chapter
of the *Wealth of Nations* (21), where he writes of inventions
being made by 'those who are called philosophers or men of
speculation, whose trade it is, not to do any thing, but to
observe every thing; and who, upon that account, are often
capable of combining together the powers of the most distant
and dissimilar objects'. His 'philosophers or men of speculation' are not just armchair speculators, although they are contrasted with men of action. James Watt, no less than Sir Isaac
Newton, is a 'philosopher', as Smith uses the term. In corresponding passages of earlier versions of this thought, Smith
refers to the 'philosopher' who invented the 'fire engine' or 'fire
machine' (J 347, 349, 492, 570). Scientists and technologists, no
less than philosophers in the modern sense of the word, are
'men of speculation' who have the leisure to observe widely and
to make connections which would not occur to others. The
connections may be physical, metaphysical, or social. In the
Wealth of Nations (674) Smith refers to Quesnay as 'a physician, and a very speculative physician', because he thought of
'the political body' after the analogy of the human body. In the

Moral Sentiments (136) Smith imagines what our reaction would be if the whole of China were destroyed by an earthquake: after initial sorrow for the widespread distress, a 'man of speculation' might 'enter into many reasonings concerning the effects which this disaster might produce upon the commerce of Europe, and the trade and business of the world in general'. If it were Voltaire thinking about the Lisbon earthquake, he would reflect on the implications for theology. If it were Adam Smith, he would reflect on the implications for the world economy.

Philosophy, science, and social science were all the same sort of activity for Smith. In the manuscript that W. R. Scott has called an 'Early Draft' of the first part of the *Wealth of Nations*, Smith has a list of different kinds of 'philosophers'— 'mechanical, chymical, astronomical, physical, metaphysical, moral, political, commercial, and critical [i.e. writers on literary theory and aesthetics]' (J 570). They all have the same sort of aim, to make connections between diverse phenomena, but they do not all pursue the same sort of method in finding the relevant phenomena. All rely on observation, their own and that of others. Most natural scientists, however, will not need to depend much on the recorded observations of the past, i.e. on history, and can often repeat in their own laboratories observations reported by others. Social scientists have to rely much more on history and on the reported observations of others in addition to their own. Adam Smith was a keen, and generally an accurate, observer but he knew very well that his own observations could supply only a minute portion of the data he needed, whether for economics or sociology or moral philosophy. In all three areas he relied heavily on historical investigation as well as on the reports of contemporary enquirers. As I have said in Chapter 2, his favoured method of finding his feet in a subject was to study its history and then, after critical examination of earlier theories, to make his own contribution by improving upon them. The purpose of Smith's historical investigations, whether he was studying the history of events or the history of theories, was to acquire the data necessary to back up or refute a generalization, a hypothesis about a possible scientific law.

Soon after the death of Adam Smith, Dugald Stewart wrote an account of his life and writings for the Royal Society of Edinburgh. It was then reprinted as an introduction to Smith's *Essays on Philosophical Subjects*, published in 1795. In the course of it Stewart coined the phrase 'theoretical or conjectural history' to describe Smith's procedure in much of his work. Stewart was led to his remarks on this topic when he came to record the printing of an essay by Smith, 'Considerations concerning the First Formation of Languages', as an appendix to the third (Stewart said the second) and subsequent editions of the *Moral Sentiments*. The essay is worked up from a shorter treatment of the subject in Smith's lectures on rhetoric. Stewart said that while this essay on the origin and development of languages was interesting in its own right for its ingenuity, it deserved attention more, in his survey of Smith's work, 'as a specimen of a particular sort of inquiry' which could be 'traced in all his different works, whether moral, political, or literary' (P 292). Stewart did not, however, suggest that 'theoretical or conjectural history' was peculiar to Smith; he said it had been pursued by several modern thinkers from Montesquieu onwards. But the phrase has stuck in subsequent discussion of Adam Smith.

The adjective 'conjectural' is misleading if taken (as it has been by some) to imply that Smith invented some of his data and called the result history. One could say this of the essay on languages, which does include a good deal of speculation based simply on logical categories—though it also makes use of empirical facts about the languages which Smith knew and it is trying to make its way towards a scientific comparative philology concerning the structure of Greek and Latin and that of modern European languages. One might also say that the four stages theory of the history of society reaches its hypothesis of historical sequence on the basis of rather scanty evidence. There is, however, very little that is speculative or conjectural in Smith's other historical discussions, whether of ethical theory, of law and government, or of science and metaphysics. Stewart explicitly mentioned Smith's essay on the history of astronomy (together with a comparable, slightly later, history of mathematics by the French scholar J. E. Montucla) as an example of what he meant by 'theoretical history'; he used the alternative adjective 'conjectural' only once, when introducing the description, and then continued with 'theoretical history' alone. There is absolutely nothing conjectural about Smith's *history* of astronomy. It consists of firm, and on the whole reliable, data of definite empirical fact about the various theories of astronomy which have been held from Eudoxus to Newton. The essay, however, can properly be called a theoretical history (or better, as Smith described the unfulfilled project which would have included it, 'a sort of philosophical history') because it draws on the history of science as evidence for a philosophy of science. Similarly, one may say, Smith uses the history of law, government, and economics as evidence for generalizations in the theory or philosophy of law, government, and economics.

The essay on the history of astronomy shows us how Smith viewed the relation between history and theory. We should remember that he, like others of his time, made no clear distinction between philosophy and science. When he used historical evidence to support generalizations in 'political economy', present-day scholars might call those generalizations theories or hypotheses in 'economic science' or 'political science'. So far as Smith was concerned, there was no difference of substance between the principles for making headway in 'natural philosophy' and those for making headway in 'moral philosophy', including 'jurisprudence' and 'political economy'. As we shall see, the process requires the use of imagination, and so one may say that Stewart's suggestion of conjecture was not altogether misplaced; but Stewart did mislead by implying that the conjecture or imagination was used to supply missing historical data. Smith's view is that imagination is needed to fill up the gaps in a proposed *system*, a theory or model which tries to unify the data obtained by observation. Moreover, it is an exercise of imagination that is to be found in science at its best.

Smith's long essay 'The History of Astronomy', in *Essays on Philosophical Subjects*, deserves to rank with the *Wealth of Nations* and the *Moral Sentiments* as the work of an outstanding mind. In writing it Smith was one of the originators of the history and philosophy of science. On the historical side the work is remarkably well informed for its time and even today its information remains largely accurate. It is also genuinely philosophical, both in the pattern which it draws out of the historical facts and even more in its explanation of the changes from one type of scientific theory to another.

Smith starts off with the traditional view of Plato and Aristotle that philosophy (or science) begins in wonder. But he immediately elaborates this into a psychological theory that intellectual discomfort with what is unfamiliar leads on to the removal of the discomfort when we can find connections again with what is familiar. A modern scholar might describe the situation with the statement that an apparently unusual event is explained by showing it to be, not an isolated individual thing, but an instance of a general law. Smith concentrates on the psychological effects, first of surprise at the oddity, and then of relief at assimilating it with the familiar after all. A scientific theory (in astronomy or anything else) satisfies by removing intellectual discomfort at oddity. But oddity is not the only reason for intellectual discomfort. If we are to feel at ease with a recurring pattern, it must be relatively simple. Once it becomes complex, the recurrences are less easy to grasp, less familiar, and so less comfortable. When a scientific theory (for instance the Ptolemaic account of astronomy) has grown very complex in order to accommodate all the observed phenomena, we are dissatisfied once more and are prepared to welcome a different, simpler, sort of theory (like the Copernican). But of course the simplicity may have to be bought at a price. In the case of the Copernican theory we have a simpler pattern but we must adjust ourselves to a new suggestion which is exceedingly unfamiliar, namely that the Earth is in motion. So we need a development of theory which will remove our discomfort, indeed our shock, at that unfamiliarity.

This psychological explanation of the development of science or philosophy is itself, for Adam Smith, a piece of philosophy. It is in line with the interpretation of philosophy that he learned from Hume. At the heart of Smith's explanation is an account of the functions of the imagination, which comes straight out of Hume but is adapted from Hume's theory of our belief in a persisting external world and is used instead to show how scientific theory builds a framework to fit on to observed phenomena. Hume had said that the imagination fills in the gaps between observed 'impressions' (the data of perception) so as to produce the supposition of a permanent object. For example, I see a white oblong shape in front of me at 10.05; I go away, and when I come back at 10.10, I see a similar white oblong shape. My imagination fills in the gaps which occur in a series of such impressions and gives me the idea of a continuing material object, a sheet of paper, which exists both when I am in this place looking at it and when I am not. Smith adapted Hume's theory so as to apply it to scientific hypotheses about unobserved entities. The imagination fills in the gaps between observed phenomena (such as the Sun, the Moon, the Planets, and the Fixed Stars) and produces the supposition of a great 'machine' (such as a system of crystalline spheres containing the observed heavenly bodies but being themselves unobservable because they are crystalline and so transparent).

Smith evidently regards all scientific and philosophical systems as products of the imagination.

Systems in many respects resemble machines. A machine is a little system, created to perform, as well as to connect together, in reality, those different movements and effects which the artist [i.e. the practical man, as contrasted with the theorist] has occasion for. A system is an imaginary machine invented to connect together in the fancy those different movements and effects which are already in reality performed. (P 66)

Scientific theories or systems are imagined structures which connect together observed movements and other events. The systems are not themselves actualities of nature, or at least we cannot know them to be such. A theory or system is preferred, Smith says, because it suits the propensities of the human mind, not because it is the only one which accommodates the observed phenomena.

He was struck especially by the change of attitude among scientists towards Descartes's theory of vortices. As Smith saw the history of astronomy, the Copernican hypothesis scored over its predecessors by its simplicity but faced an enormous psychological obstacle with its implication that the Earth was subject to two sets of motion at very high speed. The difficulty was not the mere idea that the Earth was in motion, contrary to all appearances of rest. For the learned at least, the trouble was rather that earlier theory had represented any motion of ponderous bodies as slow, while the Copernican hypothesis required us to suppose that the daily rotation of the Earth round its own axis meant, for any point on the equator, a speed of a thousand miles an hour, faster than a cannon-ball or even than the speed of sound, and that the orbital motion of the Earth round the Sun was faster still. Descartes's theory of vortices became popular because it tried 'to render familiar to the imagination, the greatest difficulty in the Copernican system, the rapid motion of the enormous bodies of the Planets' (P 96). In due course, however, Newton's system gave a more satisfying account and Descartes's theory became an 'exploded hypothesis'.

Consequently Smith was quite ready to understand that Newton's theory might not be the last word. He ended his essay by recalling, with some difficulty, that his account of science as the work of the imagination must apply to Newton's theory no less than to earlier systems.

And even we, while we have been endeavouring to represent all philosophical systems as mere inventions of the imagination . . . have insensibly been drawn in, to make use of language expressing the connecting principles of this one, as if they were the real chains which Nature makes use of to bind together her several operations. Can we wonder then, that it should have gained the general and complete approbation of mankind, and that it should now be considered, not as an attempt to connect in the imagination the phaenomena of the Heavens, but as the greatest discovery that ever was made by man, the discovery of an immense chain of the most important and sublime truths, all closely connected together, by one capital fact, of the reality of which we have daily experience. (P 105)

It was indeed a remarkable feat on the part of Adam Smith to be able, in the 1750s, to think of Newton's account of the solar system as a theory that could be replaced, and not as a statement of objective fact. He could do so because of his view that all theoretical systems depend on the imagination.

There is no reason to suppose that Smith regarded systems of economic theory as any different in this respect from systems of natural philosophy. One may be tempted to think otherwise when one recalls his remark that the physiocratic system was 'the nearest approximation to the truth' that had previously been published in economics. This seems to imply that there is a 'truth' to be reached. But it is simply a natural way to speak when you are immersed in a discussion of the relative merits of different theories in a particular discipline. Smith certainly thought that the physiocratic system was superior to mercantilism in its explanation of the observed facts, just as he thought, like everyone else, that the Newtonian system was superior to that of Descartes. He noted in 'The History of Astronomy' that he had been naturally led, like others, to speak of the Newtonian system as a discovery of objective truth. So too in the *Moral Sentiments* he wrote that a system of natural philosophy, such as that of Descartes, may be accepted for a long time 'and yet have no foundation in nature, nor any sort of resemblance to the truth' (M 313). This implies that the system of Newton does have a foundation in nature and at least a resemblance to the truth. But when Smith stands back and considers the whole class of theoretical systems, he distinguishes them from the actual, or at any rate the knowable, facts of nature.

It follows, then, that Smith would say of his own system of economics what he says of the Newtonian system of astronomy. It is sounder than its predecessors but it is still a theoretical system, a product of the imagination, not a description of 'real chains which Nature makes use of to bind together her several operations'. The 'gravitating' of market prices towards the natural price, the 'invisible hand' which 'leads' self-interested agents to promote the public interest, the apparent force of 'natural liberty' and 'natural equality'—these are all products of the imagination which help us to connect observable facts but are not themselves facts or realities that might be observable or otherwise knowable. Nevertheless they are, in Smith's view, an aid to understanding; in order to make connections, science needs its 'imaginary machines'. The author of the *Wealth of Nations* is of a piece with the philosopher who wrote 'The History of Astronomy' and *The Theory of Moral Sentiments*. The *Wealth of Nations* is his masterpiece and shines by its own light, but it is further illuminated when it is linked with the other two works.

References

8   *Letters of James Boswell*, ed. C. B. Tinker (Oxford, 1924), 46; quoted by J. C. Bryce, introduction to *Lectures on Rhetoric and Belles Lettres, 34.*

12 Edward Westermarck, *Ethical Relativity* (London, 1932), 71.

12 H. T. Buckle, *History of Civilization in England* (London, 1857–61), i. 194; cf. ii. 443.

13 John Rae, *Life of Adam Smith* (London, 1895), 5.

19 Ibid. 57.

20 Ibid. 170, quoting A. F. Tytler.

23 Ibid. 211–12.

26 Ibid. 287

29 Ibid. 405.

36 A. L. Macfie, *The Individual in Society* (London, 1967), 66.

67 The log of the *Prince George*, quoted by Ronald Faux, 'Swallowed in the Swirling Sarcophagus', *The Times*, 16 Oct. 1982, Saturday Supplement, 1.

76 J. A. Schumpeter, *History of Economic Analysis* (New York, 1954), 184–5, 187, 182

80 H. T. Buckle, op. cit. ii. 432–3, 437.

81 W. von Skarzyński, *Adam Smith als Moralphilosoph und Schoepfer der Nationaloekonomie* (Berlin, 1878), 6–7, 53.

82 Jacob Viner, 'Adam Smith and Laissez Faire', *Journal of Political Economy* xxxv (1927); reprinted in Viner, *The Long View and the Short* (Glencoe, Ill., 1958).

83 Jacob Viner, 'Adam Smith', in *International Encyclopedia of the Social Sciences* (New York, 1968).

86 Determinism and 'materialism': see Donald Winch, *Adam Smith's Politics* (Cambridge, 1978), 57, 81; and more particularly Knud Haakonssen, *The Science of a Legislator* (Cambridge, 1981), 181–7.

88 W. S. Howell, 'Adam Smith's Lectures on Rhetoric: An historical assessment', *Speech Monographs* xxxvi (Nov. 1969); reprinted in *Essays on Adam Smith*, ed. Andrew S. Skinner and Thomas Wilson (Oxford, 1975).

91   Sir Samuel Romilly, *Memoirs* (London, 1840), i. 403; quoted by
     Rae, op. cit. 436.
93   W. R. Scott, *Adam Smith as Student and Professor* (Glasgow,
     1937), xxii, 317.

Further reading

The *Wealth of Nations*, *The Theory of Moral Sentiments*, and 'The History of Astronomy' (in *Essays on Philosophical Subjects*) are all works which can be read with pleasure by non-specialists. They are edited with textual and explanatory notes and introductions in The Glasgow Edition of the Works and Correspondence of Adam Smith (Oxford, 1976–83). The *Wealth of Nations* was admirably edited for an earlier generation by Edwin Cannan in 1904 (London) and his introduction and notes are still of great value. Undergraduate students of economics will probably find it most convenient, as well as economical, to acquire the Pelican Classics volume containing Books I–III of the *Wealth of Nations*, edited by Andrew Skinner (Harmondsworth, 1970) with a long, lucid introduction.

John Rae's *Life of Adam Smith* (London, 1895; reprinted with additional material by Jacob Viner, New York, 1965) is very enjoyable. A more comprehensive and up-to-date work, *The Life of Adam Smith*, by Ian Simpson Ross (Oxford, 1995), is now the authoritative biography. The biographical chapters of *Adam Smith* by R. H. Campbell and A. S. Skinner (London, 1982) contain some information that was not available to Rae (or Viner). This book also includes clear, concise surveys of Adam Smith's writings and lectures. It can be thoroughly recommended to all readers—not only novices—who are interested in Adam Smith. A similar short book, *Adam Smith: The man and his works* by E. G. West (New York, 1969), is lively but not always accurate.

For Smith's ethics the one indispensable work of interpretation is T. D. Campbell, *Adam Smith's Science of Morals* (London, 1971).

The amount of published commentary on the *Wealth of Nations* is enormous. For relative beginners I would recommend particularly: Andrew S. Skinner, *A System of Social Science: Papers relating to Adam Smith* (Oxford, 1979, second edition 1996), and Mark Blaug, *Economic Theory in Retrospect* (Homewood, Ill., 1962, but preferably the third edition, Cambridge, 1978), ch. 2. Blaug's chapter is not only for beginners; it also relates Smith's theories to those of later economists in a fairly sophisticated way. Samuel Hollander, *The Economics of Adam Smith* (Toronto, 1973), is a more elaborate discussion, though not easy reading. *The Market and the State: Papers in honour of Adam Smith*, edited by Thomas Wilson and Andrew S. Skinner (Oxford, 1976), reviews themes of the *Wealth of Nations* as they appear in our own time.

Another collection, associated with the Glasgow edition of Smith's works, *Essays on Adam Smith*, edited by Andrew S. Skinner and Thomas Wilson (Oxford, 1975), deals with all aspects of Adam Smith's writing and teaching.

Malthus

Donald Winch

In grateful memory of
Patricia James, 1917–87

Acknowledgements

I have been extremely fortunate in being able to call upon the knowledge of two of the leading Malthus scholars of our day, Patricia James and John Pullen, whose magnificent editions of the *Essay on Population* and the *Principles of Political Economy* are now available and have set a new standard in these matters after years of neglect. In addition to using these editions in draft form, I have also had the benefit of their comments on this foray into a subject on which they have both worked for many years. I am also grateful, as on so many occasions in the past, for the suggestions for improvement made by two friends, Stefan Collini and John Burrow. Any remaining errors of fact, tact, and interpretation are my responsibility.

D. W.

Contents

Abbreviations

The following abbreviations are used when citing references in the text.

FE   The first edition of *An Essay on the Principle of Population* (1798) as reprinted in facsimile by Macmillan for the Royal Economic Society, edited by J. R. Bonar, 1926, reprinted 1966.

E   *An Essay on the Principle of Population*, Cambridge University Press for the Royal Economic Society, 1990, a variorum edition compiled and edited by P. James in two volumes.

Pr   *Principles of Political Economy*, Cambridge University Press for the Royal Economic Society, 1990, a variorum edition compiled and edited by J. M. Pullen in two volumes, the first of which contains the edition published in 1820.

P   *The Pamphlets of Thomas Robert Malthus*, Augustus M. Kelley, New York, 1970.

R   *The Works and Correspondence of David Ricardo*, Cambridge University Press for the Royal Economic Society, edited by Piero Sraffa and M. H. Dobb in eleven volumes, 1952–1973.

PJ   Patricia James, *Population Malthus; His Life and Times*, Routledge and Kegan Paul, London, 1979.

Q   Article on 'Political Economy', *Quarterly Review*, January, 1824, XXX, 214–334 as reprinted in *Occasional Papers of T. R. Malthus*, edited by B. Semmel, Burt Franklin, New York, 1963.

1 *Reputation*

Robert Malthus's name is chiefly and irrevocably linked with what he was the first to present as a universal and perpetual dilemma: he maintained that the prospects for permanent improvement in the condition of the mass of society in all countries was placed in a precarious balance by an unequal race between the hare of population growth and a tortoise representing the power to expand food production. 'Malthusian', as a result, has become a permanent part of our vocabulary, still much used in scientific and popular debate on the problems of population growth in the Third World, as well as by environmentalists who treat the balance between population and exhaustible resources as a global problem. But this book does not deal—except perhaps indirectly—with these twentieth-century dilemmas and the ways in which they have been or might be resolved. Its main focus will be on the man who, rightly or wrongly, has had his name attached to them. More especially it is concerned with the writings of Malthus (1766–1834) considered against the background, mostly in the late eighteenth century and first third of the nineteenth century, which first gave prominence and point to his ideas.

Treated as a practical demographer, as someone attempting to explain actual population trends in order to propose measures designed to achieve more desirable rates of population growth, the significance of Malthus's ideas lay primarily in their defeat of a long-standing tradition which had automatically linked a large and growing population with economic progress and national power. For Malthus, a large population might only be a reflection of earlier prosperity and a warning of imminent danger of falling living standards. After Malthus, therefore, the idea that rapid population growth was always desirable could never be upheld without an attempted rebuttal of his views; and in the process it was frequently overlooked that for Malthus too population growth could be advantageous under some circumstances. While evidence has subsequently accumulated to show that the hare has usually been far less swift than he supposed, and that the tortoise is capable of such a remarkable turn of speed in some countries that we are now embarrassed by food surpluses, Malthus is still recognized as having created the terrain over which demographic dispute continues to rage, forcing those who dislike or disagree with his conclusions to argue over issues which he was the first to dramatize.

Demography in the modern sense of the term, however, was never Malthus's sole concern, and it is certainly not the only reason for the persistent attention paid to his writings. From a broader, more political perspective, Malthus's main claim to fame, or notoriety, rests on his decisive attempt to undermine the doctrine of human perfectibility, and Utopian speculations of an egalitarian or communistic nature. He still serves as the figure most responsible for revealing the anxieties that are supposed to lie at the heart of political and economic liberalism. He marks the moment when optimism regarding the prospects for social improvement turned sour and fatalistic, serving to dampen hopes by reminding us of the narrow limits within which any progress is possible, with the result that his population theory has become the hallmark of all that is sombre and 'dismal' about the laws of political economy. Moreover, since one of the earliest conclusions which Malthus drew from his findings was a denial of the right of the poor to relief under the English Poor Laws, 'Malthusian' has become a byword for those harsh *laissez-faire* social policies which equated poverty with moral failing. A fear of falling in the social scale appeared to replace the opportunity to rise as the leading motive of men in society. Mass poverty and existing inequalities between rich and poor were seen as an indelible part of the human condition, capable only of being remedied by forms of individual prudence and self-help that were unlikely to be adopted or even to be available to the mass of society until their living standards had already risen.

As Malthus was only too well aware, we do not love the bringer of bad tidings, especially when the message concerns something as inherently controversial as family life and population. One has only to think of the enraged tone of twentieth-century debates on abortion and contraception to be reminded of this fact: members of the First World who recommend policies to control the growth of Third World populations run the risk of being charged with genocide. Malthus's position has probably generated more vituperation, vilification, and misunderstanding than that of any comparable figure in the history of social and political thought. It has driven many of those who have written about him into a defensive or apologetic stance from the outset, and his work continues to invite the rehearsal of moral outrage and superior humanity—an invitation many still find difficult to resist some one hundred and sixty years after his death.

One simple explanation for the misunderstanding and dislike provoked by Malthus lies in the sheer immodesty of his basic propositions. The principle which he enunciated with such force was a universal one, capable of explaining the past, present, and future condition of mankind, wherever it was to be found. Malthus did not claim to have discovered this principle—the idea that population expands up to the available subsistence was something of an eighteenth-century commonplace. But anyone who illustrates its operation with such thoroughness, emphasizing the vice and misery which it inevitably generates, must expect to arouse staunch counter-claims and to have his motives subjected to close scrutiny. From the outset too, the question of population was connected with a number of potentially inflammatory themes: the reasons for economic inequality; the role of self-interest as opposed to benevolence in human affairs; whether man's destiny could be described as progressive or merely as a perpetual oscillation between narrow limits; the role of the passions, especially the passion between the sexes; whether man should for some crucial purposes be assimilated to the animal or botanical world, despite his capacity for free will and virtuous conduct—a formidable version of the ancient conflict between Nature and Culture. There was also, for a Christian civilization in which Malthus, himself an Anglican clergyman, was to become a significant figure, the major question of how belief in a benevolent deity could be squared with the existence of widespread poverty and misery that was only loosely or problematically connected with sinful conduct. Many of these moral questions are matters of life and death in the most literal sense, and it is one of the more interesting features of Malthus, and certainly one that will be stressed here, that he consistently attempted to combine the viewpoint of moralist and objective scientist.

The inherently explosive quality of the topic may help to explain, even if it does not excuse, the number of fundamental untruths about Malthus's views that were given currency during his lifetime. He was accused of being an enemy to all population growth; of proposing prohibitions on marriage by the poor; of maintaining that nothing should be done to reduce infant mortality or improve health standards; of recommending war, pestilence, and disease, and other forms of vice and misery as checks; of advocating immediate abolition of the right to assistance under the Poor Laws on the sole grounds that this was necessary in the interest of reducing the burden of poor rates on the rich; and of denigrating all forms of benevolence and private charity. In addition to being accused of currying favour with the rich by relieving their consciences about the poor, he was later to be charged with being the hired spokesman of the landed gentry when he spoke in favour of the Corn Laws, a measure which he thought would have a positive effect in raising food supplies and living standards.

After his death such charges were embellished by Marx and Engels, among others, and hence have continued to feature in the works of their followers up to the present day. Thus for Marx, Malthus represented all that was retrograde in bourgeois society. He was both a plagiarist and 'a bought advocate' who elevated the temporary historical laws of bourgeois society into eternal natural laws of the human condition. His ideological role lay in diverting the attention of the working class from the true reasons for its shameful condition under capitalism. It was the continual recruitment of the 'reserve army' by means of labour-saving technology that kept the labour market over-stocked, rather than that 'insult' to the intelligence of the working class, the principle of population. The power of capital itself, rather than any attempt to regulate the supply of labour, was responsible for creating the conditions necessary for ex-ploitation. 'A shameless sycophant of the ruling classes' was thereby added to charges of having, at one and the same time, put forward a set of truisms, and depicted human nature in degrading terms—charges levelled, often in vehement fashion, by such early critics of Malthus as William Cobbett, Samuel Taylor Coleridge, Robert Southey, William Hazlitt, and Thomas Carlyle.

The list of Malthus's admirers and converts is, however, equally long and impressive. These included many of the lead-ing politicians of the day from the younger Pitt onwards, as well as most political economists, whether of a Christian or secular frame of mind. Malthus continued to answer those critics who maintained that he had perpetrated an elaborate blasphemy in calling God's word ('Be fruitful, and multiply') and beneficence into question, and he took pride in having converted William Paley—one of his teachers and the leading Anglican interpreter of the political and social order—to his views. After John Bird Sumner, later to be Archbishop of Canterbury, published his *Treatise on the Records of Creation* in 1816, a work specifically designed to show the 'consistency of the Principle of Popula-tion with the Wisdom and Goodness of the Deity', Malthusian ideas became a standard feature of the social teachings of the Established Church, attracting the interest of some lead-ing evangelical intellectuals: Edward Copleston (Bishop of Llandaff), William Otter (Bishop of Chichester), and Richard Whateley (Archbishop of Dublin). It was also from the ranks of the divines that Malthus acquired his most fervent disciple in the shape of the Scottish preacher and professor Thomas Chalmers, whose sermons and prolific writings were probably responsible for more converts than anything Malthus himself ever wrote.

Many of those who approached political economy from a more secular perspective adopted Malthus's population principle as the foundation for their position on wages, the causes of poverty, and the need for fundamental changes in the Poor Law. This was especially true of David Ricardo, James Mill, and his precocious son, John Stuart Mill. The *Edinburgh Review*, the Whig organ which became the most important contemporary arena for rehearsing new ideas on political economy, and to which Malthus contributed several articles, consistently upheld his position and attacked that of his opponents. There were respectful criticisms of Malthus's priorities and way of expressing his principle from within the orthodox political economists' camp in the 1830s, notably by Nassau Senior, later to be one of the main authors of the Report of the Royal Commission on the Poor Laws in 1834; and what amounted to a retraction of his earlier support by John Ramsay McCulloch, another of Ricardo's followers. But John Stuart Mill, reviewing the situation in the 1840s, nearly half a century after Malthus's first writings on population, put up a stout defence of the population theory against its critics, treating it as the beginning of all sound thinking on the subject of wages and mass poverty: 'Though the assertion may be looked upon as a paradox, it is historically true, that only from that time has the economical condition of the labouring classes been regarded by thoughtful men as susceptible of permanent improvement.'

Mill's influence as the leading liberal philosopher and political economist of his day ensured a renewed lease of life for the Malthusian principle as the key to higher per capita incomes during the third quarter of the nineteenth century. But his use of control over population growth as a major criterion for judging the likely future success of socialist and communist alternatives to present society was representative of a new phase in the history of Malthusianism—a phase more accurately described as Neo-Malthusianism. For Mill, like his father before him, was an advocate of birth control within marriage, a solution which Malthus regarded as immoral and likely to diminish the sum of human happiness. Moreover, in Mill's hands, an argument which began life as an attack on the viability of communistic societies became associated with the case for social experiment along just those lines.

Malthus's population principle also acquired a new career when it was revealed that both Charles Darwin and Alfred Russel Wallace were indebted to their reading of Malthus for insight into the mechanisms underlying natural selection and the struggle for survival in the plant and animal kingdom, thereby setting on foot a complex interchange of ideas between the social and biological sciences. An argument based on human ecology, showing the adaptive response of human beings to variations in their environment, and making use of strategic comparisons with the biological and botanical world, was reappropriated by biology as part of an evolutionary perspective that had, or was taken to have, considerable significance for the study of social evolution.

Population and agriculture were Malthus's main point of entry into the larger issues posed by political economy, a field of inquiry that was still dominated by Adam Smith's *Wealth of Nations* when Malthus made his first contributions to the subject. For the first two decades of the nineteenth century he was the single most prominent figure in the development of the new science. In addition to making the problem of wages and food prices under conditions of economic growth central to what subsequently became known as classical political economy, he made original contributions to the fundamental laws which were held to underlie rent, profits, and capital accumulation.

In dealing with Malthus's reputation as a political economist it is important to recognize that he was addressing himself to a number of controversial questions in a historical context which gave them special point. Thus his first *Essay on Population* (1798) appeared in an atmosphere that was still dominated by the French Revolution and all that this *événement* entailed in terms of hopes of dramatic improvement in the human condition as a result of changed political institutions. It also appeared four years after and two years before two major periods of acute scarcity in the availability of grain, the price of which was the main determinant of the living standards of most wage-earning families. In 1801 the first of the decennial censuses appeared, revealing that British population, contrary to a common belief shared by Malthus, had been growing rapidly during the second half of the eighteenth century; it was to reach its maximum rate of increase during the period in which Malthus was producing successive editions of his *Essay*. The second and subsequent editions of the *Essay* (1803–1826) also appeared during the Napoleonic Wars and their aftermath, a period characterized by a puzzling combination of economic signals: the emergence of Britain as a dominant commercial and manufacturing power under conditions of economic warfare, rising taxation, and national indebtedness; a period in which agriculture enjoyed prosperity as a result of high food prices and rents, but when it was also becoming clear that Britain had become a net importer of foodstuffs and might only be able to support her growing population from domestic sources at ever-higher prices, and by acquiescing in the unprecedented shift of occupational pattern towards foreign trade, urban employments, and manufacturing. Above all, the signs of prosperity were accompanied by burgeoning expenditure under the Poor Laws to support the growing numbers of able-bodied labourers requiring public relief. From almost every point of view, therefore, Malthus was responding to circumstances in which major and troubling structural changes in Britain's economic life were taking place; when fundamental choices were being posed between a future in which Britain might have to rely on manufacturing strength, and hence capacity to export, to support a growing population, and one in which legislative intervention might be required to achieve a balance between agriculture and industry on moral, strategic, and economic grounds. Malthus was inclined towards the latter solution, and with hindsight we can see that he was, on the one hand, the crucial figure posing the dilemmas mentioned above, while on the other hand being, broadly speaking, on the losing side in the prolonged dispute which they occasioned.

The main challenge to Malthus's ideas on political economy came from David Ricardo, and much of the history of the subject during the first quarter of the nineteenth century is contained in the remarkable public and private disputes conducted by these two close friends. The controversy covered all the main laws or principles of the infant science and their application to the urgent policy questions of the day, with Ricardo gradually establishing ascendancy—partly by a narrower form of economic logic, and partly as a result of the proselytizing activities of his followers.

One of the recurrent topics in the Malthus–Ricardo dispute concerned the explanation for post-Napoleonic Wars distress. Malthus treated this as a problem of general glut or depression, attributable to a deficiency in 'effective demand', though his diagnosis was also bound up with longer-term issues connected with the maximum rate at which capital accumulation and growth could take place. Reviewing this dispute in the light of his own concerns with unemployment in the 1930s, John Maynard Keynes saw in Malthus a worthy predecessor whose attempts to counter Ricardian ideas mirrored his own struggle to escape from economic orthodoxy. Hence Keynes's remarkable conclusion that: 'If only Malthus, instead of Ricardo, had been the parent stem from which nineteenth-century economics proceeded, what a much wiser and richer place the world would be today!' Just as Malthus played a part in stimulating Darwin during the process which resulted in the *Origin of Species* (1859), so this different aspect of his work features in the story of Keynes's *General Theory of Employment, Interest, and Money* (1936).

Whatever the merits of Keynes's judgement, he was certainly correct in suggesting that if history is only to be written from the victors' point of view a good deal will be lost, not least from the victors' case, by not understanding how the choices were originally posed. The vicissitudes of Malthus's reputation will be reconsidered in the concluding chapter, after the evidence of what he was actually contending in his various writings has been reviewed and interpreted. But first we must consider the outline of his biography, trusting that his character and the nature of the man will gradually emerge from the ensuing treatment of his opinions.

2 *Life*

Malthus was born on 13 February 1766, the second son and sixth child of Daniel Malthus, a well-to-do, eccentric country gentleman with serious, if somewhat scattered intellectual enthusiasms which included science, foreign literature, botany, and a fervent admiration for the works and character of Jean-Jacques Rousseau. Robert was educated initially by a clergyman friend of his father, but at the age of 16 was sent to the Dissenting Academy at Warrington, where he lived with and was taught by Gilbert Wakefield, a leading and controversial figure in the Unitarian movement following his resignation from the Church of England in 1779. This was an unusual step for Malthus's father to take, for although his son was not the only pupil of Wakefield to come from an Anglican background, Robert was destined from an early age to take up a career in the Church of England. The decision to send him to be educated by Dissenters with 'advanced' views is an interesting sign of his father's own position, as well as being of some consequence to the son's writings later.

In 1784 Malthus went up to Jesus College, Cambridge, the college at which Wakefield had been a Fellow. Here, too, Robert's path crossed with Dissenters of a radical turn of mind: one of his tutors was William Frend, who, just after Malthus left Cambridge, was removed from his Fellowship for publishing an attack on the civil disabilities imposed on Dissenters by the Test Acts, as well as for opposing the war with the new French Republic.

Malthus's main studies at Cambridge centred on mathematics, and he emerged as Ninth Wrangler in 1788. Despite a speech defect resulting from a cleft palate, he was ordained immediately after leaving university, and first took up a curacy at Okewood near his family's home in Albury, Surrey. In 1793 he was elected to a non-residential Fellowship at Jesus College. During the ten years that followed graduation, therefore, Malthus lived the quiet life of a country curate, carrying out the modest duties of his post, and completing what had already been a thorough yet leisurely education, while continuing to live with his parents and two unmarried sisters.

In 1796 Malthus made an abortive attempt to publish a political pamphlet entitled *The Crisis, a View of the Present State of Great Britain, by a Friend to the Constitution*. The recorded fragments of this provide a few valuable insights into Malthus's early opinions, but it was not until two years later that he managed to appear in print, though as yet anonymously, as the author of a work bearing the following title: *An Essay on the Principle of Population as it affects the future Improvement of Society, with Remarks on the Speculations of Mr. Godwin, M. Condorcet, and other Writers*. The book had humble domestic origins in a dispute with his Rousseauist father, but it was to catapult its 32-year old author into the limelight for the first time, and provide him with the subject which dominated his life and subsequent writings.

The success of what was essentially a polemical work dashed off in a fairly short time without access to many sources induced Malthus to make a more thorough investigation of the historical and demographic record in order to document his position more fully. Extended tours of Scandinavia in 1799, and of France and Switzerland in 1802, were partly undertaken in order to collect additional information on the subject of population. The result of these labours was the appearance in 1803 of a second and much enlarged edition of the *Essay on the Principle of Population* with a modified and more positive subtitle: *A View of Its Past and Present Effects on Human Happiness, with an Inquiry into our prospects respecting the Future Removal of the Evils which it Occasions*.

In the same year Malthus became Rector of Walesby in Lincolnshire, a permanent living from which he drew an income for the rest of his life. This enabled him to marry in 1804, at the age of 38; three children were born to a marriage which provided the peaceful domestic setting for the rest of Malthus's life. These facts may be of some significance when dealing with someone whose main solution to the population problem lay in deferred marriage. An equally important fact, however, was his appointment as Professor of History and Political Economy at the East India Company's College in Hertfordshire, established in 1805 for the training of boys aged 15 to 18 who wished to enter the Company's civil service. The appointment, the first of its kind in England, provided Malthus with an opportunity to make political economy his profession as well as his hobby. While this post conferred financial security, it was purchased at a heavy price in terms of the time and effort he frequently had to devote both to quelling riotous pupils and to the defence of the college's existence and autonomy against its numerous critics.

In his first *Essay*, when dealing with the contribution, as he saw it, of the English Poor Laws to the spread of pauperism, Malthus broached a policy question which was to become the chief focus of public debate on poverty in the period which led up to the Poor Law Amendment Act of 1834, an Act which he was widely considered to have god-fathered. He also contributed to a debate on another topic that was at the head of the agenda of political economy for the next three or four decades, when he published a pamphlet on the *High Price of Provisions* in 1800. In addition to producing successive editions of his *Essay* (six in all, the last appearing in 1826), he wrote topical pamphlets on the Corn Laws and the nature of rent, and articles on monetary problems and Ireland.

Although these publications established Malthus as one of the leading political economists of his day, he did not produce a comprehensive statement of his position on the principles of political economy until 1820. For some years he hoped to bring out an edition of Adam Smith's *Wealth of Nations* that would have incorporated the original ideas on political economy which he had developed in the course of his teaching at the East

India College. This project had to be abandoned in 1814 when a rival edition of Smith's classic appeared, the first of several opportunities to put his views before the public in a reasonably coherent form which Malthus either missed or mishandled—a fact which is of some significance to his reputation both then and later. Thus, while Malthus had by the end of the Napoleonic Wars in 1815 assembled in characteristically untidy fashion many of the ingredients for a distinctive set of Malthusian variations on Smithian themes, he was increasingly aware of growing divergences between his own theoretical and practical opinions and those of other political economists, notably Ricardo, with whom he had been in regular correspondence for a number of years. Ricardo had rapidly assimilated Malthus's theories of population and rent in his own contribution to the Corn Law debates in 1815, but he put them to quite different uses: first to attack, rather than defend the Corn Laws, and secondly, to construct a model of economic growth and distribution which was to provide the foundation for his *Principles of Political Economy* published in 1817, with further editions appearing in 1819 and 1823. From this point onward, therefore, Malthus found himself having to combine exposition of his own ideas with responses to those of Ricardo and his followers. His own version of the *Principles of Political Economy considered with a View to their Practical Application*, as well as two shorter books on the *Measure of Value* (1823), and *Definitions in Political Economy* (1827), became attempts to combat the theoretical and methodological presuppositions of Ricardo and the 'new school of political economy' which was being formed around Ricardo's ideas. Malthus died in 1834, having been only partially successful in this enterprise. The appearance of a posthumous second edition of his *Principles* in 1836 did little to revive a reputation that had been overshadowed by that of his friend. When John Stuart Mill undertook a comprehensive restatement of the principles of political economy in 1848, he did so along Ricardian lines, praising Malthus for his pioneering work on population, but otherwise treating him as someone who had unfortunately lent his authority to an error on a fundamental question, namely the possibility of general over-production.

As the remarks of Keynes cited at the end of the previous chapter indicate, this was by no means the final judgement on the subject. But the first question posed by Malthus's biography must be: how did this obscure and mild-mannered curate come to be the author of a work that was to scandalize so many people?

3 *Population: the first* Essay

The first *Essay*, as its subtitle makes clear, was designed as a contribution to the debate on 'the future improvement of society', and more especially as an answer to the visionary speculations of William Godwin and the Marquis de Condorcet on this subject. None of the fundamental issues raised by the debate was entirely novel: the innate characteristics of man as opposed to what could be attributed to his social circumstances and political institutions; whether his fate could be described as progressive or cyclical; the relationship between rich and poor in society; and whether population growth represented an insurmountable barrier to prospects for permanent social improvement—all this and much else that featured in the controversy had been rehearsed in detail by moral philosophers, theologians, and political speculators during the second half of the eighteenth century. But the debate which Malthus joined in 1798 had acquired heightened significance by virtue of the fact that Godwin's *Enquiry Concerning Political Justice* (1793) and Condorcet's *Esquisse d'un tableau historique des progrès de l'esprit humain* (1795) had appeared during the period of political upheaval initiated by the French Revolution.

In this respect Malthus's first entry into the lists can be compared with another famous contribution to the debate aroused by events in France, namely Burke's *Reflections on the Revolution in France* (1790). Indeed, many have seen Malthus's first *Essay* as an integral part of the campaign against pro-French or Jacobinical literature begun by Burke; as a counter-revolutionary tract for the times, delivering what is perhaps a more shattering blow to hopes of improvement in man's temporal fate through political reform than Burke's furious denunciation of those abstract thinkers who had brought such ruin on France and threatened to do the same in Britain. Both men certainly bequeathed to their successors powerful arguments in favour of the established order; and the antagonism which Burke aroused among radical circles in the 1790s was maintained against Malthus for a much longer period, and by critics drawn from a wider political spectrum which included 'romantic' conservatives and, later, socialists, as well as political radicals. When seen in this counter-revolutionary light, Malthus provides a far less defensive argument for the status quo than can be inferred from Burke's *Reflections*. The conservative forces appear to have gone onto a permanent offensive.

In a history of popular ideologies these similarities between Burke and Malthus have something to be said for them; but they do not prepare the reader for the stance adopted by Malthus in his *Essay*. For whereas Burke appeared in the guise of an enraged critic, Malthus presented himself as a calm and dispassionate seeker after scientific truth in the accepted Newtonian manner; as a friendly arbitrator in what he described as the 'unamicable contest' between those speculative philosophers who entertained dreams of unlimited improvement, and those advocates of the present order (he probably had Burke in mind) who defended abuses from a partisan perspective. Malthus spoke as one who 'ardently wished' to believe in the kind of improvements held out by Godwin and Condorcet, as someone who was 'warmed and delighted' by the portrait of man's future which they had painted. Unfortunately, his regard for scientific truth would not allow him to share their dreams. Since false hopes were being entertained on the basis of faulty diagnoses of the present state of affairs, he had reluctantly taken up his pen to oppose them.

This was not an ironical pose on Malthus's part. It consorts well with the origins of the first *Essay* in an argument with his father, and with the fact that Malthus, as a result of the peculiarities of his early education, was brought up within precisely those radical dissenting circles that were the target of much of Burke's anger and provided the background out of which

Godwin's anarchistic, free-thinking, but anti-revolutionary work emerged. Malthus should also be regarded as a seeker after scientific truth because of, rather than despite, his clear theological commitments. Although his Cambridge education was aimed at producing a clergyman, this was tantamount, in the circumstances of the day, to producing a Newtonian natural and moral philosopher capable of subjecting all theories to the test of observation and experiment. Malthus's quest for a middle way between opposed doctrines, his search for the 'golden mean', and his respect for the claims of both abstract reason and experience were characteristic of the way in which he approached all subjects in his later writings. The first *Essay*, therefore, reveals a great deal about his later work, despite the changes that were later to be made to Malthus's opinions on population and related matters of political economy.

Although written hastily and published anonymously, the first *Essay* pursues a complex polemical strategy. It begins with an exposition of the principle of population treated as a set of deductive propositions; and it then proceeds to show how historical and empirical evidence lend support to the abstract principle. Secondly, the implications for egalitarian and perfectibilist schemes in general, and those of Condorcet and Godwin in particular, are spelled out in what also amounts to a short treatise on scientific method according to the accepted Newtonian model. Thirdly, an argument is mounted against Adam Smith's theory of economic growth which is of great significance to the later development of Malthus's views on political economy, and will therefore be considered in that context (Chapter 5). Fourthly, there is a concluding exercise in theodicy designed to show why the 'disheartening' results of the operation of the natural laws previously expounded are entirely compatible with belief in a beneficent deity. Though often treated as an embarrassing and detachable part of the *Essay*, this theodicy contains essential clues to the form of theological utilitarianism which underlies Malthus's moral philosophy.

The principle of population

Malthus took his stand on three propositions. First, that population cannot increase without the means of subsistence; second, that population invariably increases when the means of subsistence are available; and third, that 'the superior power of population cannot be checked without producing misery or vice' (FE 37). The first two of these propositions he took as established truths, with the reader being referred to the writings of David Hume, Adam Smith, and Robert Wallace on this point. His own contribution to the subject lay in drawing attention to the precise ways in which population growth had in fact been limited by the operation of a series of checks which entailed vice and misery in one form or another.

The deductive argument required two postulates: the necessity of food to man's existence, and the assumption that the passion between the sexes was both necessary 'and will remain nearly in its present state' (FE 11). Malthus also posited that the power of population to grow was 'indefinitely greater' than the power of the earth to produce subsistence. He illustrated this inequality by means of a contrast between the geometric power of population increase and the arithmetic power of improvements in food production. Applied to Britain in 1798, with an assumed population of 7 million (it was actually well over 10 million), the two series would look as follows: population had the power to double every twenty-five years (from 7 to 14 to 28 to 56 million by 1883), but food production could only increase by a constant factor (from 7 to 14 to 21 to 28, half the amount that would be needed to support the population in 1883). Since the two unequal powers must be equated in some way, one should look to the means by which the difficulty in acquiring subsistence constantly exerts a check on population—a check that must fall mainly on the great mass of mankind at the bottom of society's pyramid.

The checks came in two forms, positive and preventive. The former reveal themselves in higher mortality rates and lower life expectancy, the latter operate by means of voluntary retraint on birth-rates. Both entail misery and vice, misery being a necessary consequence, vice—a category designed to hold the casualties in the eternal struggle between good and evil—being a probable result. War, pestilence, and famine were the main positive checks; abortion, infanticide, prostitution, and other 'unnatural' attempts to accommodate the constant passion between the sexes while avoiding the consequences, counted as preventive checks. The principle of population, therefore, showed that no society, present or future, could guarantee that all its members 'should live in ease, happiness, and comparative leisure', feeling 'no anxiety about providing the means of subsistence for themselves and families' (FE 17).

Here was Malthus's dilemma locked in what he sometimes treated as an 'impregnable fortress' of Euclidian logic. He then proceeded to argue, as Rousseau and other eighteenth-century writers on the theme of inequality had done, from an assumed state of simpler and purer human nature. Let us imagine a state of equality, simple manners, and virtue, a state in which misery and vice were unknown. In such a state, population, through early marriage and reproduction uninhibited by any concern for rising or falling in the social scale, would increase at its maximum possible rate, a situation that could actually be observed in the United States where population doubled every twenty-five years. It might be possible to double the production of the means of subsistence in the first twenty-five years, but could it be quadrupled in the next, as would be required if population growth continued at the maximum? Clearly not, in Malthus's opinion. And since food was necessary to existence, a widening gap could not be allowed to develop. Long before this the positive and preventive checks would be at work keeping population down to subsistence. Nor was this proposition confined to isolated states that might gain temporary relief through emigration; the analysis could be extended to cover the globe as a whole.

In the world of plants and animals unrestricted increase was counterbalanced by overcrowding and failure of the excess to survive. In man the capacity for reason and foresight acted as a preventive check. Thus in the present state of society prudence would take account of such matters as the effect of marriage and reproduction on future independence and rank, the possible need to work harder, and the life-prospects of any offspring. In some respects, therefore, there had been progress and improvement on the earlier savage state, where the positive checks operated with full force. Despite such prudential considerations, however, population increase placed the lower classes of every society under constant pressure of want and distress as a result of food scarcity, falling wages, and increasing toil.

What Malthus had in mind was a form of cycle arising from delayed responses, periods of good times associated with high wages leading to early marriage and population increase, followed by bad times in which distress brings population increase to a halt. At the bottom of the cycle the cheapness of labour would act as an encouragement to food production, thereby restoring the balance between population and resources to the original position. It is a model of 'perpetual oscillation' rather than unilinear progress, and while it is possible for the oscillations to occur around a rising trend, there was no guarantee that this would be the case. The oscillatory path entails the persistence for the mass of misery and vice at some point in each of the cycles—'the same retrograde and progressive movements with respect to happiness are repeated' (FE 31).

Why then had these permanent rhythms gone unnoticed? Malthus's answer was that the phenomenon was probably more irregular in real life than his model suggested; that the histories of mankind which had been written so far had largely concentrated on the higher classes, rather than on those whose lives were most subject to the cycles; and that in any case a proper study of the subject required 'the constant and minute attention of an observing mind during a long life' (FE 32). It entailed close attention to marriage rates, the incidence of 'vicious customs', the comparative mortality of the children born to the poor, and a general comparison of wages and the living standards of the poor over time. Moreover, the process would not be a regular one: it would be constantly spurred on or interrupted by causes of a more or less temporary nature—by agricultural and commercial success and failure; by wars and pestilence; by 'the invention of processes for shortening labour without the proportional extension of the market for the commodity' (FE 34); and by the way in which the movement of money wages usually lagged behind changes in the price of food. To this list Malthus added the operation of the Poor Laws, a subject which was later to occupy a good deal of his attention.

Malthus was quite right in believing that such an extended study of the empirical circumstances attending the lives of the mass of society had only just begun. A pioneering treatment of *The State of the Poor* by Sir Frederick Morton Eden had appeared the year before Malthus's *Essay*, but the official decennial census of population did not begin until 1801. Nevertheless, Malthus's agenda gives a precise foretaste of his own enquiries and methods of procedure during the rest of his life.

The first *Essay* draws on simple ethnographic evidence to show that the principle of population operates among North American Indians and the Hottentots, as illustrated by the constant state of war and famine in which they lived, as well as by the hardships endured by their women. The idyll of the noble savage in a conjectured state of nature would be short-lived; and the actual state of savage man fell far short of nobility.

In modern Europe, where agricultural improvements had occurred, population had grown; but in Malthus's opinion it had been growing at a slow rate (doubling over a period of 300 to 400 years). This could be accounted for by resort to the preventive check of delayed marriage by the middle and upper classes, and by the operation of both preventive and positive checks on the lower classes. Malthus drew attention to infant mortality rates and the stunted growth of children in rural England—subjects on which he could comment on the basis of his experience as a country curate. He also regarded the growth of 'unwholesome' manufacturing towns, with their crowded conditions and proneness to epidemics, as another sign of the operation of his principle. But the most striking evidence of the pressure being exerted by population in England was to be found in the growth of expenditure on poor relief, currently standing at about £3 million per annum. (It had doubled over the previous two decades and was to reach over £8 million by 1815.) In the short term, this redistribution from rich to poor, under conditions either of food scarcity or low elasticity of supply in response to price increases, merely increased the competition for available supplies. In the long term, the availability of relief as of right had the more disastrous effect of lowering wages and encouraging early marriage among those without the prospect of supporting children by their own efforts and income. Hence the conclusion that the Poor Laws 'in some measure create the poor which they maintain', and its corollary that 'dependent poverty ought to be held disgraceful' because '[a] labourer who marries without being able to support a family, may in some respects be considered as an enemy to all his fellow-labourers' (FE 86).

At this stage of his inquiry then, before any reliable census data was available, Malthus was inclined to believe that the British population was growing slowly and that, despite improvements in agriculture and the rise of manufacturing, standards of living or, more generally, 'happiness and virtue', had not improved greatly during the previous century—a conclusion which was, as we shall stress in a later chapter, in marked contrast with Adam Smith's far more optimistic account of the same phenomenon since 1688. Malthus agreed with Smith, however, in regarding the United States of America as peculiarly favoured by the abundance of cheap land and high wages, by the absence of tithes and other agricultural hindrances such as primogeniture, and by the possession of 'a greater degree of liberty and equality'. Here truly was an exception that proved the rule, a society where 'population increases exactly in the proportion that the two great checks to it, misery and vice, are removed; and [where] there is not a truer criterion of the happiness and innocence of a people, than the rapidity of their increase' (FE 107–8). Nevertheless, even new countries like

America could not expect to escape indefinitely from the principle of population. A man 'might as reasonably expect to prevent a wife or mistress from growing old by never exposing her to the sun or air' (FE 343). As we shall see, however, Malthus recognised that while 'perpetual youth' could not be sustained, it was possible, through unwise policies, to produce a state of 'premature old age'.

The anti-utopian argument

In criticizing Condorcet and Godwin, Malthus naturally concentrated on those matters on which his opponents could be found in agreement: a broadly Rousseauist attribution of social evils to imperfections in man's political arrangements; a common assumption that reason, benevolence, and greater equality were likely to characterize the society of the future; and considerable convergence in their speculations on the subject of increased life expectancy and the remoteness and remediable nature of any future population problem. Malthus was fully justified in placing the works of Condorcet and Godwin side by side as evidence of a radical Enlightenment belief that, as a result of the French Revolution and 'the great and unlooked for discoveries that have taken place of late years in natural philosophy', high expectations were being entertained 'that we were touching on a period big with the most important changes that would in some measure be decisive of the future fate of mankind' (FE 2).

Condorcet and Godwin reflected another feature of post-Revolutionary thinking that can be attributed to the violent course of events after 1792. It was expressed by Godwin in the preface to a set of essays he published in 1797 under the title of *The Enquirer*. There he spoke of the early mood induced by 'the principles of Gallic republicanism' as one of 'exaltation and ferment', when 'the friends of innovation were somewhat imperious in their tone'. He wished to announce his retreat to a 'more patient and tranquil' position. Faced with a violent present reality, one might say, it was now necessary to sustain the original hopes released by the Revolution by calmer and more philosophical speculations on the prospects for a golden future that was to be achieved by peaceful means, through reason and sincerity. There are good grounds for believing that Condorcet, living closer to that violent reality, and becoming a victim of it when he died in prison in 1794, shared Godwin's aims.

But there are also differences between Condorcet and Godwin which can best be briefly expressed by saying that Condorcet's vision was more technocratic, emphasizing the role to be played by the application of scientific knowledge to the reconstruction of society from above, an aspect of the idea of progress which he passed on to his French successors, Saint Simon and Auguste Comte, the founders of nineteenth-century sociology constructed along positivist lines. Godwin's ideal society, by contrast, is informed by an anarchistic vision which rejects authority, even when benevolently constituted, and is more ambivalent in its attitude towards economic complexity and technical progress. Moreover, Godwin's work was a contribution to the British political debate provoked by French developments: an answer to Burke, but no less so to Thomas Paine and those impetuous 'friends of innovation' whose revolutionary ideas Godwin wished to repudiate along with Burke's defence of the aristocratic status quo. In these and other respects, Malthus was more closely engaged by Godwin than by Condorcet, and was sometimes to be found in agreement with him.

Godwin's Utopia was based on a belief that government, along with legal coercion and all deferential relationships that were not based on true merit, would gradually give way to a regime based on frankness, sincerity, simplicity, transparency, and respect for individuality and privacy. Vice was merely a species of ignorance. All those corrupt institutions which prevented man's natural goodness from manifesting itself would sink under the weight of their own imperfections in the face of enlightened opinion. All inequalities between rich and poor, the main sources of crime and civil disarray, would disappear, as would the alienating effects of the division of labour and a system whereby the many were enslaved by their need to labour in order to produce luxuries consumed only by the few. In a society where 'no man is to apply to his personal use more than his necessities require', mutual benevolence would replace more possessive forms of property, which included the institution of marriage. By eliminating the artificial wants associated with inequality, and by dividing the labour of the community more equally and simply, the working day could be reduced to less than two hours for all, thereby allowing attention to be focused on the disinterested pursuit of communal rather than individual welfare.

Godwin had fully anticipated the Malthusian objection before it had been penned by answering Robert Wallace's *Various Prospects of Mankind, Nature and Providence* (1761), a work upon which Malthus was later to draw. Wallace had advanced a Utopia based on common ownership, but had forecast that under a perfect system of government there would be no constraint on population growth, with the result that, at some future point, 'mankind would encrease so prodigiously, that the earth would at last be overstocked, and become unable to support its numerous inhabitants'. In the absence of any acceptable expedient for controlling population, Wallace concluded that his Utopia would destroy itself and force a return to 'the same calamitous condition as at present'. Godwin's answer to Wallace was that various checks would prevent population from increasing beyond the means of subsistence, some involving delayed marriage, others involving abortion, infanticide, and celibacy. But if these checks proved inadequate, three-quarters of the globe was still uninhabited and there was ample scope for agricultural improvement: 'Myriads of centuries of still increasing population may pass away, and the earth be yet found sufficient for the support of its inhabitants. It were idle therefore to conceive discouragement from so distant a contingency.'

With progress, too, 'mere animal function' would be replaced by more cerebral pleasures. Condorcet had addressed himself to this problem, but had suggested birth control as a solution rather than a waning of the passion between the sexes. To both of Malthus's opponents, then, population pressure was either a remote prospect or something that could easily be overcome when it arose. It was a distinctive mark of Malthus's interpretation of the problem , however, that it was 'imminent and immediate' rather than in the future. Moreover, most of the remedies mentioned by Condorcet and Godwin entailed recourse to expedients which Malthus regarded as examples of vice and misery.

Condorcet had speculated about 'organic perfectibility', a state that would be achieved through improvements in diet, medicine, and other physical changes in modes of life. While these would not abolish mortality, they could prolong life expectations indefinitely. Godwin's hopes for the prolongation of human life centred more on the enhancement of intellectual powers and the growing hegemony of mind over body. Such conjectures were an affront to the Newtonian in Malthus; they broke a fundamental rule of scientific inquiry by reasoning from causes to possible effects, rather than from observed effects to possible causes. They were a reversion to the 'wild and eccentric hypotheses of Descartes' (FE 159). Facts should not be made to bend to hypotheses, and Nature should not be treated as mutable. Malthus could see no evidence for indefinite life expectancy; the whole speculation was based on the fallacy that because the limits of human life were undefined, because they had increased in the past, therefore they could be extended almost at will. Malthus could not help thinking that his opponents, having rejected the religious promise of eternal life, had found it necessary to invent immortality on this earth as a compensation. He also defended belief in the immortality of the soul from the charge that it was mere conjecture on a par with the speculations he had rejected. On such matters, where no scientific authority could be derived from experience , reasoning from analogy was defensible. And if we saw around us so much evidence of a supernatural power, why should we not suppose this power to be capable of resurrecting the physical body? But it is perhaps a mark of Malthus's strong commitment to the Newtonian method that he concentrated most of his attack on matters that could be settled by recourse to experience rather than revelation.

Malthus treated Godwin with great courtesy as the author of 'the most beautiful and engaging' (FE 174) system of equality produced so far. One of the features most admired by Malthus was its reliance on benevolence and 'the unlimited exercise of private judgment' rather than on solutions imposed by the community at large. In these respects Godwin had been responsive to one of the main objections raised against earlier schemes of equality, namely that individual liberty of action and conscience had to be sacrificed to the egalitarian and communitarian ideal. Godwin himself had condemned Rousseau's invocation of 'civic religion' on these grounds, and Malthus and Godwin shared a belief that human dignity derived from self-exertion and the exercise of discretionary foresight in managing personal affairs—a mark perhaps of the common Dissenting origins of their views.

Godwin's 'great error', according to Malthus, lay in 'attributing almost all the vices and misery that are seen in civil society to human institutions' (FE 176). Even so, it is worth noting that Malthus does not deny Godwin's contention that *some* institutions prolong or worsen economic conditions. Although the rich were incapable of preventing the 'almost constant action of misery upon the great part of society', and even their elimination in a state of equality would bring no respite, Malthus acknowledged that the rich were sometimes guilty of 'unjust conspiracy' (FE 36) against the labouring poor. He also accepted that the abolition of primogeniture might bring benefits by equalizing property and increasing the number of agrarian proprietors; and he conceded that the present degree of inequality could not be justified. Clearly Malthus was driven by the logic of the dispute to give as much to his opponent's arguments as possible, while still denying the conclusion. But there seems no reason to believe that he was not expressing his own opinions in making these concessions, which form a prologue to the ingenious *reductio* he was to apply to Godwin's vision.

Let us suppose a society in which all men are equal and living in a state of healthy abundance and simplicity. The ease of gaining subsistence and forming early attachments, without the constraint of monogamy, would ensure a rapid growth of population. What happens when all land is under cultivation, and all improvements have been tried? Will the spirit of benevolence and co-operation survive? Once this situation arises, the 'mighty law of self-preservation' will reassert itself with a vengeance. Scarcity and questions of desert re-enter the picture. Benevolence can no longer be exercized out of superfluity, only out of necessities. The division of land and private property would have to be invented. Exchange would replace gift relationships. Men would be held responsible for the children they had fathered, and later generations would come into a world in which everything had been appropriated. Those without property would have to offer their labour services to those with property, and accept that what they were offered depended on a demand/supply relationship based on the food surplus and the available number of workers. This outcome would not be the result of depravity but of 'inevitable laws of nature', and the end result would be a return to the fundamental features of existing society, a 'society divided into a class of proprietors, and a class of labourers, and with self-love for the main-spring of the great machine' (FE 207).

Much of Malthus's negative critique is couched in terms of this demonstration that Godwin's scheme, whereby unnecessary labour would be abolished and labour divided equally, was incapable of being realized on a permanent basis. However, a more assertive position was also being advanced which can be understood initially as a decisive, though in itself hardly novel, attack on Rousseau's argument against civilization and the corrupting effects of property, inequality, self-interest, and vanity. Here again, though, Malthus started from a position that was close to that adopted by Godwin, who had also rejected Rousseau's invocation of the savage state as an ideal.

Godwin attributed Rousseau's error to his decision to invert an infamous paradox, originally propounded by Bernard de Mandeville, whereby the advantages of civilized life (public benefits) were inextricably linked with individual pursuit of the objects of luxury and vanity (private vices). Godwin agreed thus far with Mandeville in believing that luxury and inequality was a state through which it was necessary to pass on the way to a higher form of social organization: 'But though inequality were necessary as the prelude to civilization, it is not necessary to its support. We may throw down the scaffolding, when the edifice is complete.'

It was this form of the critique of the status quo that Malthus set out to undermine with the following riposte:

It is to the established administration of property, and to the apparently narrow principle of self-love, that we are indebted for all the noblest exertions of human genius, all the finer and more delicate emotions of the soul, for everything, indeed, that distinguishes the civilized, from the savage state; and no sufficient change has as yet taken place in the nature of civilized man, to enable us to say, that he either is, or ever will be, in a state, when he may safely throw down the ladder by which he has risen to this eminence. (FE 286–7)

Malthus was answering Godwin by recourse to arguments derived from Adam Smith's more philosophically and morally respectable version of Mandeville's arguments on the connections between private vice and public benefit: his demonstration that under a system of free barter and exchange, self-love and social good could be reconciled; and that liberty, and material and cultural progress were best served by prudence and accumulation. Godwin had attacked Smith indirectly when he rejected the 'system of optimism', whereby 'seeming discords' were held to contribute to 'the admirable harmony and magnificence of the whole', and 'the intellectual improvement and enlargement we witness and hope for' was treated as 'worth purchasing at the expense of partial injustice and distress'.

Malthus simply inverted Godwin's claims by commending Smith's system of natural liberty as the only practical way of reducing inequality and dividing the necessary labour of society without employing force or having recourse to unacceptable forms of dependence. On this matter at least, Malthus was united with Condorcet, who had also endorsed Smith's system and conceded that the society of the future would still be dependent on those who maintained themselves by the sale of their labour. Acceptance of this lay behind Condorcet's proposals for a compulsory system of public insurance designed to iron out any inequalities arising from this source. Nevertheless, it is important to stress an earlier point, namely that Malthus did not proceed to give an optimistic account of man's present and future prospects. His defence of Smith on the question of self-love was in fact to be an overture to an attack on a central feature of the *Wealth of Nations*—where, paradoxically, Malthus remained close to Godwin in doubting whether economic growth was always advantageous to the mass of society.

Another of Godwin's faults, according to Malthus, lay in his over-emphasis on the intellectual as opposed to corporeal elements in man's nature, his faith that reason and truth would always prevail over man's vices and moral weaknesses. Malthus held that many of the influences which affect moral character could not be controlled; they are beyond our will. Our efforts to improve might grow stronger, but we shall not succeed in eliminating vice. Godwin had conjectured that the passion between the sexes, like all inferior passions, would wane. Malthus took the view that pure love and the sensual pleasures connected with it neither could nor should be ousted by intellectual pursuits. The latter, like any single source of pleasure, were equally subject to exhaustion or diminishing returns, and he closed this argument with one of his more pessimistic predictions, namely that 'the principle argument of this essay tends to place in a strong point of view, the improbability, that the lower classes of people in any country, should ever be sufficiently free from want and labour, to attain any high degree of intellectual improvement' (FE 217–18). How large this group would be, and under what circumstances members of the lower classes could be released from this condition, was to occupy a great deal of Malthus's attention in later editions of the *Essay*.

From Nature up to Nature's God

The 'melancholy hue' of the *Essay*'s conclusions led Malthus on, or rather back, to more fundamental questions of natural theology in a pair of concluding chapters outlining a theodicy capable of reconciling divine general providence with the existence of 'partial evils' associated with population pressure. Although some of Malthus's arguments in this theodicy departed from contemporary Anglican orthodoxy, the methodological underpinnings of the exercise conformed both with the Newtonianism of eighteenth-century natural theology, and the established principles of Anglican social apologetics. Society, no less than the physical and biological universe, was the creation of natural laws established by God with man's ultimate welfare in view. Hence the obligation to 'reason from nature up to nature's God, and not to presume to reason from God to nature'. Malthus had already charged Condorcet and Godwin with not following this precept when they speculated about 'why some things are not otherwise, instead of endeavouring to account for them, as they are' (FE 350).

Malthus maintained that this world should be seen as one in which man has been placed under the pressure of want in order to 'awaken inert, chaotic matter, into spirit' (FE 353). The wants of the body are the first stimulants to action, and necessity is the mother of invention, overcoming the listlessness that would otherwise prove destructive of improvement. Without the pressure of population upon subsistence, man would never have left the savage state; and if the pressure could ever be permanently abated, man would sink back into a state of torpor and lose all the advantages of civilization. The argument relies on a form of theological utilitarianism, proximately derived from the work of William Paley, in which pain-avoidance, as much as active pleasure-seeking, becomes the motor force of action. Pain and pleasure have their moral equivalents in the avoidance of evil and the pursuit of goodness. Moreover, when Malthus maintained that 'evil seems to be necessary to create exertion; and exertion seems evidently necessary to create mind' (FE 360), he was, once more, simply inverting one of Godwin's arguments to the effect that only savages were 'subject to the weakness of indolence'. In a civilized society, he held, 'it is thought, acuteness of disquisition, and ardour of pursuit that set the corporeal faculties at work'. Malthus was countering this mind-over-matter view with one suggesting that mind could only develop out of matter.

Malthus believed that fixed laws of nature constituted the only means by which God's progressive purpose could be achieved on earth. If God was treated as a visible presence, capable of intervening to adjust the application of laws to specific circumstances in order to mitigate their effects, the incentives to industry and the exercise of reason, foresight, and intelligence would weaken. When applied to the variety of the human condition, in which some individuals and societies were less favoured than others, fixed laws were bound to produce partial evils. But it was folly to wish that all could be placed in some medium state of climate, fertility, and prosperity. All parts were necessary to the whole, as the roots and branches of a tree were necessary to its more useful trunk. It followed that our duty lay in finding ways of reducing the incidence of evil and poverty without weakening the system as a whole. And what was true of the different parts of the globe was also true of each society: 'If no man could hope to rise, or fear to fall, in society; if industry did not bring with it its reward, and idleness its punishment, the middle parts would not certainly be what they now are' (FE 369).

Here then was the basis for a more assertive case for the established order than that contained in Malthus's *reductio*. It was not sufficient to rely, as Godwin did, on the 'enlarged motives' that could only operate in exceptional cases. 'Narrow motives' were required to inspire action on the part of mankind taken generally. Just as sorrows and distress are necessary 'to soften and humanize the heart, to awaken social sympathy', so 'moral evil is absolutely necessary to the production of moral excellence' (FE 375). A perfect, uniform, and undiversified state, containing only good, would not bring forth our active powers of mind and character: 'Evil exists in the world, not to create despair, but activity. We are not patiently to submit to it, but to exert ourselves to avoid it' (FE 395).

Acting on the advice of more senior members of the Church of England, Malthus later withdrew some of the more heterodox elements in this theodicy. Nevertheless, it expresses views which constantly recur in his writings and are essential to an understanding of the peculiarities and paradoxes of his position as a social scientist and moralist. He provided the basis on which the principle of population could be incorporated within the Anglican tradition by such theologians as John Bird Summer; and the terms on which this was accomplished help to explain why Malthus did not regard himself as being guilty of cosmic pessimism and would have been affronted by the connotations of such phrases as the 'Malthusian devil'. A natural law based on natural instincts could only be the work of a beneficent deity. Far from being a sombre and pessimistic reflection on the entire human condition, the population principle pointed out the means by which God intended to secure the happiness of the mass of society on this earth, and achieve a progressive development in man's mental and material condition. Paradoxically, therefore, Malthus's theological commitments provide him with a teleology of improvement that acts as the religious equivalent of the secular perfectibilism which his *Essay* set out to undermine.

4 *Population: the second* Essay

The enlarged version of the *Essay* that emerged in 1803 as a result of Malthus's travels and search for additional ethnographic and statistical evidence to illustrate the principle of population was in many respects, as he claimed, a 'new work'. Although everything continued to revolve around the population principle, the expanded version was also a more mature treatise on morals and politics, expounding Malthus's hopes as well as fears about the course on which British society appeared to be embarked. The alterations made to the second *Essay* over the period 1803 to 1826 provide a running commentary on Malthus's intellectual development; they embody his responses to numerous critics and his efforts to encompass events and new evidence. This chapter and its successor will deal with the more important themes to emerge from Malthus's revisions of his basic position.

Freed from the constraints imposed by the earlier polemic, Malthus was now anxious 'to soften some of the harshest conclusions' of his original statement of the consequences of the population principle. The most important change was a reclassification of the checks to population designed to focus on moral restraint as the acceptable alternative to vice within the category of preventive checks operating on birth rates. Although Malthus had acknowledged the role of prudence or foresight in the first *Essay*, moral restraint was now given considerable prominence as the ultimate solution, the response that should be actively fostered. Other forms of prudential restraint might be accompanied by vicious practices, but moral restraint meant 'restraint from marriage from prudential motives, with a conduct strictly moral during the period of this restraint' (E I 18). It meant refraining from or postponing marriage on grounds of the likely effect on the economic and social status of having to support a family, accompanied by what French commentators have called *le célibat vertueux* during the waiting period. It defines the ideal moral response to population pressure, even though, as a realistic moralist, Malthus was fully aware that less-than-ideal prudential responses were likely to be more common.

Others have argued that the entire framework of the second *Essay* was changed by the dropping of the concluding theological chapters. But it is a mistake to believe that Malthus abandoned the brand of theological utilitarianism contained in his earlier theodicy in order to become a more secular social theorist; there was no conflict between Malthus the Christian moral philosopher and Malthus the scientist. The retention of the categories of vice and virtue, alongside, indeed attached to, pain and happiness, testify to their continuing importance. Indeed, an understanding of what precisely was 'moral' about moral restraint requires constant reference to the methodological standpoint of the theological utilitarian, for whom the greatest surplus of virtue and happiness over vice and misery was the supreme criterion for judging the worth of individual actions and social outcomes.

As the reference in the subtitle of the second *Essay* to 'the future removal or mitigation of the evils' occasioned by the operation of the principle of population suggests, a great deal more space is devoted to positive solutions. In other words, even though the basic model of human motivation remains intact, together with its reliance on the spur of material necessity, greater scope is allowed to human agency and legislative prudence in mitigating its results. This trend towards giving a human power greater scope over a natural power is a persistent feature of Malthus's later revisions and writings.

One of the more controversial legislative reforms espoused by Malthus was the abolition of the Poor Laws. The subject had been broached in the first *Essay*, and it became one of Malthus's major preoccupations in subsequent editions. When taken in conjunction with moral restraint, it has led many to accept the proposition that the main tenet of Malthusian social policy is that there should be no social policy—a position that seems to echo or anticipate such well-known ideas as the Protestant work ethic, the virtues of 'self-help', even the 'survival of the fittest' and the attribution of poverty to defects of individual character. As we shall see, Malthus's views on the Poor Laws are a good deal more complex than his long term aim of abolition suggests, and while moral restraint emphasizes individual responsibility as the most dignified and effective solution to pauperism, Malthus was far too closely identified with the Enlightenment belief in the application to social affairs of general laws of a Newtonian variety to subscribe to the view that poverty was visited only on the feckless. We also need to broaden the rather anachronistic notion of *social* policy to encompass political questions connected with education and civil and political liberties which were of particular importance to Malthus.

Moral restraint

Having uncovered a natural law which operated without exception on human affairs, Malthus saw the task of the Christian moralist as one of pointing out ways of minimizing its unfortunate consequences and maximizing its benefits both to individuals and society at large. But as with all problems of maximization or minimization, marginal adjustments rather than simple all-or-nothing choices were entailed. Every non-Utopian solution to the problems posed by population pressure involved striking a difficult balance between vice and virtue, and frequently between the lesser of two vices. In addition, short-term gains or losses had to be set against long-term results.

As in the first *Essay*, Malthus treated all universal passions, impulses and wants, when considered abstractly or generally, as being natural or good; the satisfaction of such passions brought happiness. The desire to satisfy our material wants was also the impulse which underlay the process of civilization itself, and the passion between the sexes was the foundation on which the pleasures associated with conjugal affection, a prime softening agency, was based. The danger to happiness lay not in these impulses but in the 'fatal extravagances' to which they gave rise. Since it was impossible to weaken the force of our basic impulses without injuring our happiness, regulation and redirection, rather than Calvinistic suppression or diminution, was the correct response.

The utilitarian view stresses the need to weigh the mixture of good and evil consequences flowing from an action rather than the motive for action itself. In the face of population pressure man's task was to conduct himself in a manner that would mitigate the evil consequences that accompanied the benefits derived from any general law of nature. Malthus traced once more the trail of misery and vice left by the failure to check birth rates: low wages, excessive toil, indigence, irregularity of employment, loss of character, crime, vicious practices, and high mortality rates. Hence the moral duty of delaying marriage until there was a prospect of supporting children. Celibacy for a longer period would, he felt, ease relations between the sexes and enable them to establish 'kindred dispositions' before marriage. The passion between the sexes would not be extinguished, but would burn 'with a brighter, purer, and steadier flame' (E II 98). The period of delayed gratification would become a period of sobriety, industry, and economy undertaken with marriage as its prize.

Malthus envisaged a quite different form of late marriage from that which he regarded as prevailing in his own time, namely arranged marriages between those with 'exhausted' constitutions and affections, chiefly undertaken for the sake of men. Women, presumed to be the more virtuous half of society, would adjust to the new system more readily, with the normal age of marriage rising to 28 or 30, depending on circumstances. Malthus recognized that later marriage might lead to an increase in the vices connected with sex, particularly on the part of men. He held that prostitution was always attended by evil because it weakened 'the best affections of the heart' and tended 'to degrade the female character' (E I 18). But the sexual vices were by no means the only vices, and they had to be compared with those arising from mass poverty. Thus prudential restraint, accompanied by vice, was preferable to misery and premature death. Although a more secular age may find it strange that Malthus seems to have ranked contraception within marriage as equal to, or even above, prostitution in the scale of vices, he does not appear to have been a prude in sexual matters. Nor does it seem accurate to attribute to him responsibility for narrowing the term 'moral' to connote sexual morality alone. It was only after 1817 that he substituted a weaker 'there may' in the opening part of the following sentence: 'I have little doubt that there have been some irregular connections with women, which have added to the happiness of both parties, and have injured no one' (E I 19). But while such liaisons might not produce misery for the individuals concerned, the utilitarian perspective required them to be described as vicious because their general effect was 'to injure the happiness of society'.

Moral restraint was the solution 'dictated by the light of nature, and expressly enjoined in revealed religion' (E II 102). The difficulties in acting according to these dictates, as in similar cases where temptation had to be overcome, could not serve as an argument against the duty they embodied. Nor was it necessary for moral restraint to 'be universally or even generally practised': partial implementation would be accompanied by improvement in the circumstances of those who practised it, thereby reducing the sum total of misery and vice. This explains why Malthus did not regard his ideal solution as tantalizingly Utopian (one could substitute 'Godwinian'): moral restraint did not entail acting from unaccustomed motives directed at a general good 'which we may not distinctly comprehend, or the effect of which may be weakened by distance and diffusion'. Each individual, acting without co-operation and aiming only at his own happiness, would also serve the general good: 'Every step tells. He who performs his duty faithfully will reap the full fruits of it, whatever may be the number of others who fail' (E II 105). It was a duty capable of being understood by all, even those of the 'humblest capacity'; and it placed responsibility where it belonged, on the person who produces children he cannot support.

Malthus did acknowledge, however, that a process of re-education directed at all classes, but especially those prone to fall from a state of poverty to pauperism, was required. He continued to attack those critics who focused exclusively on unjust political institutions, the avarice of the rich, and inequalities in wealth as the only causes of poverty, and kept up his attack on visionary doctrines of equality and common property in all subsequent editions of the *Essay*, adding Robert Owen's communitarian schemes in the 1817 edition. The lower classes could be brought to understand that they were the authors of their own fate, provided that efforts, such as his own, were made to overcome the influence of the doctrine that early marriage and large families conferred a public benefit. Malthus also attached considerable importance to public support for education both along general lines and in order to inculcate the truth of the principle of population: 'it cannot be said that any fair experiment has been made with the understandings of the common people' (E II 106). While this remained the case, 'the errors of the labouring classes of society [were] always entitled to great indulgence and consideration' (E I 334). They did not deserve to have their condition dismissed simply as the result of personal improvidence and want of industry.

The object of those who wished to better the condition of the poor must be 'to raise the relative proportion between the price of labour and the price of provisions'. Existing policies had merely increased population and reduced real wages. Moral restraint offered a means of putting the hare of population growth to sleep, thereby giving the tortoise of food production a chance of first catching up, and then overtaking it. By such means Malthus hoped that it would be possible to inaugurate an era in which population growth would always lag behind improvements in food supply, uniting what he described as 'the two grand *desiderata*, a great actual population, and a state of society in which squalid poverty and dependence are comparatively but little known; two objects which are far from being incompatible' (E II 109). Wages would rise and poverty of an 'abject' kind would be entirely confined to those 'who had fallen into misfortunes against which no prudence or foresight could provide' (E II 97). In common with most of his contemporaries, Malthus was chiefly concerned with the number of able-bodied poor who were in receipt of relief; he might have had a more sympathetic hearing if he had always stressed the distinction between them and widows and the infirm—those whose situation could not be imputed to lack of foresight.

We find here too Malthus's answer to those who charged him with advocating a stationary or declining population. If the rate of increase could be slowed and then kept in step with provisions, he could 'easily conceive, that this country with a proper direction of national industry, might, in the course of some centuries, contain two or three times its present population, and yet, every man in the kingdom be much better fed and clothed than he is at present' (E II 111).

The Poor Laws

In the first *Essay* Malthus had argued that the Poor Laws, by attempting to guarantee a minimum level of support to all those whose income fell short of that necessary to support them and their families during periods of food scarcity and high prices, had contributed to the problem they were designed to alleviate by lowering wages, increasing the price of food, and encouraging population increase. He concluded that 'if the poor-laws had never existed, though there might have been a few more instances of very severe distress, yet the aggregate mass of happiness among the common people would have been much greater than it is at present' (FE 94). Here was another case where a balance of probabilities had to be struck, bearing in mind that on a strictly numerical basis, the lower, and hence most numerous classes, constituted 'the most important part of the human race'.

On these grounds Malthus criticized Pitt's plan to reform the Poor Laws in 1796, which would have granted relief on grounds of family size. But in 1798 Malthus's main proposals were: the abolition of the Settlement Laws, which restricted relief to those born within the parish, a policy for creating a free market in labour which had been advocated by Adam Smith in 1776; the granting of 'premiums' to those who took new land under cultivation; the removal of restrictions which kept agricultural wages artificially below those paid to urban artisans; and the establishment of county workhouses where assistance could be granted to those suffering from 'severe distress', regardless of nationality or place of residence, but on condition that work was undertaken at the going market rate.

Malthus's analysis of the unfavourable consequences of the Poor Laws rested on the assumption of fixity, or extreme inelasticity, of food supply, an assumption that was more or less valid under conditions of acute grain scarcity, when the domestic harvest fell short of what was needed to maintain existing standards of food consumption. Over the longer run Malthus conceded that the additional demand for food would act as a spur to food production, though at this point he introduced another assumption concerning the difference between food and 'wrought commodities'. Food supply was limited by the availability of fertile land and the length of time required for agricultural investments to come to fruition. Moreover, the long run was not relevant to those suffering from high prices now.

In 1800, in a pamphlet addressed to the causes of the *High Price of Provisions*, and partly designed to carry on Adam Smith's campaign to show that dealers in corn were not responsible for exacerbating scarcity, Malthus returned to the Poor Laws by adducing the recently introduced 'allowance system' as one of the reasons why grain prices had risen higher than they might otherwise have done on grounds of scarcity alone. The granting of assistance according to the gap between money wages and the cost of supporting a family at existing food prices merely placed extra purchasing power in the hands of poor families and enabled them to bid up the price of a fixed stock of food both to themselves and others not in receipt of assistance. Nevertheless, while reiterating his opposition to the Poor Laws in general, Malthus believed that in the special circumstances of the day the allowance system had been 'advantageous to the country' (P 19). By raising prices, the pressure of scarcity had implicated the whole community and brought about a general retrenchment in the use of grain. A higher price had also led to importation and greater incentives to farmers to increase next year's crop. But the episode also confirmed the diagnosis of the first *Essay*, namely that population was the underlying cause of vulnerability to periods of distress.

In the second *Essay* Malthus devoted several chapters to the subject, charging once more that the Poor Laws had alleviated individual misfortune at the expense of spreading 'the evil over a much larger surface' (E I 348). The defensible short-run features of the system were precisely those that produced the long-term drawbacks. As in his pamphlet on scarcity, he regarded the events of the previous years as confirmation of his original position. Attempts to maintain previous consumption standards under conditions of absolute scarcity had resulted in a far higher rise in prices than would have occurred if some effort had been made to economize in consumption. The brunt of the problem had fallen on those whose resources were just sufficient to make them ineligible for parish assistance, a group that was presumed to possess 'superior skill and industry' (E I 351). The additional £7 million which had been distributed as relief in 1801 was the main reason for the threefold increase in the price of grain. A permanent upward spiral had been avoided by the fact that the increase in money supply needed to support the inflationary process had come from the country banks, rather than the Bank of England. The return of peace and exceptional harvests had also reduced the need for assistance on the scale reached in earlier years. Raising wages in line with food prices would have had a more permanently damaging effect by increasing unemployment, especially in non-agricultural pursuits. Once more, however, Malthus made it clear that he was not opposing assistance: temporary aid was essential, and so were special importation and economy measures.

For Malthus's strong argument it was not only necessary to assume inelasticity in food supplies but also to maintain that in the long run the Poor Laws had encouraged population growth by encouraging early marriage and raising the birth rate. However, he acknowledged that the facts did not bear him out on this matter. Despite the unique provision of relief as of right, England did not seem to enjoy high birth and marriage rates when compared with other countries without such poor laws. Malthus attributed this to the fortunate persistence among the English poor of habits of independence and foresight which made them unwilling to rely on poor relief. Prudential if not moral restraint had come to the rescue. Adam Smith's 'desire of bettering our condition', or more relevantly, 'our fear of making it worse', was acting as a natural physic. Moreover, since each parish was obliged to maintain its own poor, those who paid the poor rates had an incentive to pull down cottages, thereby discouraging early marriage. The stringent conditions under which relief was granted also acted as a deterrent. Malthus was not contradicting his earlier support for the abolition of the Settlement Laws; he was merely pointing out that the existing system had features that were self-regulating.

On the question of workhouses, however, there was a change of position. In the second *Essay* he argued that attempts to employ the poor had failed, and where successful had driven non-parish labour out of business. No new capital was being brought into trade; it was merely being diverted from productive uses elsewhere. But he remained unwilling to press general principles too far, and so hedged his bets by saying that he could imagine circumstances in which the individual good derived from employing the poor in workhouses might overbalance the general evil.

Successive editions of the *Essay* enabled Malthus to claim that his views had been vindicated by events following the end of the Napoleonic Wars. It had proved impossible to maintain and keep all claimants in employment. The Poor Laws had not even prevented starvation, and those parishes which had been unable to cope with the demand on their rates had found it necessary to resort to voluntary charity. The poor were still being deluded by the false promises held out by the Poor Law statutes.

In the additions made to the *Essay* in 1817 and after, Malthus increasingly called upon an economic diagnosis based on cyclical deficiencies in 'effective demand' to explain recurrent bouts of distress—a diagnosis which will be considered more fully in a later chapter. The years following the peace settlement were certainly marked by severe unemployment and trade depression, which in turn were accompanied by violence and agitation for parliamentary reform. In the aftermath of the 'Peterloo massacre' in 1819, Malthus praised those who had helped to alleviate distress, and was certainly not pressing for abolition of the Poor Laws at this stage:

It is practicable to mitigate the violence and relieve the severe pressure of the present distress, so as to carry the sufferers through to better times, though even this can only be done at the expense of some sacrifices, not merely of the rich, but of other classes of the poor. But it is impracticable by any exertions, either individual or national, to restore at once that brisk demand for commodities and labour which has been lost by events, that, however they may have originated, are now beyond the power of control. (E I 368–9)

Malthus's ameliorative solution, once more, was a programme of public works, but designed this time not to compete with existing capital: road and bridge construction, and railway and canal preparation, plus some employment on the land fell into this category. Such measures would still entail disadvantage to others via the redistribution of capital, but he was willing to face up to this on the basis of a straightforward utilitarian calculus, and on the assumption that the measures would be temporary. As in the case of the steps taken to deal with scarcity in 1800, it was justifiable to spread the burden over a larger surface 'in order that its violence on particular parts may be so mitigated as to be made bearable by all' (E I 370).

During the post-war period Malthus also revised his earlier assessment of emigration as a 'very weak palliative' attended by dangers that it would merely create a vacuum into which increased population would flow. In 1817 it became a legitimate temporary device for coping with the depressed state of demand for labour. Malthus expected that the revival of effective demand after the war, taken in conjunction with a fall in marriage and birth rates, would restore full employment at good wages. Looking back on his prediction in 1826, however, he admitted that he had been proved wrong. Despite trade revival and the fall in food prices, there had been no decline in the proportion of the labouring classes needing parish support. Unlike some of his contemporaries among the political economists, Malthus was not prepared to advocate lower taxes and reduced government expenditure as a means of dealing with unemployment. Under some circumstances, he maintained, government expenditure provided a greater stimulus to demand than the same funds would have done in private hands.

But the persistence of the problem brought Malthus back to his earlier diagnosis of the role being played by population and the Poor Laws. The allowance system had prevented wages from rising in step with the price of provisions: '. . . no human efforts can keep up the price of day-labour so as to enable a man to support on his earnings a family of moderate size, so long as those who have more than two children are considered as having a valid claim to parish assistance' (E I 373). Hence his return to 'the *gradual* and *very gradual* [his emphasis] abolition of the poor laws', ('so gradual as not to affect any individuals at present alive, or who will be born within the next two years') (E I 374) as the only long-term means of raising wages and preventing large sections of the population falling into pauperism. Cautious as ever, Malthus attached another condition to the proposal: 'I should be very sorry to see any legislative regulation founded on the plan I have proposed, till the higher and middle classes were generally convinced of its necessity, and till the poor themselves could be made to understand that they had purchased their right to a provision by law, by too great and extensive a sacrifice of their liberty and happiness' (P 34). And if this condition was not met, as he plainly did not think it was in the 1820s, he was prepared to settle for 'an improved administration of our actual laws, together with a more general system of education and moral superintendance' (PJ 450).

Political agency

Malthus's caution with regard to legislative change, as we shall see in later chapters, was not connected with his polemical attempts in the first *Essay* to minimize the role played by human institutions in explaining the persistence of vice and misery. What 'appear to be the obvious and obtrusive causes of much mischief to mankind', he had said in 1798, were in reality 'mere feathers that float on the surface' (FE 177). By 1803 this image had been removed, one of a number of minor changes which indicate that Malthus wished to allow greater scope to institutions and human agency as ameliorating factors in dealing with man's moral condition.

Morals were often linked with politics by Malthus, where this connoted something more philosophically ambitious than mere party allegiance. In terms of party labels, Malthus must be firmly placed in the Whig camp—though at a time when the Whigs were divided into a number of factions, and alliances were fluid, this is not a particularly enlightening ascription. Judging his position from the fragmentary quotations from his unpublished pamphlet on *The Crisis* written in 1796, it would seem that he was then a Foxite Whig, opposed to the repressive measures taken by the Pitt Ministry to curb the pro-French, anti-war, and reformist activities of the radical corresponding societies. Malthus's Whig credentials can also be gauged from his support for Catholic emancipation, the abolition of the public disabilities attached to membership of a Dissenting sect, and from the pattern of his friendships, which included the founders of the *Edinburgh Review*, the Whig quarterly. These Whig allegiances were to survive Malthus's defection from the free trade camp over the Corn Laws, and they enabled him to welcome, albeit retrospectively, the passage of the Reform Bill of 1832.

But the nature of Malthus's Whig sympathies cannot be judged from private alliances and public measures alone. In *The Crisis* he called upon 'the country gentlemen and middle classes' to revive 'true Whig principles' by acting as an independent influence, mediating between the Pitt Ministry and the claims of the popular radicals outside Parliament. In this way he hoped that a 'safe and enlightened policy' would be pursued, namely one of 'removing the weight of objections to our constitution by diminishing the truth of them'. In the same pamphlet, and on much the same grounds, Malthus advocated the removal of civil disabilities affecting Dissenters. He was well aware, from his acquaintance with the writings of his ex-tutors, Wakefield and Frend, that radical Dissenters were prominent in the campaign against the war with France. A policy of religious tolerance would, he hoped, do much to reconcile them to the Constitution: 'Admitted to equal advantages, and separated by no distinct interests, they could have no motives peculiar to themselves for dislike to the government.'

The role of moderate reformer, anxious to mediate between executive tyranny and popular radicalism, attempting to preserve the space which would allow gradual reformation to be achieved, defines the political stance which Malthus adopted throughout his life. It was a stance that entailed a lasting sensitivity to the radical Dissenting voice, while at the same time holding 'patriotic' views on the virtuous contribution which independent 'country gentlemen' had made in the past, and could still make to the preservation of English liberties. The main threat to these liberties lay in the growth of executive power, supported in Parliament by those with official and other connections with the ministry. The antidote lay in the preser-

vation of balance between the various orders and interests represented in Parliament, and more especially in the hands of the
independent members, supported by enlightened opinion in the
nation at large, and acting as a check on executive encroachment. Malthus managed to add a 'modern' Whig position (of
the kind associated with the name of Macaulay in the period
before and after the Reform Bill) to what was an older 'Country'
Whig tradition by linking the middle classes with the country
gentlemen, and by according them a more prominent role over
time.

The clearest version of this position can be found in a chapter
in the second *Essay*, to which another was added in 1817,
debating the following question: '[whether] a doctrine which
attributes the greatest part of the sufferings of the lower classes
of society exclusively to themselves, is unfavourable to the
cause of liberty, as affording a tempting opportunity to governments of oppressing their subjects at pleasure, and laying the
whole blame on the laws of nature and the imprudence of the
poor' (E II 122). In other words, was Malthus's own view of
poverty compatible with ideas on civil and political liberty
which he also espoused? The way in which the question is
framed reveals Malthus's underlying concerns and does a great
deal to explain the persistence of his opposition to radical
doctrines and schemes of equality.

Any failure to assign the correct causes of distress among the
lower classes of society, by treating it as a simple product of
misrule, Malthus argued, provided opportunities for revolutionary demagogues to bring down governments, and in turn to be
brought down themselves when events proved that they too
were incapable of meeting popular expectations. In an effort to
end the cycle of anarchy 'the majority of well-disposed people,
finding that a government, with proper restrictions, was unable
to support itself against the revolutionary spirit, and weary and
exhausted with perpetual change' (E II 123) would place themselves under the control of the tyrant or despot. Malthus's
diagnosis of the way in which popular discontent, mob
violence, and despotism were connected draws on classical

commonplaces supplemented by Hume's ideas on the possible euthanasia, or 'easiest death', of the British Constitution in absolute monarchy. But the course of events in France after the Revolution, when taken in conjunction with the repressive measures adopted by British governments during the war, and the frequent eruption of popular unrest connected with food scarcity, machine-breaking, and post-war unemployment, gave renewed significance both to Hume's ideas and Malthus's diagnosis.

Echoing a century or more of anti-executive rhetoric, Malthus announced himself to be 'an enemy to large standing armies'; and in 1817 he declared that the British government had 'shown no great love of peace and liberty during the last twenty-five years' (E II 134). The abolition of wars resulting from competition for land and food was one of the incidental benefits that would come from recognition of the principle of population. It would also deprive ambitious politicians of offensive weapons in the form of a ready supply of soldiers: 'A recruiting sergeant always prays for a bad harvest, and a want of employment, or, in other words, a redundant population' (E II 101). One of Robert Southey's many complaints against Malthus was the effect of his teachings on this subject: 'As if we did not at the moment want men for our battles!' He was also quite right to suspect, when writing to a fellow-Tory in 1808, that 'Malthus will prove a peacemonger'.

The dilemma of Malthus's position was shared by all those who felt themselves to be caught between the extremes represented by 'general declaimers' exploiting the genuine distress and ignorance of the unpropertied mass on one side, and the upholders of executive tyranny on the other. Malthus was surely speaking directly for himself when he said that the real effect of 'indiscriminate and wholesale accusations against governments' was 'to add a weight of talents and principles to the prevailing power which it never would have received otherwise' (E II 130). Regrettably, the standing army had proved necessary during the food riots which occurred at the turn of the century, and the threat of mob violence, rather than corruption, explained why the country gentlemen, 'the appointed guardians of British liberty', had so often found themselves supporting the Crown against the people during and after the Napoleonic Wars.

The political importance of the principle of population and the lessons it taught on the true causes of, and remedies for low wages and poverty lay in its effect in undermining the support given to 'turbulent and discontented men in the middle classes of society'. For with the fear of the mob removed, 'the tyranny of government could not stand a moment' (E II 129). Necessary reforms in the Constitution could be undertaken, and proper attention could be given to the 'striking and incontestable' contribution that better government could make to human improvement. Thus while the effect of constitutional reforms on economic problems could only be 'indirect and slow', Malthus was in no doubt that a combination of civil and political liberty, fortified by an extension of educational opportunities to the populace at large through a parochial school system along the lines advocated by Adam Smith, would act as a powerful means of spreading to the lower classes all those virtues of industry, respectability, independence, and prudence which had so far been confined to the middle classes.

In espousing *embourgeoisement* as a political and economic goal for the mass of society, Malthus may not have been particularly original, even in the early 1800s, though his views on education, religious tolerance, and political representation were probably far more common among Dissenting ministers than among Anglican clergymen at that time. Of possibly greater interest is the contrast with the more 'melancholy' reflections on the same subject in the polemical first *Essay*, and the fact that Malthus, when faced with arguments by others which stressed prospective *embourgeoisement* as a reason for expecting population pressure to recede, tended to revert to his original position—the one that found endorsement in his theology. This stressed the enduring part played by the spur of necessity in God's scheme of things, and made it difficult for Malthus to accept as whole-heartedly as others did that similar results might be achieved by forethought based on anticipated as opposed to established gains. His unwillingness to countenance birth control, as well as his scepticism towards such measures as emigration considered as a long-term solution, have a similar origin.

5 From population to political economy

Malthus's interest in population had its origins in a dispute over perfectibilism and the moral and political consequences of inequality and mass poverty, but he was quickly drawn into the ambit of Adam Smith's wider speculations on the wealth of nations—those questions of economic circulation, growth, and stability which were to remain central to classical political economy until the last third of the nineteenth century. On all these matters Malthus was to sustain a distinctive, sometimes isolated, position; and as a result of the way in which he entered this domain, namely in the course of an inquiry into the relationship between increased food production and population growth, there was always an aspect of his thinking which will have to be loosely described for the moment as an agrarian bias.

As population theorist, he was, after all, as much concerned with the possibilities (and difficulties) of expanding food production as with containing population growth; and his supposition that, once land had become scarce, food production could only expand at an arithmetic rate implied a version of what became known as the law of diminishing returns—an empirical or historical generalization thought to have special relevance to agriculture, which could be extrapolated into the future under certain assumptions about technical change and improvements in agricultural organization. Malthus's name was to become as closely associated with this law or tendency as any other contemporary political economist's; and his writings are replete with references to the peculiarities of agricultural production and the special difficulties under which it operated in attempting to absorb investment and respond to market stimuli.

But the starkness of the contrast between the arithmetic and geometric ratios of food and population, though useful in dramatizing the operation of checks and limits, tends to conceal another important feature of Malthus's thinking on all subjects: his 'doctrine of proportions', the search for *optimal* conditions or relationships, that 'golden mean' or precise balance of forces which would produce the best result under changing circumstances. Malthus expressed this concern in such homely analogies as that involving the hare and the tortoise, but he put it more precisely when he called upon his knowledge, acquired as a Cambridge mathematician, of calculus or the theory of fluxions: 'Many of the questions both in morals and politics seem to be of the nature of the problems *de maximus et minimis* in Fluxions; in which there is always a point where a certain effect is the greatest, while on the other side of the point it gradually diminishes' (P 119). Such an approach required distrust of solutions which appeared to depend on unidirectional change in any single variable. As he put it in another homely expression, 'there is no argument so frequently and obviously fallacious as that which infers that what is good to a certain extent is good to any extent' (E II 70).

Thus, while much of the polemical force of Malthus's first *Essay* derived from its emphasis on the crude physical limits posed by food supplies, it soon became apparent that the problems of agricultural production were intimately bound up with the other variables that underlay economic growth, notably capital accumulation, the relationship between agriculture, manufacturing, and foreign trade, and the connections between rents, profits, and wages, and the prices of goods and services. In moving from population theory to political economy, therefore, Malthus moved from the optimal relationship between food and population growth over time to a larger question involving the most desirable course that economic growth and the occupational pattern of the British economy should take.

While this describes the broad direction taken, it does not capture some of the special features of Malthus's approach. It may not be surprising to find that the systematic theories of morals and politics which he deployed in dealing with population were carried over into his contributions to the narrower and, as Malthus saw it, subordinate field of political economy, though his practice in this regard was increasingly out of tune with that of many of his fellow-economists. Malthus was also more persistent in following Smith's example in attempting to place his interpretation of British economic problems against a comparative-historical background which brings out the plural emphasis of any inquiry into the wealth of nations. Furthermore, he remained closer to the political and cultural themes expounded by Smith in his historical treatment 'of the different progress of opulence in different nations', which dealt with the mutual interaction of town and country, manufacturing and agriculture, showing it to be essential not simply to economic growth, but to the 'silent revolution' which had overthrown feudal society in Western Europe, and which had placed liberty, defined as security under the rule of law and the disappearance of dependent relations between individuals and ranks, within the grasp of the majority for the first time.

Again, Malthus's attachment to these wider features of eighteenth-century debate on the origins of modern commercial or civil society, these attempts to establish the connections between commerce, 'luxury', and manufacturing on one side, and liberty, independence, national power, and political stability on the other, was also increasingly uncommon among his contemporaries. Such features formed part of a general inquiry into the benefits and drawbacks of modern civilized society when compared with its agrarian or feudal predecessors; and while improvement or progress provided an underlying motif, this did not rule out concern with possible 'seeds of decay'—sources of potential stagnation and decline. As political economy became more closely focused on the urgent, often short-term problems plaguing British policy-makers during the first quarter of the nineteenth century, such matters came to be seen, perhaps, as irrelevant or unproblematic by the new generation of economic commentators. This was never Malthus's position.

The sources and meaning of Malthus's agrarian bias are usually sought in more obvious places. In the course of developing his mature position, Malthus sometimes appeared to be questioning Smith's dismissal of those ideas, normally associated with his French predecessors, the *Economistes* or Physiocrats, which gave priority or special prominence to agriculture as the source of a nation's wealth and power. Malthus certainly returned to some of the issues which had featured in Smith's modifications to the Physiocratic conception of the relationship between agriculture, commerce, and manufacturing in the process of circular economic flow and growth. Smith had replied to the Physiocratic emphasis on the uniquely 'productive' qualities of agriculture by extending the term to cover all activities, including commerce and manufacturing, in which labour was employed productively by capital. The return on capital—interest and profits—thereby became, like rent, a source of economic surplus potentially available for future accumulation and economic growth. Malthus had no quarrel with this conclusion, but he did entertain serious doubts about Smith's stress on the universal benefits and self-regulating qualities of the process of capital accumulation, especially when the notion of the invisible hand was taken up in more doctrinaire form by other followers of Smith.

The most obvious mark of Malthus's agrarian sympathies, however, is normally taken to be his support for the Corn Laws, his defence of agricultural protection as a legitimate exception to the principles of free trade. In the eyes of many of his readers, even some of his friends, this established his reputation as an apologist for agricultural interests, especially those of the land-owning aristocracy. This reputation was compounded later when he maintained, on the basis of his theory of effective demand, that the 'unproductive' expenditure of those in receipt of rent incomes might be necessary to sustain full employment and economic stability. The elements were thereby assembled for a portrait of Malthus as the ideological spokesman for an agrarian order increasingly under threat from industrialization and free trade.

The precise nature of Malthus's agrarian bias, and the way in which he developed his position, will be considered here. The story begins with a pair of chapters in the first *Essay* (16 and 17) which were enlarged to four and later six chapters in subsequent editions (Book III 8–13). These comprise a self-contained treatise on the optimal relationship between agriculture and manufacturing under different national circumstances; and they provide important clues to the final position adopted by Malthus on a number of key topics in political economy. They also furnish the background to his controversial decision to come out more firmly and publicly in favour of agricultural protection in 1815.

Agriculture versus manufacturing

In the first *Essay* Malthus employed the self-interest principle and Smith's system of natural liberty to counter Godwin's Utopian ideas, but he was not prepared to endorse Smith's optimistic views on the consequences of economic growth. Indeed, his initial foray into this territory consisted of a major attack on one of Smith's main conclusions—the idea that capital accumulation, in itself, could always be presumed to confer material benefits on society at large. According to Smith, these would accrue chiefly in the form of an expanding demand for labour, higher money wages, increased per capita output, and lower prices of those goods on which wages were mostly spent. Malthus questioned this essentially smooth account of the growth process by taking a polar case in which capital accumulation was applied solely to the employment of labour in manufacturing. While this might raise wages and be counted, on Smith's definition, as an increase in annual riches, the output of agricultural products would remain static. In such circumstances the rise of wages would be accompanied by an increase in the price of food, the main wage-good, thereby depriving the labouring classes of any improvement in real living standards.

Malthus was also casting doubt on Smith's interpretation of the historical record, his assessment that economic growth in Britain since the Revolution of 1688 had bettered the condition of the mass of society. According to Malthus the concentration of investment in trade and manufacturing had meant that wealth had been increasing faster than 'the effectual funds for the maintenance of labour'. Wealth was not, therefore, increasing the happiness of the mass by improving their condition. 'They have not, I believe, a greater command of the necessaries and conveniences of life; and a much greater proportion of them, than at the period of the revolution, is employed in manufactures, and crowded together in close and unwholesome rooms' (FE 313). Hence his belief, in 1798, that population had been increasing very slowly throughout the eighteenth century due to the equally slow increase in domestic food production. The rise in money wages had preceded the rise in the price of food, thereby raising costs ahead of revenues and impairing the ability of domestic agriculture to respond to the price rise. Enclosure and other improvements in agricultural technology had mostly been concentrated on grazing rather than arable wheat production, and fewer people were now employed on the land. In short, population would have increased faster if manufacturing and commerce had not expanded so rapidly at the expense of agriculture.

By means of such arguments Malthus sought to emphasize the possibilities of conflict between economic growth and the 'happiness and comfort of the lower orders of society'. Real wages might not increase and many wage-earners might suffer in the process of exchanging a stable and healthy form of life in agriculture for an 'unwholesome' existence in manufacturing occupations and towns, where they were exposed to the risks of vice and unhealthy surroundings as well as to greater uncertainties 'arising from the capricious taste of man, the accidents of war, and other causes' (FE 310). As Malthus said of manufacturing occupations in the first *Essay*, 'I do not reckon myself a very determined friend to them', (FE 293) and while he became distinctly friendlier towards them over time, this was a case where the conclusions of his science of morals took precedence over the science of wealth narrowly conceived. If vice and misery could be reduced by slowing down the growth of manufacturing, this should be made part of the moral calculus, even if it entailed lower per capita incomes on aggregate.

Malthus was proposing a major qualification to Smith's system of natural liberty, and doing so along lines that supported the Physiocratic conclusion concerning the priority, or especially 'productive' qualities, of food production. The chain of reasoning which he employed, however, was his own. He was suggesting that while investment in manufacturing might be advantageous to individual capitalists, it was less so to society—the reverse being true of agriculture. This opened up the possibility of socially-beneficial intervention by the government, though in the first *Essay* Malthus did not spell out what form this might take, apart from some hints that 'superior encouragement' had been given to commerce and manufacturing.

It is important, however, not to confuse Malthus's emphasis on the priority of agriculture and what would now be called the 'social' costs of industrialization with the position adopted by, say, his 'romantic' critics, Coleridge and Southey, who despised the commercial spirit of the age and entertained both feudal and bucolic visions. The social costs might be remediable (Malthus certainly noted improvements on this front in later writings), and the balance between agriculture and manufacturing might also, with greater difficulty, be adjusted in the right direction. Moreover, as a good Whig, albeit one with 'Country' sympathies which emphasized the beneficial oppositional role played by 'independent country gentlemen', Malthus was as conscious of the wider social and political benefits associated with the rise of commerce and manufacturing as Smith had been earlier:

Yet though the condition of the individual employed in common manufacturing labour is not by any means desirable, most of the effects of manufactures and commerce on the general state of society are in the highest degree beneficial. They infuse fresh life and activity into all classes of the state, afford opportunities for the inferior orders to rise by personal merit and exertion, and stimulate the higher orders to depend for distinction upon other grounds than mere rank and riches. They excite invention, encourage science and the useful arts, spread intelligence and spirit, inspire taste for conveniences and comforts among the labouring classes; and, above all, give a new and happier structure to society, by increasing the proportion of the middle classes, that body on which the liberty, public spirit and good government of every country must mainly depend. (P 118)

In the second and subsequent editions of the *Essay* Malthus's position on agriculture versus manufacturing underwent considerable development—so much so that he entertained the notion of publishing as a separate work the six chapters on the subject which eventually appeared in the 1817 edition. The flirtations with Physiocratic categories and definitions introduced in 1798 and extended in 1803 were largely excised three years later. But an expanded treatment was given to the comparative and historical dimensions of the issue in order to focus on the peculiarities of a 'large landed nation', such as Britain, experiencing a rapid shift towards commerce and manufacturing under conditions of war. Many of the negative remarks on manufacturing occupations were qualified or withdrawn, but Malthus made an additional effort to articulate his anxieties concerning possible sources of long-term stagnation arising out of the course on which the British economy was now fully embarked. Finally, the policy implications of his position, particularly with regard to agricultural protection, were spelled out more openly.

In 1798 Malthus was inclined to believe that population had been rising very slowly throughout the eighteenth century. The census evidence which became available after 1801 made it necessary for him to recognize that population was rising quite rapidly. He also had to come to terms with the evidence that

Britain had not only ceased to be a net exporter of grain products, but was on the verge of becoming a consistent net importer—a situation fraught with both short- and long-term dangers, especially under conditions of war. Indeed, the fact that Britain was almost continually at war with France until 1815 was a major consideration in Malthus's thinking. Napoleon's attempted economic blockade gave added point to worries about security in food supply. War had also imparted an 'artificial' stimulus to her commercial and manufacturing capacity by conferring near-monopoly status on many of her exports.

According to Malthus's new diagnosis, Britain had been an agricultural nation until the middle of the previous century, and everything would have proceeded smoothly if trade and manufacturing had grown at the same rate as agriculture. No 'germ of decay' (E 1803 ed. I 400) could be found in such a system of balanced growth. But Britain was becoming a predominantly commercial nation, and one mark of this was the recurrence of food scarcity and the need to import a larger proportion of her food needs in response to rising population and higher wages. He did not believe it was possible or desirable for a 'large landed nation' to adopt food importation as a long-run expedient. The short-term cost would be a rise in food prices in line with wages, and in the long term this would place a limit on the capacity to support a larger population. But the real danger to future prospects lay in the fact that economic pre-eminence based on commerce and manufacturing could be eroded through competition from newly industrializing nations. As the examples of Holland, Hamburg and Venice showed: 'In the history of the world, the nations whose wealth has been derived principally from manufactures and commerce, have been perfectly ephemeral beings, compared with those, the basis of whose wealth has been agriculture' (E 1803 ed. I 395). Malthus was adding a new twist to the argument between ancients and moderns on the question of whether 'luxuries' were inimical or beneficial to a nation's survival: he was endorsing the position of the moderns, but maintaining that, carried to excess in the way he had diagnosed, dependence on manufacturing could contain 'seeds of decay', even though it might take a couple of centuries or more for them to develop.

The argument involved Malthus's doctrine of proportions. Conceding that commerce and manufacturing provided a market for agriculture, and hence a necessary stimulus to food production, he was seeking to define the point at which the growth of manufacturing could become excessive. Under war conditions Britain seemed to be approaching that point, with capital being attracted away from agricultural improvements by a combination of high profits in manufacturing, high interest rates due to war loans, and the slow and risky returns on capital employed in agriculture—factors which impaired the capacity of domestic agriculture to respond to the rise in wages and food prices. Any attempt to deal with the problem through cheaper food imports would further damage agriculture without much prospect of reducing money wages, which Malthus believed to be fairly inflexible in a downward direction.

The solution favoured by Malthus was a return to the situation in which Britain possessed the capacity to produce on a stable basis more than was normally consumed at home. Since he had shown that normal market processes did not produce the optimal solution, he was forced to conclude that a departure from Smith's free-trade principles was called for in order to deal with the fact that 'the body politick is in an artificial, and in some degree, diseased state, with one of its principal members out of proportion to the rest' (E 1803 ed. I 408). The expedients he favoured from 1803 onwards were a bounty on corn exports and restrictions on corn imports. This meant that he had to overthrow Smith's arguments on this subject which suggested that such measures would have no effect in raising agricultural profits and hence production. He also had to face up to the fact that agricultural protection might retard the progress of manufacturing, and he did so quite openly by accepting that it was desirable 'to sacrifice a small portion of present riches, in order to attain a greater degree of security, independence, and permanent prosperity' (E 1806 ed. I 423).

The mature version of Malthus's position on the relative merits of agricultural, commercial and manufacturing, and mixed societies can be found in the fifth and sixth editions of the *Essay* (1817, 1826) and in his *Principles of Political Economy* (1820), where the comparative dimension was further developed to the point where it became the framework for a treatise on nations classified according to the degree of their dependence on agriculture or manufacturing, and the different stages which they occupied in the development process. For example, the existing state of such 'feudal' economies as that of Poland, Russia, and Turkey provided ample material for speculation centring on the causes of agrarian stagnation, where the causes lay in their failure to have undergone the 'silent revolution' described by Smith when dealing with the political and economic benefits attributable to the opening up of commerce between town and country. Ireland, which was increasingly to occupy the attention of Malthus as the most striking and potentially dangerous contemporary illustration of the principle of population, provided a case of rapid population increase based on the ease with which subsistence derived from potato cultivation could be acquired. This situation was compounded by political and religious difficulties, and the lack of alternative employment in commerce and manufacturing. The contrast with a far more prosperous America, another agrarian state also undergoing rapid population growth, was obvious when placed within the new Malthusian framework.

Britain, however, still occupied the polar position as a nation with a growing population and the capacity, unlike Holland or Venice, for growing its own food, but increasingly reliant on commerce and manufacturing to support its population. Malthus continued to uphold the virtues of balanced growth, the dangers of dependence on unstable manufacturing activities, and the risks of forfeiting manufacturing pre-eminence to latecomers with greater capacity to support their populations from domestic sources. But while the limits of progress were never far from his mind, there were also signs of an increasing accommodation to the contemporary facts of British economic life and the benefits associated with manufacturing. Britain seemed to be no nearer to the end of its resources in the 1820s; in fact Malthus began to be worried by the ease with which she made good the ravages of war through capital accumulation. He also accorded greater recognition to the fact that standards of living depended as much on the conveniences and comforts which were increasingly available to the lower classes as on cheaper food. Indeed, he added yet another twist to the luxury debate by claiming that its benefits were greater precisely when luxuries were consumed by the mass of society. His reasons for believing this were connected with a realization that the availability of such goods had permanently beneficial effects on the habits of the populace at large; they were a powerful stimulus to both industry and prudence, and therefore helped to create, along with education, and civil and political liberty, the conditions for *embourgeoisement*.

As on the question of population, therefore, Malthus had come a long way from the pessimistic conclusions of 1798. From a starting position that involved being unfriendly to manufacturing occupations on moral and economic grounds, he gradually accepted that they could bring permanent benefits.

The Corn Laws

No reader of the above arguments on agriculture and manufacturing in the *Essay* should have been surprised when Malthus came out in favour of the retention of that measure of protection conferred by existing Corn Laws in 1814–15. He made his first contribution to public debate in a pamphlet entitled *Observations on the Effects of the Corn Laws, and of a Rise or Fall in the Price of Corn on the Agriculture and General Wealth of the Country* in 1814; and in this work he rehearsed the arguments for and against the Corn Laws in a spirit of 'strictest impartiality'. Despite this, he was regarded by freetraders as having weakened the barriers against error and prejudice. By this time the issue had become a far more divisive one, for not only was there a presumption, which Malthus shared,

that 'artificial' systems of bounties and restrictions ran counter
to the principles of political economy, but a large body of public
opinion had come to regard protection as involving a sacrifice of
public interest (especially that of manufacturers, wage-earners,
and consumers) to special interests—chiefly those of a land-
owning aristocracy that also happened to enjoy legislative privileges. Hence both Malthus's courage and moderation in arguing
as he did: pamphlet contributions to public debate carried more
risk than expressing similar views in a scientific treatise.

As in the *Essay*, Malthus had to counter Smith's authority on
the subject by arguing that bounties and restrictions could
increase and actually had increased production by raising agricultural prices and profits. At the same time he had to expose
fallacies in the case put forward by supporters of the Corn Laws,
by employing more orthodox reasoning to show that free trade
possessed 'striking advantages' and, consequently, that protection (even maintaining an existing system rather than creating
it anew) involved 'sacrifices' (P 124).

Malthus made two more contributions to the debate in the
following year; the first, an *Inquiry into the Nature and
Progress of Rent*, was an indirect contribution, more scientific
in tone and purpose, while the second, *Grounds of an Opinion
on the Policy of Restricting the Importation of Foreign Corn*,
was intended for more popular consumption. They revealed
that Malthus was now a more whole-hearted supporter of the
case for retaining protection, and they opened up a rift between
him and his Whig and radical friends, especially those responsible for the *Edinburgh Review* and other orthodox devotees of
political economy, most notably his friend Ricardo and his
two lieutenants, James Mill and J. R. McCulloch. From this
moment on Malthus was denied the pages of the *Edinburgh
Review* as an outlet for his views on any subject apart from
population; he also became the object of hostility from within
the political economists' camp, especially from McCulloch and
the young John Stuart Mill. This meant that he had to make use
of the pages of the *Quarterly Review*, a Tory periodical that had
attacked his population views earlier, and that his version of

political economy became suspect, incapable of being made the basis for various popular versions of the subject that were appearing at that time, the most significant being the articles on political economy topics in the supplement to the *Encyclopaedia Britannica*.

The new factors which had brought Malthus down from the fence were: evidence of the extent of new investment in agricultural improvement that was likely to be thrown out of employment by any sudden fall in corn prices; the risk of adding to the deflationary effect resulting from a further increase in the value of money; and his belief that such foreign suppliers as France, who now possessed, or so Malthus believed, a permanent cost advantage in grain products, would restrict the export of corn when domestic scarcity threatened. Free-trade principles had to give way in the light of knowledge concerning the quantitative impact of changes in legislation, as well as in the face of the realities of other nations' likely policies.

Malthus's new position emphasized the beneficial effect on wage-earners' living standards of maintaining a high and steady price for food, a case that ran directly counter to the normal argument in favour of cheap foodstuffs. The case required him to maintain that as long as the general demand for labour (and hence levels of employment) remained buoyant, and once money wages were adjusted to the higher corn price, the wage-earner would be able to exert greater command over the non-agricultural 'conveniences and luxuries of life'. Apart from the intrinsic gains involved, Malthus also believed that a combination of high wages and corn prices was more likely to act as a restraint on population growth than low wages and cheap corn. The chief gainers from free trade would be those capitalists who were engaged in foreign trade; but against the possible expansion in demand for British goods abroad associated with free trade had to be set the likelihood of an even larger decline in home demand and employment associated with the fall in agricultural incomes resulting from the influx of foreign corn and declining corn prices.

It was in this context that Malthus introduced his argument for placing a high priority on the 'unproductive' consumption out of rental incomes accruing to landowners. By stressing this source of demand, and by comparing it favourably with that associated with a small minority of stockholders in receipt of incomes from interest on the national debt who might benefit from a fall in the general price level, Malthus upheld, via a different route, a conclusion with which Smith would have agreed, namely that though landowners 'do not so actively contribute to the production of wealth' as other classes, their 'interests are more nearly and intimately connected with the prosperity of the state' (P 162).

Malthus's second pamphlet, though still cautiously argued, conveyed (to free-traders at least) an air of proving too much, both with respect to the benefits to wage-earners and, more especially, with regard to the long-term hopes for food prices. The law of diminishing returns, or the idea that 'in every rich and improving country there is a natural and strong tendency to a constantly increasing price of raw produce, owing to the necessity of employing, progressively, land of an inferior quality', (P 152) provided the basis for the theory of rent which he advanced in *An Inquiry into the Nature and Progress of Rent*. Nevertheless, in *Grounds of an Opinion* Malthus allowed himself to speculate about the possibility of a fall in the price of domestically produced food as a result of improvements in technology.

Rent

The public interest in the Corn Law question had provided Malthus with an excuse for publishing his views on the nature of rent—a subject left in an ambivalent state by Smith, and one on which Malthus had formed a distinctive and original position of his own in the course of his teaching duties. Malthus defined rent as the return to landowners after other costs of production had been met, which meant that the proximate cause of rent was the excess of food prices over costs of production. In some parts of the *Wealth of Nations* Smith had adopted this view, but had also treated it as a kind of monopoly return to the owners of a scarce resource. Malthus was opposed to such an interpretation, especially when it was espoused and elaborated by other writers such as Jean-Baptiste Say, Sismondi, and David Buchanan. To the last of these writers, for instance, the clear implication was that the return to monopoly was at the expense of the consumer; and that rent could therefore be considered as a kind of transfer payment from one class of income recipient to another.

Malthus agreed that there were affinities with natural monopoly based on the limited supply of fertile land available. This justified the term 'partial monopoly', but it was not the end of the story. Another reason for the price of food being above costs was what Malthus sometimes called 'the bounty of Nature', or 'the bountiful gift of Providence'. Land yielded more to labour than was necessary to support those working on land. It was the

source of all power and enjoyment; and without which, in fact there would be no cities, no military or naval force, no arts, no learning, none of the finer manufactures, none of the conveniences and luxuries of foreign countries, and none of that cultivated and polished society, which not only elevates and dignifies individuals, but which extends its beneficial influence through the whole mass of the people. (P 191)

Moreover, the peculiar feature of the necessaries of life was that their supply created demand—another way of expressing the population principle. In other truly natural monopolies demand was 'exterior to, and independent of, the production itself', (P 189) but in the case of food, as opposed, say, to rare wines, 'the demand is dependent upon the produce itself'. As labour and capital became cheaper in the process of growth, so the pressure on land and hence the price paid for its use became greater. What was originally a gift came at a higher and higher price to those who arrived late in the Garden of Eden, but it was still a gift because it took the form of surplus. Rent, therefore, was a creature of progress, and would arise whenever a nation attained to any considerable size of population or accumulation. The rent level was a kind of barometer of progress to Malthus, as others had chosen to treat the rate of interest earlier, and Ricardo was to treat profits later. Rising rents were simply the other side of a coin on which accumulation of capital, rising population, extension of cultivation, and a rising price for raw produce were written. It followed that any attempt to bring down the price of produce in order to reduce rent would be accompanied by a withdrawal of cultivation from all but the very best of lands, a movement back along the scale of progress.

In this way Malthus proved that 'the actual state of the natural rent of land is necessary to the actual produce'. The price of food at any given time was equal to the cost of producing it on the least good land. It followed that 'the very circumstance of which we complain, may be the necessary consequence and the most certain sign of increasing wealth and prosperity' (P 209). Nor should we complain on behalf of those most affected by high food prices. The essentials to their well-being were to be found in a combination of prudential habits with regard to marriage and an expanding demand for labour: 'And I do not scruple distinctly to affirm, that under similar habits, and a similar demand for labour, the high price of corn, when it has had time to produce its natural effects, so far from being a disadvantage to them is a positive and unquestionable advantage' (P 215).

The episode reveals a remarkable degree of convergence among political economists upon a theory of rent that was the simultaneous discovery of several authors. Apart from Malthus, Edward West, Robert Torrens, David Buchanan, and Ricardo all reached similar conclusions on the nature and causes of rent based on the law of diminishing returns to marginal land and capital. Nevertheless, in the case of Malthus and Ricardo especially, differing structures were eventually to be erected on the same foundations, which explains not merely the different conclusions which they came to on the subject of the Corn Laws, but, as we shall see in the next chapter, their differences on a wide range of other questions as well. Since the Ricardian alternative against which Malthus found himself increasingly having to argue also originated during the Corn Law debates, it may be helpful at this stage to look at its outlines.

Ricardo's contribution to the Corn Law controversy, his *Essay on the Influence of a Low Price of Corn on the Profits of Stock* (1815), was in part a reply to Malthus, and it was to become the basis for remoulding the shape of political economy which he undertook two years later in his *Principles of Political Economy*. According to Ricardo's view of things, profits throughout the economy were determined by those received by the farmer working on the least fertile land where no rent could be earned. It followed from this that if Britain relied on domestic agriculture to support a growing population, diminishing returns would raise rents and reduce profits, the main motive and source of capital accumulation, thereby impeding future growth. Ricardo's theory also underlined the divisive conclusion of such authors as Buchanan by suggesting that 'the interest of the landlord is always opposed to the interest of every other class in the community' (R IV 21). Anything that raised the price of food, whether it was increasing population, agricultural protection, or poor agricultural methods, increased the share going to the receivers of rents. There could be no more decisive break with the common assumption of eighteenth-century writers, including Smith, that the interest of landowners was always at one with that of the nation under progressive conditions.

Ricardo's answer to Malthus's fears concerning dependence on foreign suppliers was that a stable policy of import would create a reliable British market for foreign suppliers, and that this would lower the price of imported corn. Fluctuations in prices would also be lessened by recourse to a variety of sources, not likely to be moving in the same direction at the same time. Ricardo was proposing what to a large extent happened in Britain later in the century, namely that she should specialize in manufactured goods and rely on her exports of such goods to pay for cheap imports of food and raw materials. Britain's capital would be employed where the return was greatest, a principle of free trade or natural liberty which had been established by Smith under different circumstances. It follows that Ricardo could not share Malthus's anxieties about unbalanced growth.

Hence too Ricardo's difficulty in understanding why Malthus bemoaned the loss of capital involved in any shift away from domestic agriculture. 'We might just as fairly have been told, when the steam-engine, or Mr. Arkwright's cotton-machine, was brought to perfection, that it would be wrong to adopt the use of them, because the value of the old clumsy machinery would be lost to us.' There would be losers in abolishing the Corn Laws, especially those farming on the less fertile land, 'but the public would gain many times the amount of their losses; and, after the exchange of capital from land to manufactures had been effected, the farmers themselves, as well as every other class of the community, except the landholders, would very considerably increase their profits' (R IV 33). Notice also that Ricardo's interpretation of the rent doctrine opened up another rift, namely between capitalist farmers and their landlords.

How could Malthus answer such a persuasive case, one built on principles that he himself upheld on general grounds? One answer was implicit in all his earlier writings, namely that legislative wisdom lay in forsaking wealth whenever the cost in terms of 'happiness' and 'virtue' were found to be excessive. He continued to maintain this position, but he obviously felt the need to provide stronger arguments from within political economy itself, rather than rely on exceptions of a political and moral kind. The germs of his reply can be found in his argument that higher food prices could be advantageous to wage-earners. On this Malthus could rely on his population doctrines: a high price was more likely to curb population growth. But in order to provide an accurate account of all the consequences involved, Malthus also needed to find an alternative answer to Ricardo's belief in the natural equilibrating effects on income and employment levels of markets operating under freely competitive conditions. This eventually entailed a reconsideration of the effect of different policies on the distribution of income, and hence on the level of effective demand, the subject of the next chapter.

It may also be worth pointing out, in conclusion, that while Malthus was, so to speak, on the winning side in 1815—a protective Corn Law was passed, though not necessarily for the reasons given by Malthus—he was not entirely happy with the result. A familiar pattern of popular unrest accompanied the passage of the Bill, and these events clearly shook the moderate politician in Malthus so much that he concluded that the people should not have a divisive measure imposed upon them. Again, the conclusions of his science of politics took precedence over his principles of political economy, but it was characteristic of Malthus that he continued to suffer agonies of conscience throughout his life for the part he may have played in undermining the general principle of non-intervention to which he was deeply attached.

6 The political economy of stable growth

A long and fairly tortuous story precedes the publication of both editions of Malthus's *Principles*, and only slight exaggeration is involved in saying that most readers of the work have had almost as much trouble in deciding what kind of book it is as Malthus had in writing it. During the course of his teaching he had compiled a great deal of material embodying commentary and qualifications to the positions developed by Adam Smith in the *Wealth of Nations*. He made several attempts to publish this material, and the *Inquiry into Rent* and the fifth edition of the *Essay* published in 1817 contain some of the distinctive views on political economy which he had developed in the course of his teaching duties. After Ricardo's *Principles* appeared, Malthus redoubled these efforts to put his views before the public. But it was never his intention to compile 'a new systematic treatise', largely because he did not think the time was ripe for such an ambition. Hence in great measure his difficulties in settling on a title for his response to Ricardo; and while he eventually settled on *The Principles of Political Economy considered with a view to their Practical Application*, it might have been better if he had stuck to the idea of tracts or essays, connected disquisitions on disputed matters. Those who were led to expect that 'practical' meant 'policy' found that they had to make an effort to follow a good deal of deductive theorizing, albeit fleshed out, in Malthusian fashion, with broad historical and empirical material.

The same might be said of two shorter works which were written during the last decade of Malthus's life when he was still trying to codify his thoughts: *The Measure of Value Stated* (1823) and *Definitions in Political Economy* (1827). Modern readers who have not developed a taste for economic reasoning may find they still have to make an effort, but it cannot be avoided in any attempt to understand Malthus's preoccupations, and there may be some consolation in the fact that translating Malthus's ideas into the language of modern economics (largely avoided here) would not ease their problem.

The *Principles* was based on Malthus's belief, in contrast to Ricardo, that 'the science of political economy bears a nearer resemblance to the science of morals and politics than to that of mathematics' (Pr 2); his conviction that one of the chief faults of economists lay in their 'precipitate attempt to simplify and generalize' (Pr 6)—their unwillingness to recognize the multi-causal influences at work in the world and to modify principles in the light of evidence that had accumulated during the half-century that had elapsed since Smith's work first appeared. Once again we see Malthus the moderate at work, attempting to curb 'premature generalisations' by subjecting them to the test of experience, and by constantly stressing the lessons of the doctrine of proportions. In this respect there are similarities between his attitude to Ricardo's doctrines and his attack on Godwin and Condorcet in the first *Essay*. For as he said in a concluding peroration to the *Principles*, although 'we cannot make a science more certain by our wishes or opinions', it was possible to 'make it much more uncertain in its application, by believing it to be what it is not' (Pr 515).

It should now be clear that from the outset of his career as a political economist Malthus was prepared to question the un-qualified application to policy of any single system or principle, however distinguished its lineage, and regardless—as in the case of the population principle—of whether he had formulated it himself. Hence the frequent charges of inconsistency brought against him by fellow-economists. Moreover, if general allegiance to the system of natural liberty, as interpreted by Smith and upheld under the different circumstances by some of his followers, is the hallmark of an orthodox political economist during the first half of the nineteenth century, Malthus occupies a decidedly ambivalent position.

As the opponent of Godwin and others who proposed wholesale departures from a society based on private property and employing competition and self-interest as its chief guiding principles, Malthus was anxious to demonstrate that this form of society was the only one capable of providing the incentives that would guarantee a surplus over basic needs and make rising standards of living possible; that it led to the best available solution by preventing production from going beyond what was economically sustainable, even when this solution fell short of the maximum level of output that was physically possible. This was more than an argument against the feasibility of egalitarian and communitarian schemes of reformation: China and other countries in which population had been 'forced' up to the physical limits of their natural resources served as dire warnings of what could happen if these propositions were ignored.

On the other hand, no other orthodox classical economist pursued quite so many lines of inquiry based on the notion that, for a variety of reasons, economic systems operating under competitive market conditions were not likely to be self-adjusting—or, what amounts to the same thing, capable of adjusting in ways and over time-periods that were acceptable on economic or moral grounds. It was this concern with what happens in the process of adjusting from one constellation of economic forces to another which lends a consistently dynamic dimension to Malthus's work as a political economist. Nor did any other contemporary economist of similar prominence lay so much emphasis on the limits to stable growth arising from the failure of effective demand to expand in harmony with an economy's aggregate supply or capacity to produce. Although Malthus's proposals for institutional change and state intervention to overcome these problems of maladjustment, whether of a temporary or more deep-seated variety, were fairly tentative (his opponents described them as hesitant and vacillating), the underlying preoccupations cannot be ignored in any attempt to understand his method of approach and choice of questions that needed to be answered. Malthus's political economy manifested a persistent concern with fluctuations, instability, limits to growth, possible sources of stagnation, and ways in which the plans and expectations of individuals and groups of economic actors could be frustrated or left unfulfilled in ways that imperilled the continuity of economic life.

Cycles

The earliest signs of this interest are to be found in the treatment given to 'perpetual oscillation' in the first *Essay*—to the cycles, perhaps of some sixteen to eighteen years' duration, which arose from the delayed response of population to the rise or fall in real wages. This helped to explain periodic oversupply, unemployment, and general distress. Ricardo put his finger on a major difference between himself and Malthus when he observed that Malthus always had in mind 'the immediate and temporary effects of particular changes', while he concentrated on the 'permanent state of things which will result from them' (R VII 120). In agreeing with this observation, while noting implicitly that 'temporary effects' might not be confined to a few months or even years, Malthus defended his priorities by saying that: 'I really think that the progress of society consists of irregular movements, and that to omit the consideration of causes which for eight or ten years will give a great *stimulus* to production and population, or a great *check* to them, is to omit the causes of the wealth and poverty of nations—the grand object of all enquiries in Political Economy' (R VII 122). The final paragraph of the *Principles* shows the same concern, with Malthus complaining that 'theoretical writers' (which usually means Ricardo and his followers) have overlooked the consequences, judged by utilitarian standards, of these 'serious spaces in human life':

They amount to a serious sum of happiness or misery, according as they are prosperous or adverse, and leave the country in a very different state at their termination. In prosperous times the mercantile classes often realize fortunes which go far towards securing them against the future; but unfortunately the working classes, though they share in the general prosperity, do not share so largely as in the general adversity. They may suffer the greatest distress in a period of low wages, but cannot be adequately compensated by a period of high wages. To them fluctuations must alway bring more evil than good; and, with a view to the happiness of the great mass of society, it should be our object, as far as possible, to maintain peace, and an equable expenditure. (Pr 522)

The reference here to peace signals the connection with the prolonged period of economic distress that followed the cessation of hostilities in 1815. In seeking explanations for this phenomenon—a topic they were still actively debating in the 1820s—Malthus and Ricardo revealed all their main differences on matters of theory and policy. For it was when advancing his diagnosis and remedies for post-war depression that Malthus further developed the principle of 'effective or effectual demand'. We have noted his use of this principle in various arguments put forward in the later revisions to the *Essay* and in his Corn Law pamphlets—arguments to the effect that when the demand for labour was expanding it was possible for the poor to be rich in the midst of general dearness. This was a precondition for his belief that a combination of high food prices and wages was beneficial to wage-earners. The 1817 edition of the *Essay* also enabled Malthus to incorporate his diagnosis of post-war depression: the conditions most conducive to improvements in the condition of wage-earners, a buoyant effective demand for the products of labour, yielded, by inversion, an explanation for what had gone wrong after the war.

According to Malthus the post-war depression was triggered by the fall in corn prices after exceptionally good harvests in 1814–15. The resulting fall in the incomes of landowners and farmers, accompanied by a failure of money wages to fall in line with food prices, had led to a reduction in agricultural employment and a fall in the home demand for manufactured goods. This in turn had led to export markets being over-supplied and a consequent decline in mercantile incomes. The extent of the depression was partly connected with the immense stimulus given to population and production during the war, and partly with special factors connected with demobilization of the military, high taxes and national debt, and a decline in the general price level due to a reduction in the money supply. Here was a situation in which rents, profits, wages, and prices were simultaneously depressed, and redundant capital was being driven to find employment abroad.

Malthus felt that this evidence was incompatible with two of Ricardo's leading doctrines: his explanation for profit decline in terms of higher wages resulting from diminishing returns in agriculture (a limiting but not a determining condition in Malthus's view): and his diagnosis of the depression as one involving partial rather than general glut. The latter position relied on a proposition associated with the names of Jean-Baptiste Say and James Mill to the effect that aggregate supply or output was always capable of generating a level of aggregate demand that would ensure the sale of all goods produced. According to this proposition, while the markets for some goods could be overstocked, an equivalent understocking would be taking place elsewhere—an idea which Malthus thought was comparable to the assertion 'that every man in the streets of London who was observed to have his head covered, would be found upon examination to have his feet bare' (Q 204).

Whereas Ricardo treated post-war depression and unemployment as a problem of maladjustment due to a mismatch in the demand and supply of individual commodities, Malthus regarded it as evidence of a general deficiency of demand in relation to supply, leading to all markets being overstocked and profits being depressed across the board. Ricardo's solution was to restore prosperity by encouraging investment, chiefly through a reduction in taxes and the burden of national debt, and by allowing market forces to bring about a realignment of the detailed pattern of demand and supply. Although Malthus agreed that cycles had self-correcting features, he also felt that the war stimulus, followed by a severe post-war check to prosperity, had unusual features which warranted special ameliorative action. He was opposed to Ricardo's idea that what was needed, above all, was an increase in capital accumulation under circumstances in which it was manifest that profits and trade were generally depressed.

In order to clarify his position on this point Malthus drew parallels between periods of redundant population and redundant capital. Each was subject to cycles arising from an over-response to earlier conditions of high wages and profits. And just as there were limits to the rate of increase in population which could be sustained without damaging living standards, so there were limits to the volume of savings that could be invested with any hope of obtaining a return that would cover costs and give an adequate incentive to continue production: 'it is equally vain, with a view to the permanent increase of wealth, to continue converting revenue into capital, when there is no adequate demand for the products of such capital, as to continue encouraging marriage and the birth of children without a demand for labour and an increase of the funds for its maintenance' (Pr 375).

The population parallel also consorted well with Malthus's attitude to short-term remedies. For just as the Poor Law and other emergency measures could be justified during exceptional periods of rising food prices, so short-term measures were warranted in order to bring the economy through a cyclical downturn involving an excess of productive potential over effective demand. Addressing himself specifically to the peculiarities of the post-war period, Malthus was not in favour of any sharp reduction of taxes, retirement of debt, and further cuts in public expenditure. This would increase the risk of reducing effective demand in conditions where the productive potential of the economy had been greatly increased during the war. He advocated caution in the removal of protective duties on goods that were competitive with the products of domestic industries, and was anxious to find ways of affording relief to the unemployed by encouraging those capable of increasing the demand for 'unproductive labour' to do so. These could either be 'landlords and persons of property' who might be induced 'to build, to improve and beautify their grounds, and to employ workmen and menial servants'; or relief might take the form of activities, 'the results of which do not come for sale into the market, such as roads and public works' (Pr 511). Such diversions of expenditure away from productive employments, though not justifiable under conditions of full employment, were 'exactly what is wanted' as a counter-balancing factor when there was 'a failure of the national demand for labour' connected with a sudden shift, under conditions of general glut, from the unproductive labour of war towards productive employment. Contrary to the views of some pro-inflationist writers, however, Malthus was not in favour of increasing the quantity of money as a means of raising prices on grounds of the temporary nature of the stimulus and the secondary role played by money in the process of wealth expansion and contraction.

On all these matters Malthus found himself in stark conflict with Ricardo's thinking. An increase in expenditure on unproductive labour, Ricardo commented, was 'just as necessary and as useful with a view to future production, as a fire, which should consume in the manufacturer's warehouse the goods which those unproductive labourers would otherwise consume' (R II 421). And as for public expenditure: 'What could be more wise if Mr. Malthus doctrine be true than to increase the army, and double the salaries of all the officers of Government?' (R II 450). Malthus did not reply to these jibes directly in the second edition of the *Principles*, one reason being that in the context of depression produced by a general over-supply of commodities, consumption meant for him exactly what Ricardo was ridiculing, namely 'used up' or consumed as in a fire. Similarly, while Malthus would not have approved of an increase in the wages or salaries of those employed by public funds as a remedy for depression, he was in favour of increasing public employment in fields that did not add to the existing excess supply of goods. Since Ricardo and all those who adopted the Say–Mill view of things denied the possibility of general glut, it is no wonder that they were bemused by Malthus's heterodox solutions to what they regarded as a non-existent problem.

Effective demand and stable growth

Sharp though these disagreements over both diagnosis and remedies for post-war depression were, they were largely by-products of an issue which is more central to Malthus's *Principles*, namely the discovery of 'the most immediate and effective stimulants to the continued creation and progress of wealth'. This interest in long-run growth prospects, in those institutional and other factors which explained progressive, stationary, and retrograde states of society, was also present in the treatment given to agricultural, manufacturing, and mixed states in the *Essay*. But Malthus gave the theme greater unity and prominence in the *Principles* by focusing on effective demand as one of the essential guarantors of stable and sustainable growth. The significance and peculiarity of Malthus's position on unproductive labour and consumption is also more readily appreciable when placed within the context of these long-run concerns.

Here too Malthus found himself in conflict with the implications of the Say–Mill Law of Markets, as it has come to be called, namely that if capital accumulation and the aggregate supply of goods were increasing over time, the appropriate level of aggregate demand would follow in its train. Once goods had been produced, both the power and the will to consume them existed; economic growth and full employment were entirely compatible. Ricardo's model envisaged, as a theoretical possibility at least, the existence of a 'stationary state' at which profits would be reduced by rising food costs and wages to a level at which there would be no further incentive to invest— a state in which all further growth would cease. But he was anxious to deny that this condition was near at hand, or had actually been reached by Britain, and that it entailed any breakdown in market processes. He was especially anxious to deny any suggestion that the prolonged conditions of post-war depression heralded the arrival of 'a retrograde state of society'. Once the economy had adjusted to post-war conditions, once taxes and the burden of debt had been reduced, and certain unwise policies such as agricultural protection had been abandoned, Ricardo believed that Britain enjoyed almost unlimited scope for further investment and growth.

It is not difficult to see how an argument about partial as opposed to general gluts could become confused with another one involving the distinction between temporary and permanent stagnation. On the surface at least, post-war depression lent support to both positions. The evidence immediately available did not allow a distinction to be made between a situation that was partial and temporary, and one that was general and presaged a permanent retardation. Neither Ricardo nor Malthus succeeded in keeping the problems of short-term cycles and long-term growth prospects separate. There are signs too that Malthus believed—when writing during the post-war period slump at least—that cyclical depression might have more permanent effects. But in order to understand the nature of Malthus's challenge it is helpful to treat the short-term cycle as an acute or special (rather than a chronic or generic) case of principles he had worked out to deal with long-run problems. He was not so much contesting Ricardo's basic optimism about Britain's growth prospects as drawing attention to an important set of preconditions for stable growth that played no part in Ricardo's account. Malthus's main divergence centred on whether the progress or retardation of wealth could be understood simply in terms of the physical factors underlying the productive potential or aggregate supply side of the economy— its labour force, capital stock, and command over natural resources and technology. To this needed to be added, he believed, an account of the variables which determined the level of effective demand, where the main connections between aggregate supply and demand could be found in a distribution of income and expenditure that favoured continued growth.

The problem was largely one of how to sustain economic motivation, a problem which Malthus regarded as being crucial and constant, not merely in poor and what would later be called underdeveloped economies, but in countries like Britain as well. This was a reflection of assumptions about the constancy of human nature that were displayed in the first *Essay* when arguing for the Newtonian character of the social world. It featured in his debate with Ricardo as a question of whether the existence of the *power* to produce and consume guaranteed that the *will* to produce and consume would automatically follow, and if not, what kind of stimulants were needed to make it do so. Whereas Ricardo held that 'will is very seldom wanting when the power exists', Malthus maintained that the inertial forces of 'indolence' were ever-present and had to be overcome by new stimuli, new wants, and new incentives to acquire additional wealth. Ricardo and Malthus were agreed that in theory wants were insatiable; the question at issue was whether, and under what circumstances, the main actors in the economic drama would be prepared to make the necessary sacrifices in terms of leisure forgone in order to obtain the additional goods that would satisfy these wants; whether, in the terminology Malthus employed, luxuries would always be preferred to indolence. Ricardo found such concerns otiose; they might explain slow growth or stagnation in the past, and in China, Latin America, and Ireland in the present, but they were irrelevant to a country like Britain 'with a dense population abounding in capital, skill, commerce, and manufacturing industry, and with tastes for every enjoyment that nature, art or science will procure' (R II 340).

Malthus's answer to this and other questions can be found in a long chapter 'On the Immediate Causes of the Progress of Wealth', which first reviews the factors which underlie the power to produce—population, capital accumulation, fertility of the soil, and 'inventions to abridge labour'—in order to show that, in themselves, acting separately or in combination, they were incapable of generating sustained growth. The missing element was effective demand, which in turn depended on the way in which the total product of society was distributed between the different economic classes, and on whether production was adapted to the wants of consumers. The conditions for effective demand were satisfied when a level of prices existed that was capable of covering all production costs and of giving a return on capital sufficient to serve as an incentive to continue production.

The concept of effective demand rested on the distinction between productive and unproductive consumption which we have already encountered when dealing with Malthus's diagnosis of the post-war depression. Capital accumulation entailed the use of revenue or income for purposes of productive consumption. Although it referred to a form of expenditure on material goods, and was not, therefore, the exclusive province of any class of income recipient, much of the discussion between Malthus and Ricardo was conducted on the assumption that capital accumulation was chiefly an activity or propensity associated with capitalists, those in receipt of profits as opposed to rents and wages. It involved the translation of savings into investment in order to employ labour with a view to producing further profit from the sale of material goods. Unproductive consumption entailed either the purchase of labour services as an end in itself, or the production of material goods that were not intended for sale on the market. The former activity was usually taken to be the main propensity of landowners or rent-receivers, with those in receipt of interest from their holdings of public debt being added, particularly after a war in which such holdings had grown considerably. Again though, it was the nature of the expenditure rather than the form of income from which it derived that mattered most. Although unproductive consumption did not create wealth, it was, according to Malthus, an essential ingredient on the demand side acting as a stimulus to wealth-creation. Maintaining the correct balance between these two activities, therefore, contained the clue to a healthy state of effective demand. It explains Malthus's unorthodox belief, hinted at in his criticisms of Smith in the first *Essay* and developed in opposition to Ricardo in the *Principles*, that 'the principle of saving, pushed to excess, would destroy the motive to production' (Pr 8). While investment of the savings of capitalists (productive consumption) undoubtedly increased the demand of those who were in receipt of wages from such employment, this needed to be supplemented by unproductive consumption to ensure that the increase in output associated with investment was purchased at prices capable of covering the costs of production. If this condition was not met, Malthus believed that the expectations of all savers/investors could be frustrated: there would be insufficient demand to ensure that profits were realized and that production at the new, higher levels would continue. If the doctrine of proportions was not observed in this matter, growth could be impeded rather than facilitated by increased saving/investment.

When Malthus diagnosed an excess of aggregate supply over demand, resulting in a level of output that could not be sold at cost-covering prices, he naturally thought of repairing the deficiency by increasing the level of unproductive consumption by those in receipt of rental and *rentier* incomes. Rents were particularly suitable for this purpose, being earned as a result of the contribution of a natural resource to production, but not for any specific contribution which the ownership of land made to output. Similarly with some public works; they generated incomes and employment without increasing the supply of goods to what might be an overstocked market in which prices and profits were already depressed.

In upholding this position, Malthus has been treated, as he was by Ricardo and his followers, as committing a version of a common 'underconsumptionist' fallacy—the fallacy of believing that, under circumstances which could be either temporary or permanent, the conversion of savings into investment might not be matched by a sufficient volume of demand, either for goods or services, to ensure continued success. The employment of wage-earners resulting from additional investment, though a positive contribution to aggregate demand, might need to be supplemented from other sources to achieve balance. Malthus did not treat saving as 'hoarding' (an increase in idle money balances and hence a subtraction from the income flow), and he endorsed Smith's conclusion that 'the produce which is annually saved is as regularly consumed as that which is annually spent, but that it is consumed by a different set of people'—a concession which Ricardo regarded as being at odds with everything else Malthus wished to contend on this subject. The answer to the apparent contradiction seems to be that Malthus was not raising doubts about unrequited leakages from the annual circular flow, so much as pointing to the fact that an economy in which productive capacity was growing would need ever-higher levels of aggregate demand to secure full employment. This was not a simple matter of fallacious reasoning; rather it was a case of adopting a more pessimistic or cautious view of the opportunities for expanding effective demand sufficiently over time. Malthus's position clearly made sense during the post-war depression, but, with the benefit of hindsight at least, Ricardo's more robust attitude to the ease with which new wants could be released has more to be said for it over the longer period. In recommending that under some circumstances it might be necessary to practice a form of moral restraint with regard to investment, Malthus seems, once more, to be cast in the role of a Cassandra proved wrong by subsequent developments.

Yet this cannot be the last word on the subject, any more than it would be correct to think of Malthus as entertaining dismal views on the impossibility of ever achieving a combination of rising population and living standards. First one must bear in mind the size of the historical and geographical canvas on which Malthus painted. As a historical analysis of the barriers to economic growth in the European past, and as a diagnosis of the difficulties that had to be overcome in Africa, Asia, and Latin America, Malthus's approach, as Ricardo conceded, had a great deal to commend it. It amounted to saying that, in addition to some essential institutional requirements connected with security of property and political stability, a steady expansion of demand, bringing with it rising prices and profits, was a major precondition for sustainable growth. In this respect Malthus remained closer to Hume and Smith in paying more attention to political and moral variables affecting economic habits, and to expansive forces connected with wider markets and the spread of market incentives.

This becomes obvious when Malthus turns to consider those ways in which the distribution of incomes arising from economic activity affect economic growth, favourably or otherwise. The treatment given to this subject is basically a re-examination of some of the topics Smith had dealt with when describing the causes and consequences of the breakup of feudalism, and when illustrating his proposition that the division of labour, and hence the productive powers of society, were dependent on ever-wider extensions of the market.

Malthus's account is organized under three main headings; the division of landed property; the spread of internal and external commerce; and the maintenance of a body of unproductive consumers. Only on the last of these does Malthus depart from Smithian premises. The 'unequal and vicious' division of land under feudalism, creating a small number of wealthy consumers and a large body of poor producers, was highly unfavourable to effective demand, to incentives, and to the adoption of improved methods of production. The subdivision of land, by creating a larger number of smaller consumers and producers, had been an essential step towards making continuous growth possible. This was the solution which Malthus had recommended in the later editions of the *Essay* to the problems of such countries as Russia and Poland. The doctrine of proportions, however, suggested that this process could be carried too far. Thus, Malthus was not in favour of Britain following the French example in abolishing primogeniture, which could lead to a peasantry living at bare subsistence levels and vulnerable both to food shortage and 'military despotism' (Pr 434). Economic and political considerations could not be separated in a matter of this importance.

Primogeniture had swelled the ranks of effective demanders by forcing younger sons (like himself, it might be added) to seek incomes from commerce, manufacturing, the professions, and from dividends on private shares and public debt. What was referred to earlier as Malthus's 'Country' Whig allegiances have a role to play here in disposing him to believe that English liberties depended on the continued existence of a landed aristocracy. But it is a sign of the direction in which his thoughts were moving that in the second edition of the *Principles* he added the middle classes as guardians of liberty when endorsing the benefits of the Reform Bill of 1832 in extending the franchise. He also welcomed the likely further effect of an increase in the size of the manufacturing and commercial sector in generating greater equality, and he attempted to neutralize the connotations of his discussion of unproductive labour by referring instead to a demand for 'personal services'. Landowners, and an 'idle' *rentier* class generally, were no longer the sole source of what Ricardo thought of simply as wasteful expenditure. The demand for any kind of services that generated employment would increasingly come from a wide variety of sources of income.

The expansion of markets through improved internal and external communications has a more obvious basis in Smith's views on extension of the market and the division of labour. The only novelty in Malthus's discussion of this factor lies in his attempt to combat Ricardo's more restricted account of the gains from trade based on his theory of profits. Whereas Ricardo felt that the chief gain would come through a reduction of wages as a result of the importation of cheaper grain products and a consequential rise in profits, Malthus adhered to Smith's more common-sense view that anything which increased the foreign demand for domestic products would raise both wages and profits. With regard to imports, Malthus stressed their 'tendency to inspire new wants, to form new tastes, and to furnish fresh motives for industry', a species of gain which was not of a once-and-for-all variety, and consequently one which 'even civilized and improved countries cannot afford to lose' (Pr 470).

In this case, therefore, Malthus might be said to have adopted a more dynamic, and possibly a more optimistic, view of foreign trade than Ricardo. The same is true of his views on the introduction of machinery, a subject on which Ricardo had dismayed his followers by withdrawing his original opinion that machinery always benefited wage-earners. Given Malthus's belief, expressed as early as 1798, that 'the invention of processes for shortening labour without the proportional extension of the market for the commodity' (FE 34) could be damaging, he might have been expected to follow Ricardo's newer, less optimistic position. In fact, however, Malthus stated that Ricardo had gone too far in a pessimistic direction; there were many circumstances in which new machinery cheapened the product, expanded the market, and led to increased employment: the growth of Manchester, for example, testified to the fact that the demand for the products of the Lancashire cotton industry, as cheapened by machinery, had proved to be elastic.

Most of what Malthus has to say on the balance between productive and unproductive consumers, between savers and spenders, the purchasers of material goods and those who bought personal services has been covered earlier. The only observation worth making in conclusion is that to understand Malthus's position it is necessary to bear in mind not merely the post-war depression, but the fact that he was combating a doctrine of Ricardo's to the effect that the *only* limits to further growth were to be found in the difficulties of procuring food. Since the origins of Ricardo's model are to be found in his case for abolishing the Corn Laws, a conclusion resisted by Malthus, an element of polemical exaggeration on this point should perhaps be entered on both sides of the account. Over the whole spectrum of subjects in dispute, however, which included more metaphysical topics such as the measure of value as well as theories of wages, rent, and profits, the differences are more readily attributable to genuine differences of intellectual style and opinion, where again the participants showed considerable awareness of the source of their divergence. Ricardo put the matter thus:

If I am too theoretical, which I really believe is the case, you are too practical. There are so many combinations, so many operating causes in Political Economy, that there is great danger in appealing to experience in favour of a particular doctrine, unless we are sure that all the causes of variation are seen and their effects duly estimated. (R VI 295)

Malthus recognized the inescapable role played by theory and the impossibility of solving complex problems by simple appeals to practical common sense. But he lacked Ricardo's confidence in thinking that economics was 'a strict science like mathematics' (R VIII 331), and his commitment to experience as the ultimate arbiter was consequently stronger, whatever the result might be in terms of tidiness.

It is not difficult to understand why Keynes, looking back on this dispute from the vantage point of the 1930s, another period of severe depression, found much that was congenial in Malthus (see Chapter 1). But it also seems important to recognize that Malthus's challenge, first to Smith and later to Ricardo, includes, but goes well beyond the kinds of questions which Keynes was to make his own a hundred or so years later. It was not simply that Malthus, like Keynes, was responsive to those 'serious spaces in human life' which may get overlooked in the search for the 'permanent state of things', believing, as Keynes memorably put it, that 'in the long run we are all dead'. Malthus was also concerned about growth prospects over periods of time in which we *are* each likely to be dead.

7 Conclusion

Much of this book has been devoted to answering a deceptively simple historical question: what was Malthus attempting to say to his contemporaries? What, in effect, was he trying to *do* in his various writings on population and political economy? The question of whether he was right in what he contended or did, where 'right' could connote either scientific or moral truth, has been a lesser concern. Yet to those for whom the study of a past thinker must be made subservient to present preoccupations if it is to avoid the sin, harmless or otherwise, of antiquarianism, these priorities may seem perverse, even evasive. What does Malthus have to say that is both new and true to a late twentieth-century audience? That seems a simpler, certainly a blunter way of getting to the heart of matters; and in the case of someone who was self-consciously striving to advance the claims of a science that was capable, in principle at least, of explaining events occurring at all known times and places, it may not only seem to be the most appropriate question, but one that is capable of being answered in a fairly straightforward fashion.

In order to do so, however, one has to begin, in deference to the modern academic division of labour, by distinguishing between Malthus the population theorist and Malthus the political economist, despite the historical fact that the latter role emerged directly from the concerns of the former. One also has to separate Malthus the moralist from Malthus the social scientist, or, more precisely, from Malthus treated as a social scientist according to some influential current interpretations of what a modern social scientist should look like. Having rearranged the intellectual landscape to suit modern tastes, it is then possible to consider Malthus's merits and demerits as a guide to the problems of his own day and ours, praising his pioneering qualities in some cases, but also pointing out the numerous ways in which his formulation of the issues has been improved on, and his predictions falsified—a process which can be carried out with varying degrees of sympathy, often largely depending, in the case of his demographic ideas, on whether the interpreter believes that population pressure in some form is, or is not, a major issue in some part of the world today.

The demographer

As a guide to demographic trends in his own society during the first three decades of the nineteenth century, Malthus has been criticized for paying insufficient attention to the quantitative evidence that was available to him, and for misinterpreting it when he did. His account of the effects on marriage and birth rates of the old Poor Law, the incompleteness of his system of checks as a model for the variables affecting fertility, notably with respect to age-structure and sex-composition, and his assignment of the causes of population growth have all been subject to attacks of this kind. In recent years, however, it has been acknowledged that the connections, or feed-back mechanisms, which he envisaged between food supply and the response of population are more sophisticated than polemical versions of the doctrine suggest. Historical demographers are also willing to grant that he provides a valuable guide to the behaviour of population in pre-industrial societies, thereby adding an element of historical irony to his career: his views were published just as they were about to be made irrelevant, first by the industrial revolution, the discovery of non-land-using raw materials, and the subsequent fall in the price of foodstuffs produced by new suppliers in North America and Australasia, and later by the more widespread use of contraceptive methods. The Malthusian trap was escaped by two exits, one of which he thought was guarded by a tough retaining spring (food supplies), while the other involved the use of methods which he believed to be 'unnatural', immoral, and likely 'to remove a necessary stimulus to industry' (E II 235).

Considered as a predictive device, the dramatic use of the geometric and arithmetic ratios has always given rise to criticism by friends and foes alike. As Malthus himself revealed, the geometric ratio can be reformulated as a fruitful negative hypothesis—why does something *not* happen which an abstract law suggests is possible? The arithmetic ratio is more difficult to rescue, particularly when treated as a *law* of diminishing returns—whatever sense it may have made when interpreted as an inductive inference based on the state of the agricultural arts over a short-run period during the early years of the nineteenth century. But judged in terms of predictions licensed by the crudest form of the Malthusian principle, the whole system has long been exploded. Our capacity to increase food production has been nearer the geometric ratio, and our rate of population increase has been far lower than the maximum posited, though never claimed as an observation, by Malthus. Neither food production nor the supply of natural resources generally, seem capable of acting as a *permanent* constraint on growth rates and living standards. If we contrast the technocratic visions of Godwin and Condorcet with Malthus at his gloomiest, Malthus's opponents appear to have had the last laugh. Whether one appreciates the joke, however, still depends on where one lives in the world, and within which stratum of society.

Some critics have taken the matter further by suggesting that Malthus was guilty of a less venial crime, that of confusing moral and scientific categories, of allowing the former to influence his understanding of the latter, and of propounding a theory that was inherently untestable by virtue of its deductive, even tautological features. They are not impressed by the mass of historical, statistical and ethnographic material which he assembled, or by the fact that towards the end of his life he became a founder-member of the Statistical Section of the British Association for the Advancement of Science and of the London Statistical Society. The material used by Malthus merely becomes, in this light, a set of confirmatory illustrations of propositions which were arrived at by means that have little to do with observation, and, more seriously, were incapable of being subjected to scientific proof or rejection. Thus, when Malthus acknowledged that contemporary evidence did not square with his original prediction that the Poor Laws would encourage early marriage, he concluded that moral restraint must have been more widely practised than he had dared to hope. But instead of being regarded as an example of honesty in the face of facts that ran contrary to one of his predictions, this move is taken to be an attempt to save theoretical appearances by invoking the operation of a moral variable that could not be independently measured. No mitigation of sentence is apparently allowed for the fact that Malthus himself regretted the lack of information that would have allowed him to assign precise weight to the different checks operating singly.

Although such questions could be the essential ones for modern demographers, agronomists, human ecologists, and development specialists, they are certainly not the only ones that can be asked of Malthus. Indeed, it is not clear that they require very much knowledge of Malthus to be answered. They do, however, possess an advantage in their capacity to be framed in fairly precise terms; and in this respect they are less tendentious than those questions which are asked, often on the basis of a presumptively unified twentieth-century morality, about whether Malthus was morally and politically right or wrong in proposing the solutions that he did. As in Malthus's day, this still describes a large body of modern criticism, where the object is basically a recruiting or labelling exercise designed to assign white or black hats to the various historical cowboys.

Given that such questions are suspect or arbitrary, how ought we to look at his work? It has been suggested here that he is best seen as someone committed to the enterprise of constructing and applying a science of politics and morals. This is a reversal of Keynes's description of the trajectory of Malthus's career—'from being a caterpillar of a moral scientist and chrysalis of an historian, he could at last spread the wings of his thought and survey the world as an economist'. Although most economists have understandably been grateful to accept this description, it has been argued here that the population principle and the various ideas on political economy which Malthus advanced were intended more as contributions to the larger and higher scientific vocation of moral scientist. This meant that he was engaged over a wider front than most modern social scientists, including some of his contemporaries. Thus, in Ricardo's eyes Malthus was prone to confuse matters of economic analysis with moral considerations. For example, with regard to rent treated as a gift of a benevolent Creator, Ricardo protested that 'in a treatise on Political Economy it should be so considered. The gift is great or little according as it is more or less, not according as it may be more or less morally useful. It may be better for the health of my friend, that I should restrict him to a pint of wine a day, but my gift is most valuable if I give him a bottle of wine a day' (R II 210). Similarly with Malthus's argument based on the moral advantages of a high price of corn, Ricardo regarded this as an example of failure to recognize that it was the duty of the political economist 'to tell you how you may become rich, but he is not to advise you to prefer riches to indolence, or indolence to riches' (R II 338).

As a guide to individual conduct, Malthus would probably not have disagreed with this proposition; he was not so much preaching individual morality as pointing out the social benefits, largely in terms of stable economic progress, associated with the preference for riches over indolence. He came closer to the preaching role on the subject of moral restraint, though even here he claimed to be taking 'man as he is, with all his imperfections on his head' (E II 222). Preaching morality was secondary to the role of moral scientist capable of elucidating principles, assessing their application to the real world, and attempting to gain support for them. In this, as in so many other respects, he was combining the role of scientist and Christian moralist, and answerable under both rubrics. This distinguishes him from his more secular-minded friends and other political economists who were either without religion or kept it in a separate compartment; but it does not mark him out from other contemporaries who were attempting to create a specifically Christian version of political economy—John Bird Sumner, Richard Jones (his successor at the East India College), Richard Whateley, William Whewell, and Thomas Chalmers. And once a science of morals is understood to be the main point of the exercise, it may be possible to pass a less anachronistic verdict on Malthus's successes and failures. Although social scientists sometimes attempt to measure what Malthus would have regarded as 'moral' variables, and there are, of course, recognizably Christian positions on moral questions, it is rare in the twentieth century to hear anyone speaking of a *science* of morals in the straightforward sense available to Malthus. Whether the relinquishment of such explicit claims represents an advance or not would require another book to answer.

Having brought Malthus's cloth into the reckoning, it is also necessary to confront the uses that have frequently been made of the clerical card. One can either join Marx and Engels in saying that it virtually establishes his credentials as sycophant of the ruling classes, or maintain that the Reverend Malthus was a more humanitarian figure who sometimes came to the rescue of that hard-hearted animal, Population Malthus. With regard to the latter view, there seem to be no good reasons for assuming that Malthus was any more or less humanitarian than anybody else, including his modern critics, and I have given other reasons for doubting the existence of a split personality. As a sincere Christian, committed both to natural theology and the truths of revealed religion, it was Malthus's duty to engage in apologetics, technically defined, namely to illustrate and explicate the essential wisdom and beneficence of God's design for mankind. But was he an apologist in some more ideological sense entailing the conscious or unconscious defence of established interests from a perspective that could not be justified on grounds of science?

That apologetic uses, in this sense, were made of some of his ideas can hardly be denied. Long before Marx posed the charges in what has become the classic ideological form, Nassau Senior gave this as a reason for being prejudiced against Malthus's population principle: 'I found that principle made the stalking-horse of negligence and injustice, the favourite objection to every project for rendering the resources of the country more productive.' Malthus himself complained that he had been unfortunate in his followers: his doctrines had 'by no means the gloomy aspect given to them by many of my readers'. His speedy withdrawal of the polemical passage in the second *Essay* which suggested that those who came to 'nature's mighty feast' (E 1803 ed. II 127) without the means of paying for their meal had no right to sit at table is an indication of his desire to combat such readings, unavailing though this attempt was. The appendices which he added to the *Essay* in answer to his critics are further proof that he was conscious of the problems of misuse and did his best to overcome them. He also had to face similar charges when he announced his support for the Corn Laws and defended incomes derived from rent, both cases where he was accused of selling out to the landowning interest, and where, by inversion, his opponent Ricardo was thought to have injected a radical and anti-aristocratic political bias into his views.

Was the disagreement between Malthus and Ricardo really one about politics and relative degrees of fondness or antagonism to the landed classes? In explaining their differences over the Corn Laws and rent, perhaps some weight should be allowed to this factor. Malthus's brand of Whig politics did stress the political virtues which attached to the historical role played by the country gentry as the guardians of English liberties, though as his remarks on feudalism and the concentration of landownership show, this should not be confused with an unalloyed belief in the virtues of the landed aristocracy. For his part, Ricardo, who became a follower of the 'philosophic radical' line on the reform of Parliament—a line which relied heavily, particularly in James Mill's hands, on antagonism to the aristocratic principle and the kind of Whig politics which Malthus epitomized—might also seem to have had larger political goals in view. But Ricardo was never as fervent on such matters as his political mentor; he certainly denied animus towards the recipients of rental incomes when it was put to him by Malthus. On the divisive political issue posed by the Corn Laws, Malthus always maintained that the private interests of farmers and landowners, or any other producers' pressure group, were irrelevant to the question of public interest which it was the object of the science of political economy to establish: 'The sole object of our consideration ought to be the permanent interest of the consumer, in the character of which is comprehended the whole nation.' And just as Ricardo defended his friend from charges of political bias, so Malthus took pleasure in pointing out that:

It is somewhat singular that Mr. Ricardo, a considerable receiver of rents, should have so much underrated their national importance; while I, who never received, nor expect to receive any, shall probably be accused of overrating their importance. Our different situations and opinions may serve at least to shew our mutual sincerity, and afford a strong presumption that to whatever bias our minds may have been subjected in the doctrines we have laid down, it has not been that, against which perhaps it is most difficult to guard, the insensible bias of situation and interest. (Pr 222–3)

On the subject of the Poor Laws Malthus stated that: 'If all could be completely relieved, and poverty banished from the country, even at the expense of three-fourths of the fortunes of the rich, I would be the last person to say a single syllable against relieving all, and making the degree of distress alone the measure of our bounty' (E II 161). Neither of these statements, of course, has prevented others, both then and since, from treating him as being insincere or deluded in his protestations.

Judged by later nineteenth-century standards, those of 'self-help' and even the 'survival of the fittest', Malthus has often been seen as having all the necessary qualifications for a full-blown progenitor of a harsh *laissez-faire* position that attributes poverty to weakness of individual character alone. He has certainly been accorded this status by those who place this construction on Darwin's acknowledgements of his indebtedness to Malthus at a crucial stage in the working-out of his theory of natural selection. But, for reasons given in an earlier chapter, the Newtonian in Malthus outweighs the proto-Social Darwinist. However heavily Malthus's God may appear to have loaded the scales in favour of Nature as opposed to Culture, and however much individual prudence was expected to be one of the main agencies for delivering man from its unavoidable evil consequences, Malthus's God was still a Newtonian—meaning that poverty had to be the product of general laws acting on mankind in general rather than visited only on the morally unworthy by a ruthless struggle between individuals or classes. Some of Malthus's poor may be indolent, but they share this characteristic of human nature with the rich. Moreover, just as there is no scope for moral restraint in the natural world, so there is no Darwinian equivalent for indolence where all creatures are straining to compete. As a practical moralist, Malthus wished to show that the suffering produced by poverty was remediable rather than therapeutic. He was fully aware of the crucial differences between man and his fellow creatures in the animal world. Attempts to foster on to him post-Darwinian notions connected with eugenics, racism, genocide, and sociobiology are frequently a sign of the need to provide our scapegoats with a lineage.

When awarding moral prizes or penalties, much seems to turn on the degree of optimism or pessimism displayed by our heroes, though hopes unaccompanied by good reasons for hope, one would have thought, come fairly cheaply. For what it is worth, Malthus envisaged a society in which the only poverty that would remain would be confined to those 'who had fallen into misfortunes against which no prudence or foresight could provide', a society in which there were 'fewer blanks and more prizes' (E II 195). It was not visionary to encourage and expect success to attend efforts to increase food supplies ahead of population; but it was still essential, in Malthus's opinion, to issue warnings about the need for prudential restraint to achieve any permanent improvement in the condition of the mass of mankind. He described this vision as 'very cautious', concluding that

> though our future prospects respecting the mitigation of the evils arising from the principle of population may not be so bright as we could wish, yet they are far from being entirely disheartening, and by no means preclude that gradual and progressive improvement in human society, which, before the late wild speculations on the subject, was the object of rational expectation. (E II 202)

He was still hoping, as in the first *Essay*, to re-establish a pre-Revolutionary Enlightenment belief in gradual improvement.

The political economist

The fluctuations in Malthus's reputation as an economist, when judged by modern practitioners, have followed much the same course described when speaking of his standing as a demographer. It has risen whenever later preoccupations have coincided, or appear to have coincided, with those which inform his work. This meant, for example, that by the end of the nineteenth century, Malthus, though given his due as the author of some crucial propositions, shared in the decline of interest which attached to classical political economy generally. With the law of diminishing returns recognized as being perhaps permanently in abeyance, the attention paid to land-ownership and rents seemed excessive. Reform of the Poor Laws in 1834 and abolition of the Corn Laws in 1846 had long removed these questions from their former prominence on the agenda of British economists. Population trends and their influence on food prices, wages, and standards of living were also demoted, treated as being no longer so central to a form of economic inquiry which was increasingly preoccupied with the allocation of given, rather than augmenting or diminishing, resources. Only economists, such as Alfred Marshall, who were deeply influenced by post-Darwinian ideas on evolution, kept up the older concerns in new guise, and Marshall's interests in this aspect of economics were not passed on to the next generation.

The classical concentration on economic growth and the tripartite division of national income between the aggregate shares going to rents, profits, and wages no longer seemed relevant for another reason, namely that the behavioural assumptions which underpinned this division were less valid. Landlords were not simply and solely spenders rather than savers, the reverse of profit-recipients. Perhaps they had never been so single-minded, even in Malthus's day, though it was a common eighteenth-century assumption taken over by most of his early nineteenth-century contemporaries. Wage-earners were no longer confined to a spending role by their incomes, and their savings were beginning to be more significant than the sums deposited, with Malthus's encouragement, in the savings banks that were established to encourage working-class thrift in the early nineteenth century. In Britain at least, the rise in population had become steady rather than dramatic, and the process of *embourgeoisement* which Malthus and Ricardo had hoped for and partially analysed, was, as the rise in real incomes demonstrated, closer to becoming a reality. Comforts, decencies, and even luxuries were now part of many working-class budgets, and the whole class, or rather its male representatives, was becoming, as Malthus hoped it would, an integral part of the political nation.

With the advent of the new type of macro-economics associated with Keynes in the 1930s and beyond, there was renewed interest in the issues which underlay Malthus's dispute with Ricardo over general gluts. When Keynes decided that the doctrine underpinning Ricardian or 'classical' orthodoxy, namely Say's Law, was still one of the hidden presuppositions which made it difficult for his contemporaries to come to terms with general unemployment of the kind experienced in the inter-war period, he was naturally drawn to Malthus's challenge to this doctrine a century earlier. The resulting attempt to rehabilitate Malthus by rescuing him from the shadow cast by Ricardo and the orthodox line of thought he originated marks the beginning of the modern revival of interest in Malthusian economics. And this move was compounded by the post-war revival of interest in the economics of development and underdevelopment, where it was found that the dynamic aspects of classical thinking had much to offer that had been obscured by subsequent changes in modern economics. For these reasons Malthus's stock has been rising steadily during the last fifty years. It is now recognized that even his failures and inconsistencies were on a grand scale; that he posed many issues that are of continuing interest to economists, even if he lacked the mathematical and statistical techniques that would have enabled him to state or resolve them adequately.

This revival of interest frequently tells us more about present-day economics than it does about Malthus, though it is associated with other work in recent years which has helped us to appreciate, much better than most of his contemporaries were able to do, the relative merits of Malthus's analysis of the problems facing his own society when compared with that advanced by Ricardo and his followers. The jury is still sitting on many of these matters, but a few predictions of their verdict can be ventured. Malthus provided a better diagnosis of economic fluctuations in general and of the post-war slump in particular; his capacious, perhaps overly-capacious concept of effective demand enabled him to grasp some features of unemployment, the role of public spending, and the expansive forces needed to guarantee long-term growth prospects, better than the tidier, more aggregate supply-oriented ideas of his opponents. He also perceived some of the genuinely precarious aspects of the 'unbalanced' growth path followed by Britain during its take-off period.

But it is still necessary to return to a different kind of historical question by asking why contemporaries had so much difficulty in grasping Malthus's position, let alone its relative merits. The complaints on this score from reasonably fair-minded readers are too numerous to be ignored. Robert Torrens, for example, followed up an excessively harsh assessment ('Mr. Malthus scarcely ever embraced a principle which he did not subsequently abandon.' (PJ 265)) with one that is perhaps more judicious: 'As presented by Mr. Ricardo, Political Economy possesses a regularity and simplicity beyond what exists in nature; as exhibited by Mr. Malthus, it is a chaos of original but unconnected elements' (PJ 293–4). The same might be said of two later remarks by Walter Bagehot, namely that 'there is a mist of speculation over [Malthus's] facts, and a vapour of fact over his theories', followed by a more generous conclusion that 'he has connected his name with the foundation of a lasting science which he did not plan, and would by no means have agreed in'.

Despite Malthus's efforts to make post-Smithian political economy more applicable to a new age, he was, in contrast to Ricardo, unwilling or unable to create a new 'system' capable of commanding the allegiance of a dedicated, though small group of disciples whose writings, for a time at least, constituted an orthodoxy. Moreover, on some crucial questions of theory and policy he took a direction which had unacceptable political connotations to the Whigs and radicals who made up the bulk of the *cognoscenti* of the new science. Ricardo's theoretical system can hardly be described as an easy one to grasp, but it proved capable of being popularized and its policy recommendations were far less cluttered with qualifications. Malthus's opponents offered the application of a more straightforward logic involving free trade and competitive markets and requiring fewer, and often what seemed like *ad hoc*, exceptions to the system of natural liberty. Malthus appeared to be advancing an eclectic, idiosyncratic, even, in the case of his views on general over-production, a subversive mixture of doctrines that was only capable of being rendered systematic by later generations.

The delayed and untidy sequence of Malthus's publications and revisions to his position did not help in this regard, and some of the policies which he endorsed required detailed empirical assessments of what Ricardo dismissed as 'temporary inconveniences'—assessments which it was easier to call for than to carry out. Malthus's adherence to his doctrine of proportions made him both more cautious and more sensitive to the circumstances surrounding legislative action; and this was to prove a handicap in one so committed to 'practical applications'. It enabled him to attack contemporary issues squarely and to modify his views in the light of experience. But it also led to hesitancy when he found it impossible to come up with specific conclusions that would meet his exacting criteria for locating the golden mean. A science of morals and politics so frankly vague must always be close to accepting what was expedient, or adopting a *post hoc ergo propter hoc* view of the relationship between science and the art of legislation. By contrast with these retrospective judgements, the Ricardian and Benthamite alternatives were more clear-cut; they seemed to promise those responsible for making urgent decisions with delivery of a prospective guide to outcomes, a set of unambiguous criteria for accepting or rejecting policies in advance of their implementation. That kind of confidence based on theoretical tidiness was not Malthus's strong suit, even if it is less possible, at this distance in time, to believe that this suit was capable of winning all the available tricks.

Just as some of Malthus's Whig political beliefs were beginning to seem a little old-fashioned to the new generation of Whigs that emerged in the period running up to the 1832 Reform Bill and beyond, so the same might be said of the practical moralist in Malthus, the person anxious to weigh moral and material benefits and losses in the same scale, to take account of prejudices and the state of opinion when advocating policies, invoking larger comparative and historical themes when necessary. In the eyes of more secular devotees of political economy, who were increasingly attracted by the firmer distinction between 'is' and 'ought' statements, between science and the art of legislation, Malthus's approach seemed outdated.

In all these respects Malthus was more conditioned by an eighteenth-century upbringing than many of those with whom he was dealing. The person who in 1798 had joined a debate which could be traced back to Mandeville and Rousseau, to Hume, Wallace, Smith, and others, remained very much in evidence. Hence Malthus's interest in the institutional preconditions for economic success, and his persistent concern with those moral or psychological factors which determined whether a society possessed what Hume described as 'the quick march of the spirits', the constant spark of ignition that would consistently make riches preferable to indolence. Ricardo and his followers took such matters for granted, at least as far as Britain was concerned. This Malthus was unwilling to do: economic man could not be assumed, he had to be nurtured. In theory wants might be infinitely expanding, but people had to *want* to want, and the wants had to be adapted to production possibilities. This accounts for a persistent source of disagreement with others on the subject of those stimulants that might be needed to overcome indolence, to prevent man from slowing down or falling backwards on the path of improvement. Malthus's disagreement with Ricardo, with Nassau Senior, and others still has these echoes of his original disagreement with Godwin. The young curate who, paradoxically, made his name with an anonymous yet striking pamphlet near the turn of the century was father of the man who died in 1834.

Notes on sources

Chapter 1: the brief quotations from Marx and Engels can be found in R. L. Meek, *Marx and Engels on Malthus*, Lawrence and Wishart, 1953. The quotations from Keynes in this and the final chapter are taken from the essay on Malthus cited under Further reading. The quotation from John Stuart Mill appears in *Essays on Economics and Society*, volume I, p. 366, part of the *Collected Works of John Stuart Mill*, edited by J. M. Robson, University of Toronto and Routledge, 1963–91 (new edition, 1996).

Chapter 3: the quotations from Godwin are taken from *The Enquirer*, 1797, and from his *Enquiry Concerning Political Justice*, book VII, chapters 2–9, edited by I. Kramnick, Pelican Classics, 1976.

Chapter 4: the quotations from *The Crisis* are taken from the paragraphs cited in William Empson's article on Malthus for the *Edinburgh Review*, January 1837, LXIV, 469–506. Southey's comment on Malthus as a peacemonger can be found in a letter to G. C. Bedford in 1808, cited in O. Williams, *Life and Letters of John Rickman*, London, 1911, p. 148.

Chapter 7: Nassau Senior's remarks can be found in his *Two Lectures on Population with a Correspondence between the Author and T. R. Malthus*, 1829, as reprinted in *Selected Economic Writings by Nassau W. Senior*, Augustus Kelley, New York, 1966, p. 89. Bagehot's comments on Malthus are taken from his *Economic Studies*, London 1908, pp. 193–5.

Further reading

Malthus's published works have just become available in scholarly editions. There is a complete edition of *The Works of Thomas Robert Malthus* (Pickering and Chatto, 1986), edited by E. A. Wrigley and David Souden in eight volumes. For scholarly purposes, however, the second *Essay* is best studied in the edition produced by Patricia James (Cambridge, 1990), which shows all the modifications made over the period 1803 to 1826 and fully identifies Malthus's sources. John Pullen has done the same for the *Principles* (Cambridge, 1990), bringing together the 1820 and posthumous 1836 edition, as well as other manuscript material. Given the price of the Pickering-Chatto edition, it seems likely that most readers will still have to rely on cheaper editions, notably of the first *Essay* and *A Summary View of the Principles of Population* (for example that edited by Anthony Flew in the Pelican Classics series). *The Pamphlets of Thomas Robert Malthus* are available as a Kelley reprint, and were first published in 1970. A similar collection of Malthus's articles for the periodical press can be found in *Occasional Papers of T. R. Malthus*, with an introduction by Bernard Semmel (Burt Franklin, 1963).

Patricia James has provided us with the first comprehensive biography, *Population Malthus; His Life and Times* (Routledge & Kegan Paul, 1979), which, in addition to its other qualities as a guide to Malthus's life and period, incorporates a large number of previously unpublished letters. For the famous correspondence with Ricardo, however, it is necessary to consult Piero Sraffa's edition of *The Works and Correspondence of David Ricardo* (Cambridge, 1952–60), volumes 6 to 9. Of interest for other reasons is Keynes's essay on Malthus, reprinted in his *Essays in Biography*, and now as a paperback version of volume 10 of *The Collected Writings of John Maynard Keynes* (Macmillan for the Royal Economic Society, 1972).

Much of the secondary literature is variable in quality, but a few particularly useful and reliable items can be mentioned. Despite its age, J. R. Bonar's *Malthus and his Work* (first edition, 1885, second edition, 1924, and now available from Frank Cass, 1966) is still worth consulting. W. Petersen's *Malthus* (Harvard, 1979) covers a great deal of ground, but is marred by animus towards some of Malthus's opponents. J. R. Poynter's *Society and Pauperism; English Ideas on Poor Relief, 1795–1834* (Routledge & Kegan Paul, 1969) is a classic study of its subject matter. One of the best studies of its kind is D. E. C. Eversley's *Social Theories of Fertility and the Malthusian Debate* (Oxford, 1959). For a representative sample (good and less good) of modern research on Malthusian topics by an international group of scholars see *Malthus Past and Present* (Academic Press, 1983) edited by J. Dupaquier, A. Fauve-Chamoux, and E. Grebenik. A more distinguished collection, concentrating on demographic developments since Malthus, can be found in *The State of Population Theory; Forward from Malthus* (Blackwell, 1986), edited by David Coleman and Roger Schofield.

On some of the more specialized topics covered in this book the following selection from a vast literature can be mentioned. On Malthus's theology see J. R. Pullen, 'Malthus's theological ideas and their influence on his principle of population', *History of Political Economy*, 13 (1981), 39–54. The same author has written on 'Malthus and the doctrine of proportions and the concept of the optimum', *Australian Economic Papers*, 21 (1982), 270–86. On 'Malthus, Darwin and the concept of struggle' see the article by Paul Bowler in *Journal of the History of Ideas*, 37 (1976), 631–50. An early attempt to relate Malthus's ideas on population and political economy can be found in J. J. Spengler, 'Malthus's total population theory; a restatement and reappraisal', *Canadian Journal of Economics and Political Science*, 11 (1945), 83–110, 234–64. On the changes in Malthus's position towards economic growth and manufacturing see G. Gilbert, 'Economic growth and the poor in Malthus's *Essay on Population*', *History of Political Economy*, 12 (1980), 83–96. One of the latest and most interesting treatments of Malthus's views on effective demand and economic growth can be found in Walter Eltis, *The Classical Theory of Economic Growth* (Macmillan, 1984), chapter 5.

Keynes

Robert Skidelsky

To William

Acknowledgements

I would like to thank Peter Oppenheimer, Liam Halligan, and Clive Lennox for their incisive comments. All the imperfections are mine.

Contents

Abbreviations

Keynes's economic writings, including all his books, much of his published essays and articles, and a large proportion of his hitherto unpublished correspondence, have been published in thirty volumes by Macmillan in conjunction with the Royal Economic Society as *The Collected Writings of John Maynard Keynes* (1971–89), ed. Elizabeth Johnson and Donald Moggridge. Most of his private papers remain unpublished and, together with the originals of the published materials in the *Collected Writings*, are deposited at King's College, Cambridge. All references to quotations from the *Collected Writings*, unpublished private correspondence, and lecture notes are given in the text. All other references appear on pp. 129–31. The following abbreviations are used for Keynes's work:

CW   *The Collected Writings of John Maynard Keynes*

GT   *The General Theory of Employment, Interest, and Money*

KP   Keynes Papers

Rymes   *Keynes's Lectures, 1932–35*: Notes of a representative student, transcribed, edited, and constructed by Thomas K. Rymes (1989).

Introduction: *The man and economist*

Keynes's fundamental insight was that we do not know—cannot calculate—what the future will bring. In such a world money offers psychological security against uncertainty. When savers become pessimistic about future prospects they can decide to hoard their savings rather than invest them in businesses. Thus there is no guarantee that all income earned will be spent. This amounts to saying that there is no natural tendency for all available resources to be employed. 'Men cannot be employed', he wrote in *The General Theory*

when the object of desire (i.e. money) is something which cannot be produced [employ people in its production] and the demand for which cannot be readily choked off. There is no remedy but to persuade the public that green cheese is practically the same thing and to have a green cheese factory (i.e. a central bank) under public control. (*CW* vii. 235)

When Keynes talked about money rather than goods being the 'object of desire', was he being frivolous or was he saying something profound in a playful way? How seriously was one to take his suggestion that one should make money go bad, like 'green cheese'?

People have debated these matters ever since. Was Keynes merely a speculator in ideas or was he a saviour who brought a diseased world a new hope of health? The Fabian Beatrice Webb wrote: 'Keynes is not serious about economic problems; he plays a game of chess with it in his leisure hours. The only serious cult with him is aesthetics. To Russell Leffingwell, a US Treasury official who negotiated with Keynes at the Paris

Peace Conference in 1919, Keynes was 'always perverse, Puckish . . . a bright boy, shocking his admiring elders by questioning the existence of God, and the Ten Commandments!' However, for the economist James Meade, who knew him both as a postgraduate at Cambridge and as a civil servant in the war, Keynes 'was not merely a very great man; he was a very good man also'. For young economists generally, *The General Theory* shone out as a beacon of light in a benighted world. 'What we got was joyful revelation in dark time,' recalled David Bensusan-Butt, who came up to read economics at King's College, Cambridge, in 1933. 'Keynes's reformed capitalism had everything and more the Fabian generation had looked for in socialism: it was morally speaking egalitarian, it was fully employed, it was generous and gay. . . .' Another student, Lorie Tarshis, wrote: 'And finally what Keynes supplied was *hope*: hope that prosperity could be restored and maintained without the support of prison camps, executions and bestial interrogations. . . .'

These stereotypes have persisted. To anti-Keynesians Keynes is someone who produced fertile, but ultimately unsound and distracting hypotheses; to Keynesians he offered a profound insight into the way economies behave, permanently valuable tools of economic policy. The stereotypes are true but incomplete. Keynes had many sides; different people saw different aspects of him. He also changed, so that different generations saw him in different lights. He did love to play with ideas in a reckless way, but, as his friend Oswald Falk remarked, 'in this manner, in spite of false scents, he caught up with the march of events more rapidly than did others'. He was a striking phrasemaker, and used words deliberately to rouse people from their mental torpor. But 'when the seats of power and authority have been attained there should be no more poetic licence' (*CW* xxi. 244). About his ultimate seriousness of purpose there can be no real doubt. The real question is whether the concepts he bequeathed were the right ones to make sense of his world, and beyond that, of our world.

Keynes's ideas were rooted in time and place. He was born in 1883 and died in 1946. He was born into a world which assumed peace, prosperity, and progress to be the natural order of things, and lived long enough to see all these expectations toppled. When he grew up, Britain was the centre of a mighty empire: in the last months of his life he was handing round the begging bowl in Washington. His life spanned not just the collapse of British power, but the growing enfeeblement of the British economy. It spanned the passage from certainty to uncertainty, from the perfumed garden of his youth to the jungle of his mature years, where monsters prowled. In 1940 he wrote to an American correspondent: 'For the first time for more than two centuries Hobbes has more message for us than Locke' (KP, PP/57, JMK to Sterling P. Lamprecht, 19 June 1940).

Keynes was a product of decaying Victorian conventions. This is what made the problem of behaviour, personal and social, so central for him. But before the First World War this very decay produced a great surge of cheerfulness in Keynes and his contemporaries. They saw themselves as the first generation freed from Christian 'hocus-pocus', the creators and beneficiaries of a new Enlightenment, who could work out their ideals and maxims of conduct in the pure light of reason. Their ideals were aesthetic and personal; public life was rather depressing, because the great victories of progress, it seemed, had all been won. Experiment was the order of the day in the arts, in philosophy, in science, and in life-styles, rather than in politics or economics. Diaghilev was born in 1872, Picasso in 1881, Gropius in 1883, James Joyce and Virginia Woolf in 1882, Russell in 1872, G. E. Moore in 1873, Wittgenstein in 1889, Einstein in 1880. Only Freud, of those who moulded early twentieth-century consciousness, comes from an earlier generation, born in 1856.

Then came the First World War, and everything changed. After 1914 there was the management of the world to attend to—a world which, after 1914, seemed to be spinning into chaos. Here the problem was one of control, not liberation.

Civilization, Keynes acknowledged in 1938, was a 'thin and precarious crust' (*CW* x. 447). The men of power took over, determined to impose their versions of order on chaos: Stalin was born in 1879, Mussolini in 1883, Hitler in 1889. Modernism lost its innocence, as playfulness gave way to horror. And Keynes began to wonder about his early creed. 'I begin to see', he said to Virginia Woolf in 1934, 'that our generation—yours & mine ... owed a great deal to our fathers' religion. And the young ... who are brought up without it, will never get so much out of life. They're trivial: like dogs in their lusts. We had the best of both worlds. We destroyed Xty & yet had its benefits.' But the important point is that he never succumbed to the politics of cultural despair. Despite everything, that Edwardian cheerfulness survived. Uncertainty could be managed, not by brute force, but by brains, by the exercise of intelligence, and gradually the harmonies might be restored. This was his ultimate credo, his message, if there is one, for our time.

He was well qualified to convey it. Bertrand Russell has written that 'Keynes's intellect was the sharpest and clearest that I have ever known. When I argued with him, I felt that I took my life in my hands, and I seldom emerged without feeling something of a fool.' Others, like Kenneth Clark, felt he used his brilliance too unsparingly: 'he never dimmed his headlights.' But it was his liquidity of mind which chiefly struck his contemporaries: its tendency, as Kingsley Martin put it, to 'run round and over an obstacle rather than dispose of it. Like a stream he often appears travelling in opposite directions.' The jibe that wherever five economists were gathered there were six opinions and two of them were Keynes's was already familiar in his lifetime. 'But the charges of caprice and inconsistency so often levelled against him signify very little,' Kingsley Martin wrote, 'except that his mind deals swiftly and somewhat cavalierly with practical difficulties, offering one possible solution after another in a way that is terrifying and bewildering to the cautious and solidly rooted.' The irony, as Kurt Singer noted, was that someone who 'seemed to find rest only in motion ... [able] to build and to discard in one afternoon a memorable number of equally attractive conceptual schemes' should have bequeathed to the world 'the Book of a new faith'.

Yet it would be wrong to say of him, as he said of Lloyd George, that he was 'rooted in nothing'. He was born a Victorian, and traces of 'Victorian values' remained with him throughout. He had a strong inherited sense of duty, even though, like Sidgwick, he found it difficult to justify it philosophically. He believed in government by a benevolent clerisy, or intellectual aristocracy. There was in this notion a mingling of the social and intellectual which reflects the very Victorian rise of Keynes's own family, through brains and business acumen, into the circle of the governing class. He was a 'thinking' patriot, though his patriotism was free of any trace of jingoism. He was a firm believer in the virtues of the *Pax Britannica* and reluctant to believe that any other country could take on Britain's world role. He was pro-German, anti-French—another nineteenth-century inheritance.

Nonconformity was a powerful factor in Keynes's formation. It comes out in his frugality. People found his entertainments 'very economical', and at the end of his life he regretted he had not drunk more champagne. He became very wealthy, but he lived comfortably, not grandly or ostentatiously. As an economist, his imagination was much more excited by people's propensity to hoard than to splash; and he would turn this cultural, or psychological, defect in his own class background into a paradoxical explanation of why capitalist economies could run down.

He came from a family of preachers, especially on his mother's side. He was of the first generation of unbelievers untroubled by 'doubts', but theology was in his bones, and the distance between theology and economics much less than it is today. He had to the full the Nonconformist capacity for indignation and protest; his economic essays are secularized sermons. The 'unsurpassed individualism of our philosophy', to which he referred in 1938, rested on the belief that human beings (at least in England) had been sufficiently moralized by Victorian values that they could be 'safely released from the outward restraints of convention and traditional standards and inflexible rules of conduct, and left, from now onwards, to their own sensible devices, pure motives and reliable intuitions of the good' (*CW* x. 447).

Keynes's social sympathies were not wide, though they widened as he grew older. His family had pulled themselves up by their bootstraps, and in general he expected others to do the same, provided there were enough jobs to go round. For the residue there was the Charity Organisation Society, and other typical mid-Victorian associations for helping the unfit and alcoholic. Keynes's hereditary Nonconformity was weakened by social acceptance. He had been to Eton, as a Colleger (as Eton scholars are called), and was increasingly at his happiest in the company of clever Old Etonians. He enjoyed the company of the rich and well-born, though he indulged it sparingly. As he grew older Keynes became more conservative, an apostle of continuity and evolutionary change. The social conclusions to which his economics pointed, he wrote at the end of *The General Theory*, were 'moderately conservative'. Capitalism, for which he had a moral distaste, could survive, under improved management.

What remained intact from his childhood were his work habits. Keynes was one of the most efficient working machines ever created. Thus he imposed his own order on a disorderly world. It enabled him to lead as many lives as he did, and to show zest for each one. Every nook and cranny of the day was packed with multifarious activities and projects. He got through all his business with astonishing expedition. He had an amazing capacity to switch from one thing to another; and despite all he did he seemed unhurried, with plenty of time for friendship, conversation, and hobbies.

It was Keynes's 'queer imaginative ardour about history, humanity' which endeared him to Virginia Woolf, his 'mind working always', overflowing 'vigorously into byepaths'. He had a universal curiosity, and could not touch any topic without weaving a theory about it, however fanciful. 'England could not have afforded Shakespeare had he been born fifty years earlier,' was one favourite saying. This attractive habit of rushing in where slower minds feared to tread, and relying on quick invention to get him out of tight corners, often affronted experts and gave him the reputation of an amateur, even in economics. But it was not all after-dinner chatter. Keynes could get totally obsessed by intellectual concerns apparently remote from the mainstream of his work. Early in life he tried to work out a formula for predicting colour-blindness, based on Mendelian genetics; in the 1920s he succumbed repeatedly to his 'Babylonian madness'—an essay on the origins of money. 'It is purely absurd and quite useless,' he wrote to Lydia Lopokova on 18 January 1924, 'But just as before I became absorbed in it to the point of frenzy . . . The result is I feel quite mad and silly. With a lunatic kiss and a wild eye, Maynard.'

Even his efficiency could not save him from constant fatigue. He was always overworked. As a young man he went to spend a restful weekend with the Russells, and twenty-six unexpected guests arrived, most of them, Russell implies, summoned by Keynes. Later in life brief-cases full of paper always accompanied him on his holidays abroad. He spent years of what he himself called 'Chinese torture' on college and university committees from which he could easily have escaped. 'Is it necessary?' 'Why do we buzz and fuzz?' 'Why do I do it?' Did Keynes have any identity in solitude? He does not give the impression of being at ease with himself. He thought he was ugly. He loathed his voice. His Bloomsbury friends complained of his lack of fastidiousness, and mocked his taste in pictures and furniture. The 'masks' which he put on were physical as well as mental. The playful eyes and sensuous mouth were covered up by the conventional disguises—the military moustache, the dark suits and Homburgs which he wore even on picnics—of the 'man of affairs'. He sought his identity in mastery of the external world.

In his attitude to his fellow humans, Keynes was a mixture of benevolence and intolerance. He had a great capacity for affection, and, unlike most fellow members of the Bloomsbury Group, was exceptionally loyal to his friends. He appreciated mental quirks, oddities, obsessions, which he often saw as containing interesting possibilities. He revered genius, a word which he used in its original sense of a 'free spirit'. Like many intellectuals he respected practical expertise, even of the humblest. He was quick to excuse the faults of youth and inexperience. He was not a patient man, but he could take enormous trouble with the affairs of his friends, and those he thought deserving of it.

At the same time he could be devastatingly rude—especially to those he thought ought to know better. He had the curse of Oxbridge, believing that all the cleverness of the world was located in it and its products. With this went a profoundly Anglocentric view of the world, more typical then than now. He often got away with rudeness because of his ready command of repartee and the technique of *reductio ad absurdum*. But he could also wound. The American economist Walter Stewart wrote that

In conversation Keynes was frequently brilliant and not infrequently unkind. He could not resist scoring a point and would look around the circle of listeners to see whether others had noticed the arrow hit the mark. Some of his sharpest wit was used against those who could not easily defend themselves and even against the absent.

It was not a style calculated to endear. The Americans never took to it. Keynes's 'Open Letter' to Roosevelt in 1933, sounded, writes Herbert Stein, 'like the letter from a school teacher to the very rich father of a very dull pupil'. In Savannah, in March 1946, for the inaugural meeting of the International Monetary Fund, Keynes made a speech in which he hoped that 'there is no malicious fairy, no Carabosse' who had not been invited to the party. The reference was to Tchaikovsky's ballet, *Sleeping Beauty*, but Frederic Vinson the US Secretary of the Treasury, took it personally. 'I don't mind being called malicious, but I do mind being called a fairy,' he growled.

Kurt Singer leaves a kinder picture of Keynes in action. He evoked 'by gesture, eye and word . . . the figure of a bird, of incredible swiftness, drawing circles in high altitudes but of deadly precision when suddenly sweeping down on some particular fact or thought, able to coin unforgettable word-formulas for what he saw, forcing his intellectual booty with iron grips even on the unwilling'.

It was not predetermined, either by background or abilities, that Keynes would make economics his life's work. His father was a logician and economist, but his career was not a good omen for his son: it ended in university administration. Keynes's mind was too wide-ranging, his spirit too active, for highly-specialized academic work. In writing his *Treatise on Probability*, he exhausted his serious interest in logic: it was too narrow for his mind. One must be able to use one's brains aesthetically and practically. The psychology of money, and stock-exchange gambling, fascinated him from an early age; his administrative talents might have made him a high imperial civil servant; he was a wonderful writer. In the end he was able to use economics as the vehicle for all his obsessions and talents, but it was the uncertain state of a war-shocked world which made economics his vocation.

II

What sort of economist was Keynes? The most striking thing about him is the combination of gifts he brought to the subject. It is impossible to believe that he did not have himself in mind when he wrote, in his essay on Marshall,

the master-economist must possess a rare *combination* of gifts . . . He must be mathematician, historian, statesman, philosopher—in some degree. He must understand symbols and speak in words. He must contemplate the particular in terms of the general, and touch abstract and concrete in the same flight of thought. He must study the present in the light of the past for the purposes of the future. No part of man's nature or his institutions must lie entirely outside his regard. He must be purposeful and disinterested in a simultaneous mood; as aloof and incorruptible as an artist, yet sometimes as near the earth as a politician. (*CW* x. 173-4)

His wife, Lydia Lopokova, wrote that Keynes was 'more than economist'; he himself felt that 'all his worlds' fertilized his economic thinking. He fits that old-fashioned label, difficult to define, of political economist, someone who sees economics as a branch of statesmanship rather than a self-enclosed discipline with invariable laws. One of his interlocutors on the Macmillan Committee on Finance and Industry asked: had not social security benefits prevented 'economic laws' from working? 'I do not think it is any more economic law that wages should go down easily than they should not,' Keynes replied. 'It is a question of facts. Economic law does not lay down the facts: it tells you what the consequences are' (*CW* xx. 83-4). In middle age he used to complain bitterly that young economists were not properly educated—they were not able to draw on a wide culture for the interpretation of economic facts. Here is a clue to what has gone wrong with economics, and indeed with the Keynesian revolution. Keynes lit fires in technicians—but they remained technicians. They used his tools, but failed to update his vision.

In his essay on Thomas Malthus, Keynes claimed for 'the first Cambridge economist', a 'profound economic intuition' and 'an unusual combination of keeping an open mind to the shifting picture of experience and of constantly applying to its interpretation the principles of formal thought' (*CW* x. 108). This expressed his own philosophy of economics in a nutshell. Economics, he told Roy Harrod in 1938, is 'a science of thinking in terms of models joined to the art of choosing models which are relevant to the contemporary world . . . Good economists are scarce because the gift of using "vigilant observation" to choose good models . . . appears to be a very rare one' (*CW* xiv. 296-7). In his essay on Isaac Newton, Keynes quoted de Morgan's verdict of him: 'so happy in his conjectures as to seem to know more than he could possibly have any means of proving' (*CW* x. 365). Keynes, too, felt sure of the result long before he had supplied the proof.

Keynes was the most intuitive of economists—using 'intuitive' as people talk, or used to talk, of 'feminine' intuition—a feeling of certainty apart from rationality. (One of his biographers, Charles Hession, traces his creativity to a synthesis of female intuition and masculine logic.) Intuition in this sense must be distinguished from philosophic intuition in which Keynes also believed—the view that knowledge arises directly from introspection. Keynes had an extraordinary insight into the *Gestalt* of particular situations. He had in marked degree the scientific imagination he ascribed to Freud, 'which can body forth an abundance of innovating ideas, shattering possibilities, working hypotheses, which have sufficient foundation in intuition and common experience' (*CW* xvii. 392–3). His favoured objects of contemplation were economic facts, usually in statistical form. He used to say that his best ideas came to him from 'messing about with figures and *seeing* what they must mean'. Yet he was famously sceptical about econometrics—the use of statistical methods for forecasting purposes. He championed the cause of better statistics, not to provide material for the regression coefficient, but for the intuition of the economist to play on.

A crucial source of Keynes's understanding of business life was his personal involvement in money-making. 'It was his understanding of the speculative instinct which made Keynes such a great economist,' noted his friend and fellow financier Nicholas Davenport.

The academic economist never really knows what makes a businessman tick, why he wants sometimes to gamble on an investment project and why he sometimes prefers liquidity and cash. Maynard understood because he was a gambler himself and felt the gambling or liquidity instincts of the business man. He once said to me, 'Remember, Nicholas, that business life is always a bet.'

Keynes's generalizing passion was often at odds with his uncanny sense of the significant particular. He strove always

'To see a World in a Grain of Sand . . . And Eternity in an hour'.
It was Keynes's very ability to 'touch the abstract and concrete
in the same flight of thought' which is such a dazzling, but also
bewildering feature of his economics. People were never sure at
what level of abstraction he was working. In his review of *The
General Theory*, his Cambridge colleague Pigou complained of
Keynes's desire to 'reach a stage of generality so high that
everything must be discussed at the same time'. Schumpeter
said much the same thing. *The General Theory* was a book
which offered 'in the garb of general scientific truth, advice
which . . . carries meaning only with reference to the practical
exigencies of the unique historical situation of a given time and
country'; it constructed 'special cases which in the author's
own mind and in his exposition are invested with a treacherous
generality'.

From another Cambridge colleague, Dennis Robertson, came
a related criticism summed up in the phrase 'successive over-
emphasis'.

May I suggest that I—managing to keep throughout in touch with
all the elements of the problem in a dim and fumbling way—have
been a sort of glow worm, whose feeble glimmer lands on all the
objects in the neighbourhood: while you, with your far more powerful intellect, have been a lighthouse casting a far more penetrating, but sometimes fatally distorting, beam on one object after
another. (*CW* xxix. 166–7)

Marshall criticized Jevons in much the same way as many
criticized Keynes: 'His success was aided even by his faults
. . . he led many to think he was correcting great errors, whereas
he was really only adding important explanations.'

There is obviously room to wonder whether, as Kurt Singer
suggests, Keynes's 'general theory' is 'not in fact tailored to fit
a very particular situation dominated by the political vicissitudes and their psychological consequences of that uneasy
weekend between the two world wars; and whether [Keynes]
was not in fact dealing with a phenomenon not likely to recur'.
On the other hand, it is hard to explain the American collapse

of 1929 in these terms; the extent of the 'uncaused' American depression, as we shall see, was the overwhelming fact which *The General Theory* was designed to explain.

III

In the final analysis, the shift from 'classical' to 'Keynesian' economics cannot be isolated from the larger transitions in politics, international affairs, science, philosophy, and aesthetics through which Keynes lived. They were all refracted in Keynes's luminous and mysterious mind. He remained an Edwardian, in the sense that his beliefs about the world were crystallized in the early years of the century. He adapted his creed to the grimmer realities which followed. In his economics, he strove not for the truth but for the attainable idea necessary to the conduct of lives in a world which had lost its moral bearings. He never succumbed to despair. In his darkest moments, cheerfulness kept breaking though. Shortly before his death, he gave a toast to economics and economists— 'trustees, not of civilisation, but of the possibilities of civilisation'. Only someone with a fine sense of language, and an Edwardian sense of life's purpose, would have chosen exactly those words.

1 *The life*

I

Keynes set out to save what he called 'capitalistic individual-ism' from the scourge of mass unemployment, which, he saw, if left unchecked, would make 'authoritarian state systems' the norm in the Western world. He was born on 5 June 1883 into a very different era of 'capitalistic individualism': one in which economic progress was taken for granted; a liberal oligarchy of land and money manned the state; and Britain's position seemed secure as the head and heart of a world trading system. That this was an age which was dying was apparent only to a few. The doubts of the Victorians were still more religious than material, though there were premonitions of danger to the established order of things—the rise of the mass democracy at home, the challenge of Germany abroad, a certain loss of economic vitality, the growing amplitude of industrial fluctuations. The word 'unemployment' first appeared in the *Oxford English Dictionary* in 1888—a sign of things to come.

Maynard Keynes was the product of a not unusual Victorian success story. He was the eldest of three children of a well-off Cambridge academic family, living at 6 Harvey Road. The Keynes family traced their descent back to a Norman knight who had come over with William the Conqueror. But it was Maynard Keynes's paternal grandfather who rescued the family from poverty by making a small fortune as a market gardener in Salisbury. His only son, John Neville, established himself at Cambridge in the 1870s as a Fellow of Pembroke College. He was a philosopher and an economist who wrote standard texts on logic and economic method; later he became Registrary of the University. In 1882 he married Florence Ada Brown, daughter of a well-known north-country Congregational minister, and a schoolmistress mother devoted to the cause of women's education. Both families' antecedents were 'chapel and trade': the move to Cambridge was part of the assimilation of provincial Nonconformity into the Establishment of Victorian England.

Keynes's parents embodied the Victorian virtues in relaxed form. John Neville Keynes indulged himself in a variety of hobbies. From him Maynard Keynes took intellectual precision and administrative efficiency combined with a certain playfulness, though he was mercifully free from his father's anxiety. Florence Keynes took up 'good causes' but never at the expense of her family. She—and the Browns generally—represented the 'preaching' and 'do-gooding' side of Maynard's inheritance; they also had a streak of intellectual fancy. Keynes's genius was his own, but he felt he had a social and intellectual tradition to live up to.

The family atmosphere at 6 Harvey Road was high-minded. The Keynes circle included some of the foremost economists and philosophers of the day—Alfred Marshall, Herbert Foxwell, Henry Sidgwick, W. E. Johnston, James Ward. As a young man Maynard played golf with Sidgwick, and wrote of him with wicked accuracy (to his friend Bernard Swithinbank on 27 March 1906): 'He never did anything but wonder whether Christianity was true and prove that it wasn't and hope that it was.' Cambridge was less worldly than Oxford. Although Maynard would mingle with the world, his standards remained unworldly. He judged his own life, and others', by intellectual and aesthetic criteria. He imposed himself on the world of affairs by force of intellect and imagination, but was not absorbed by it.

He accepted without question the high value his father and mother placed on academic excellence. Indeed, he never rebelled against his parents, though he had a larger range of sympathies. His family home, where Neville and Florence Keynes continued to live after Maynard had died, gave his life stability and continuity. His social thinking had a precise reference to his family's circumstances. He saw himself as a member of the 'thinking' middle class. He thought that escape from poverty was always possible in pre-war Europe 'for any man of capacity or character at all exceeding the average' (CW ii. 6). And he never lost his belief in the duty of a capable and right-thinking clerisy to give leadership to the masses.

In 1897 he gained a scholarship to Eton, Britain's top school. He was an outstanding schoolboy, though in no narrow way, winning an enormous number of prizes, being elected to 'Pop', Eton's exclusive social club, and even performing creditably in College's incomprehensible Wall game. What is already noticeable is the extraordinary range of his interests and aptitudes. Mathematics was his best subject, but he excelled in classics and history too. He got through his work at lightning speed. He won the respect of scholars *and* athletes, just as later he would win over both academic economists and practical men. Keynes realized from an early age that cleverness guilefully deployed was the road to success in dealing with adults. Cleverness was the alternative to submission or rebellion: through cleverness one could manipulate any situation to one's advantage. What was also noticeable was a certain mismatch between his capacities and his sympathies. He was developing into the logical, statistical, administrative, arrogant Keynes; but he was also the 'Maynard' whom his intimate friends knew, craving affection, drawn to writers, artists, and dreamers, losing himself in medieval poetry or abstruse speculations. Later he would see the practical purpose of economics as providing a protective belt for civilization against the forces of madness and ignorance.

In 1902 he went up to King's College, Cambridge, on an open scholarship in mathematics and classics. Mathematics, his best subject, had never given him much pleasure, and he gave it up with relief after gaining a first-class degree in Part I of the Mathematical Tripos. He had spent most of his undergraduate time doing other things—studying philosophy, writing a paper on the medieval logician Peter Abelard, speaking at the Cambridge Union (he became its President in 1905), playing bridge, and indulging his passion for friendship. In 1906 he came second to Otto Niemeyer in the Civil Service Examination, entering the India Office as a junior clerk. In two years of routine work he picked up a sound knowledge of India's financial system, which led to his appointment as a member of the Royal Commission on Indian Finance and Currency in 1913. But he spent most of his office hours writing a dissertation on probability which, after one failure, got him his fellowship at King's College in 1909. Cambridge University remained his academic home for the rest of his life.

While he was thus laying the foundations of his career, a shift in values had been taking place which carried him far beyond the confines of his parents' relaxed Victorianism. Victorian morals had been sustained by religious beliefs which were collapsing. Keynes and his undergraduate friends were militant atheists; but, as with so many thinking Nonconformists, the loss of beliefs which they regarded as false had not removed the need for beliefs which they could regard as true. They looked to moral philosophy to tell them how to live their lives. The philosopher G. E. Moore gave them what they wanted—a justification for breaking with the social and sexual codes of their parents. His *Principia Ethica* (1903) was the manifesto of modernism to Keynes's generation: later Keynes described it as 'the opening of a new heaven on earth'.

Keynes had fallen under Moore's influence when, in his second undergraduate term, he was elected a member of the Cambridge Apostles, a selective and (at the time) secret philosophical discussion society. Through the Apostles he made some of the great friendships of his life, notably with Lytton Strachey; in the late 1900s he became a member of the Bloomsbury Group, a London commune of Apostles, their friends, and male and female relations. It was a circle of young writers and artists who found in the freer life of the unfashionable Bloomsbury district of London an escape from the stuffy conventions of their parents' households. In this partly admiring, partly disapproving, frequently malicious group of talented friends, Maynard Keynes found his emotional home before his marriage.

Moore convinced them of the supreme value of aesthetic experiences and personal friendship. He swept away the melancholy of the previous generation who could find no convincing reasons for doing their duty. He reintroduced cheerfulness into moral discussion, erecting a new argument for unworldliness on the foundation of Cambridge analytical philosophy. It was a shift possible only for those in privileged circumstances, and for whom politics was a minor interest, lacking the power to disturb 'good states of mind'—something certainly true of Keynes before 1914. But it was immensely liberating.

'One's prime objects in life', wrote Keynes in 1938 of his pre-war days, 'were love, the creation and enjoyment of aesthetic experience and the pursuit of knowledge. Of these love came a long way first' (*CW* x. 436–7). To Keynes and most of his Apostolic friends, love meant homosexual love, initially of a somewhat spiritualized kind. Keynes's lover from 1908 to 1911 was the painter Duncan Grant, a cousin of Lytton Strachey, whom he 'stole' from the latter to much perturbation in Bloomsbury. Until after the First World War all his emotional attachments were to young men. But Keynes was no more an extremist in love than in economics or politics. His homosexuality did not exclude the capacity to fall in love, and enjoy a happy sexual relationship, with the right woman; and she duly appeared after the First World War.

Beauty for Keynes and his friends meant chiefly post-impressionist painting, Russian ballet, and the new styles of decorative art influenced by both. For those with money, taste, and domestic servants (and one did not have to have much money to afford servants), London just before the First World War was an exciting place. The British philistinism of which Matthew Arnold had complained was being undermined by the artistic *avant-garde*. The idea that preposterous figures in Central Europe might be able to close down civilization in pursuit of great power ambitions and ethnic rivalries seemed unthinkable. It was a world, also, completely cut off from the ordinary experience of the masses, for whom, nevertheless, automatic economic progress was believed to be producing a better life, too.

Pursuit of knowledge for Keynes meant philosophy and economics, and more the first than the second. Most of his intellectual energy before 1914 went into turning his dissertation into the *Treatise on Probability*, not published till 1921, in which he tried to widen the field of logical argument to cover those cases where conclusions were uncertain. This work spilled over importantly into his economics. At Cambridge he lectured on money. He was an orthodox Marshallian quantity theorist, and did little to extend the frontiers of the subject, though his first (and only pre-war) book, *Indian Currency and Finance* (1913), was a lucid attempt to apply existing monetary theory to the reform of India's currency system. It was notable for its expert knowledge of the working of financial institutions, its endorsement of the gold-exchange standard, and its advocacy of an Indian central bank—details of which Keynes worked out as a member of the Royal Commission on Indian Finance and Currency the same year.

He was just as interested, though, in the problem of knowledge in economics, engaging, in 1911, in an acrimonious debate with Karl Pearson about the influence of the alcoholism of parents on the life chances of their children. Keynes rejected Pearson's use of inductive methods to establish social truths. This reflected his more general scepticism about the value of statistical inference, in line with his rejection of the statistical, or frequency, theory of probability. Economics could not be an exact science, because the number of variables was too great, and stability of variables over time could not be guaranteed. As he was to put it later, it is better to be roughly right than precisely wrong.

II

Keynes was 31 when the First World War broke out. The war changed his life-style, career, and ambitions, though not his ultimate values. After playing an important part in averting the collapse of the gold standard in the banking crisis of August 1914, he joined the Treasury in January 1915, remaining there till his resignation in June 1919. In January 1917 he became head of a new 'A' division, managing Britain's external finance. Over the period he helped build up the system of Allied purchases in external markets, which were being largely financed by Britain. He proved, in fact, to be a great Treasury official, adapting naturally to Whitehall, endlessly fertile in applying basic principles to concrete situations, able to turn out, at lightning speed, short, lucid memoranda, so invaluable to overworked Ministers. Whitehall also satisfied that part of his nature which craved for mastery over the material world. He enjoyed his work and delighted in the company of the great and powerful which his position as a Treasury mandarin, brilliant, personable, single, good at bridge, full of amusing gossip, gave him.

Yet this, the face displayed by Sir Roy Harrod in his official biography, was a mask which hid a profound inner conflict. Keynes and his circle had been shocked by the outbreak of the war, which extinguished their hopes for a 'new civilization'. As it progressed, they came to believe in it less and less. Keynes played his part in the war effort to growing criticism from his Bloomsbury and pacifist friends, and with growing unease of conscience. He justified his position in a number of ways. From the summer of 1915 to January 1916, he provided the Chancellor of the Exchequer, Reginald McKenna, with economic arguments against conscription. His case, set out in powerful memoranda, was that Britain should concentrate on subsidizing its Allies by earning foreign exchange, rather than squandering men and munitions on the Western front. This was a rational argument, based on the principle of the division of labour. But underlying it was a growing hatred of the war, and a desire to keep it away from his friends. It also earned him the hostility of Lloyd George, who believed in the 'knockout blow'.

When conscription came in January 1916, Keynes wanted McKenna, Runciman, and other leaders of Asquithian liberalism to quit the government, and proposed to go into opposition with them. When they stayed on, he stayed on too, but not before he had applied for exemption from the Military Service Act as a conscientious objector—a symbolic gesture, as he was automatically exempted by his Treasury work. Over the next six months he used his official position to help Duncan Grant and others get exemption from military service by testifying, as he put it, 'to the sincerity, virtue and truthfulness of my friends'. Keynes and his circle were not pacifists on principle, but they were liberals who held that the state had no right to make people fight. They had also come to believe that this war was not worth fighting, and that every effort should be made to end it by a compromise peace. In December 1916 Lloyd George became prime minister, in the midst of a financial crisis which threatened to deprive Britain of the means of paying for any more war purchases in the United States. Keynes wrote to Duncan Grant on 14 January 1917: 'God curse him [Lloyd George] . . . I pray for the most absolute financial crash and yet strive to prevent it—so that all I do is a contradiction to all I feel.'

Keynes's growing hostility to the war was influenced by the fact that it was making Britain dependent on the United States. With the depletion of its own assets it needed to borrow from America to supply its own Allies, especially Russia. On 24 October 1916, above the initials of Reginald McKenna, Chancellor of the Exchequer, appeared the words, almost certainly drafted by Keynes: 'If things go on as at present . . . the President of the American Republic will be in a position . . . to dictate his own terms to us' (*CW* xvi. 201). This fixes the moment when financial hegemony passed across the Atlantic. The same story was to be repeated in the Second World War. Consciousness of Britain's (and Europe's) decline relative to that of the United States gave an added urgency to Keynes's quest for a negotiated peace; it shaped much of his post-war thinking.

In September 1917 Keynes went to Washington for the first of his loan negotiations, and did not like the experience. 'The only really sympathetic and original thing in America is the niggers, who are charming,' he wrote to Duncan Grant. He was not a success with the Americans either, making 'a terrible impression for his rudeness out here', according to Basil Blackett, a Treasury colleague at the British Embassy. It was the start of a troubled relationship which lasted till Keynes died.

By the end of 1917 Keynes was convinced, as he told his mother, that the continuation of the war would mean 'the disappearance of the social order we have known hitherto . . . What frightens me is the prospect of *general impoverishment*. In another year's time we shall have forfeited the claim we have staked out in the New World and in exchange this country will be mortgaged to America.' This summarizes the mood which dominates his *Economic Consequences of the Peace*, his elegy on a vanished age and polemic against the Treaty of Versailles, published in December 1919. By that time Russia had succumbed to Bolshevism, revolution had broken out in Germany and Hungary, inflation was rampant, much of Europe was starving. Yet all the peacemakers could think about was 'frontiers and sovereignties'. As chief Treasury representative at the Paris Peace Conference, Keynes had tried hard to get Lloyd George to agree to a moderate figure for German reparations. When he failed, he resigned in disgust on 7 June 1919. He wrote his book in the summer of 1919 at Charleston, the Sussex home of Vanessa Bell and Duncan Grant.

The Economic Consequences of the Peace denounced the folly of the peacemakers in trying to extort from Germany an indemnity it could not possibly pay. He foresaw that attempts to make it pay would destroy the economic mechanisms on which the pre-war prosperity of Continental Europe had depended. He predicted a war of vengeance by Germany. There were memorable portraits of the leading peacemakers, Georges Clemenceau and Woodrow Wilson, though he left out the sketch of Lloyd George on Asquith's advice.

Keynes's main proposals were to cancel all inter-Ally war debts; limit Germany's liability for reparation to a modest annual sum, payable to France and Belgium; and restore Germany as the economic powerhouse of the Continent—Russia would be rebuilt 'through the agency of German enterprise and organisation' (*CW* ii. 186). The cancellation of inter-Ally war debts was designed to de-couple American finance from Europe. Keynes supported American loans to get European industry restarted, pay for essential food imports, and stabilize currencies. But he was adamantly opposed to Europeans borrowing from the United States to service deadweight debt.

His book became an international best-seller, had a profound effect on post-war thinking, and made Keynes world-famous. It would be far too simple to say it *created* the mood of appeasement of Germany: revulsion against wartime propaganda had already started. What it did was to turn attention from great power politics to the conditions of economic prosperity. Keynes put economics on the map for the informed general public, and it has been there ever since. The view that capitalism needed managing also started to sink in. Keynes did not emerge from the war a socialist, much less a Bolshevik. Socialism, he started to say, was for later—after the economic problem had been solved: a curious link with classical Marxism. He remained a Liberal till he died. The task he set himself was to reconstruct the capitalist social order on the basis of improved technical management.

The war also brought about a rearrangement in his personal life, which finally shed the undergraduate flavour which had persisted till 1914. He was now a great man, a world authority on international finance, whose writings caused currencies to tremble, whose counsel was sought by financiers, politicians, and public officials in all countries. He returned to Cambridge in October 1919, but Cambridge was no longer the centre of his life. He was resident only in term-time, and even then only for long weekends (usually Thursday evenings to Tuesday mornings) into which he packed his much-reduced teaching duties, his College committees, and a social life which revolved round his family at 6 Harvey Road and a few close friends among the younger dons. Between the wars he was the spectacularly successful investment Bursar of King's College, boosting the capital of the College 'Chest' from £30,000 in 1920 to over £300,000 by 1945.

His London base was 46 Gordon Square, the Bloomsbury Group's *monument historique*. Here he spent mid-weeks in term-time, and the first part of each vacation. London life was even more packed with activity. At various times he was on the Boards of no less than five investment and insurance companies, the chief one being the National Mutual Life Assurance Company, whose chairman he was from 1921 to 1937. From 1923 to 1931 he was chief proprietor and chairman of the board of the weekly journal, the *Nation and Atheneum*, working closely with its editor, Hubert Henderson. His editorship of the *Economic Journal* (1911–37) was also conducted from London. London was crucial to Keynes as a base of influence. He had direct access, for much of the inter-war years, to prime ministers and chancellors. In the 1920s his evolving ideas on economic policy permeated the official mind through monthly meetings of the Tuesday Club, a dining club of bankers, Treasury officials, economists, and financial journalists started by the stockbroker Oswald Falk in 1917; in the 1930s he sought to influence policy through his membership of the prime minister's Economic Advisory Council.

In the 1920s Oswald Falk was Keynes's main partner in money-making. They started speculating on currencies immediately after the war, and continued in commodities. Despite three major reverses—in 1920, 1928–9, and 1937–8—Keynes increased his net assets from £16,315 in 1919 to £411,238— £10m. in today's values—by the time he died. Over the inter-war years his investment philosophy shifted from currency and commodity speculation to investment in blue-chip companies in line with his changing economic theory. The failure of his 'credit cycle' investment theory to make him money led him to the 'animal spirits' theory of investment behaviour of *The General Theory*, and to a personal investment philosophy of 'faithfulness'. (To counter investment volatility he urged that the relationship between an investor and his share should be like that of husband and wife.) Journalism was another major source of money-making, especially in the early 1920s. Three major coups between 1921 and 1922, plus other journalistic earnings, netted him today's equivalent of £100,000. His successes in money-making in turn financed his activities as a collector of pictures and rare books, in homage to his youthful ideal of the good life.

The most dramatic sign of the reorganization of his life was his marriage. He first met the ballerina Lydia Lopokova in October 1918, when the Diaghilev ballet returned to London; he started wooing her at the end of 1921 when she danced in Diaghilev's magnificent, but commercially unsuccessful, production of Tchaikovsky's *Sleeping Beauty* at the Alhambra theatre. Diminutive and pert, with a turned-up nose, and a head which reminded Virginia Woolf of a plover's egg, Lydia was an outstanding artist in her own right, with a bawdy sense of humour, a genius for refashioning the English language (she once referred to 'Jesus fomenting water into wine at Cannes'), and strong and secure intuitions, directly expressed. Keynes was captivated by her, and they were married on 4 August 1925. Possibly only a woman as exotic as Lydia, and coming from right outside his own social milieu, could have won the heart of a man whose affections were basically directed towards his own sex. Despite much Bloomsbury foreboding, she proved a perfect wife for him. She gave his life the emotional stability it had lacked for many years, and which provided the necessary background to sustained intellectual effort. In 1925 he acquired Tilton, a farmhouse in East Sussex, close to Charleston. Here he and Lydia passed his vacations, with friends and relations coming to stay; in a rather damp annexe to the main house he wrote most of his two major theoretical works, *A Treatise on Money* and *The General Theory of Employment, Interest, and Money*.

Keynes had always been a busy man. In the inter-war years his activity spilt out in masses of new directions. Contemporaries knew him as the man with the bulging brief-case, hurrying from one place, one meeting, to another. His life was embedded in a dense mass of miscellaneous activities which both fertilized and distracted him from his writing. His failure to produce a major work of theory till 1930, when he was almost 50, was the price he paid. But perhaps it was just as well, in the 1920s, to keep one's intellectual investments reasonably liquid. Economic theory was in a state of flux. It took the inter-war 'shocks' to the capitalist system to crystallize the indictment of old-fashioned understandings of economic behaviour. Keynes's growing fame and involvement in public affairs also narrowed the circle, and quality, of his friendships. Outside his marriage, there was less time for 'personal moments'. 'Doing good' took precedence over 'being good'. But he never renounced the ideals of his youth; and though he was always busy, the speed and efficiency with which he got through his work gave the impression of unhurried calm.

III

The spur to Keynes's theoretical and practical efforts between the wars was his fear for the future. The pre-war mood of sexual and cultural freedom, made possible by the expectation of 'automatic' progress, had given way to a sense of the extraordinary precariousness of capitalist civilization. This was reinforced by the catastrophes of the inter-war years—especially the Great Depression of 1929–33 and the triumph of Hitler in Germany. Belief in the stability and resilience of the market system was replaced by the view that the nineteenth-century era of *laissez-faire* was a unique episode in economic history, dependent on special conjunctures which were no more; that, despite technical progress, mankind was in danger of retrogressing from the plateau of prosperity and civilization it had achieved in the Victorian age. One way of interpreting Keynes's forebodings is to see them as a delayed reaction to the nineteenth-century fear of life without God. In 1925, after a visit to Soviet Russia, Keynes wrote that 'modern capitalism is absolutely irreligious. . . . Such a system has to be immensely, not merely moderately, successful to survive' (*CW* ix. 267). This was the spiritual and psychological background to the Keynesian 'mood'.

In the years immediately following the war, Keynes's attention focused on two things: the international financial disorganization which the war had brought about, and which the peacemaking at Versailles had worsened, and the deterioration in the equilibrium terms of trade between Europe and the New World. At existing productivity levels, Europeans would have to accept a lower standard of life than before the war, since a given quantity of manufactured exports was buying less food and raw materials from abroad than hitherto. This range of concerns can be followed in Keynes's contributions to the *Manchester Guardian Commercial*'s Reconstruction Supplements, the twelve issues of which he edited between 1922 and 1923. The 'neo-Malthusian' strand in Keynes's thinking has not been sufficiently noticed. It was at the heart of his argument for a devaluation of the main European currencies against the dollar.

Despite his resignation from the Treasury, and the odium which *Economic Consequences of the Peace* had aroused in some 'official circles', Keynes played a far from negligible role in sorting out the mess left by the peacemakers. He contributed directly to the British Treasury plan for settling the reparation problem at the end of 1922; and, through his friendship with the Hamburg banker Carl Melchior, acted almost as unofficial adviser to the German government in 1922–3, a curiously underresearched role.

Until 1923 Keynes was not specially concerned with British problems, which seemed trivial in comparison with those of the Continent. However, the emergence of persisting mass unemployment turned his attention to this unique feature of the British situation. He attributed the bulk of the abnormal British unemployment of the 1920s to monetary mismanagement. Refusal to raise bank rate soon or high enough had allowed the inflationary boom of 1919–20 to get out of hand; the maintenance of punitive real rates of interest right through the subsequent period of falling prices, output, and employment had made the depression far deeper than it need have been. Keynes attributed the second phase of policy to the desire not just to eliminate the post-war inflation (which he shared), but to lower the price level sufficiently to put the pound back on the gold standard at its pre-war parity with the dollar: £1 = $4.86. Like all economists, Keynes expected British employment to recover to 'normal' (as measured by pre-war standards) when prices 'settled down' in 1922. But unemployment remained obstinately stuck at above 10 per cent. It was its failure to come down much below this rate for the rest of the 1920s which alerted Keynes to the possibility that the employment costs of a savage deflation might be more than 'transitional', with the economy remaining 'jammed' in a low-employment trap. To explain how such an 'underemployment equilibrium' could occur would be the main object of his theoretical writing.

A Tract on Monetary Reform (1923) was an attempt to design what would now be called a monetary 'regime' which would allow reasonable steadiness of economic activity. Keynes rejected the gold standard as the appropriate regime. The requirement that domestic currency should be convertible into gold at a fixed official price did not guarantee the stable domestic price level which Keynes considered essential for stable business expectations, because the value of gold itself was liable to fluctuate in terms of goods, depending on its scarcity or plenty. Further, given the actual and prospective distribution of the world's gold reserves, returning to the gold standard would be to surrender Britain's control over its own price level to the Federal Reserve Board in Washington. Britain should remain free to manage its exchange rate in accordance with the needs of its domestic economy. Such a system of domestic monetary control would, Keynes argued, be consistent with short-run exchange-rate stability. But exchange-rate stability would be a consequence of stable domestic prices, not an independent, much less overriding, objective of policy.

A Tract on Monetary Reform identified Keynes as the foremost intellectual opponent of the 'official' policy of returning sterling to the gold standard at the pre-war parity with the dollar. But his plea for a 'managed' currency found little favour. Winston Churchill, the Chancellor of the Exchequer, put sterling back on the gold standard at $4.86 on 20 April 1925. Keynes immediately attacked the decision in a memorable pamphlet, *The Economic Consequences of Mr. Churchill*. He argued that the revaluation of sterling required a 10 per cent reduction in British wage costs, which could be achieved only by 'intensifying unemployment without limit'. Implicit in this argument was the notion that the cost of labour was the main influence on the price level: under modern conditions of trade-union-led wage bargaining, a reduction in the quantity of money led directly to a reduction in the quantity of employment. He predicted that actual monetary policy would shrink from the attempt to restore equilibrium by this method. Interest rates would be kept high enough to attract foreign funds to London; but not pushed so high as to break trade-union resistance to a reduction in the money-wage per worker employed. The result would be a low-employment economy. So it proved. Despite the defeat of the General Strike in 1926, employers made little effort to reduce money-wages, which remained steady for the rest of the 1920s although the price level sagged. Keynes was the first to realize and state clearly that an overvalued currency would be a weak, not a strong, currency.

The events surrounding the General Strike shifted Keynes's political allegiance from Asquith to Lloyd George, as well as bringing about a greater sympathy for the Labour Party. Between 1926 and 1929 he played a notable part in shaping the policy of the Lloyd George Liberal Party. Lloyd George looked to Keynes to provide the economic programme which would win the Liberals at least a share of power; Keynes saw Lloyd George as the most promising instrument for 'conquering unemployment'. Keynes's service on the Liberal Industrial Inquiry in 1927–8 marked the high point in his involvement in politics. It was also the one period of his life when he thought deeply about the structural problems of British industry. The product of this phase was his political philosophy of the Middle

Way, first outlined in his pamphlet *The End of Laissez-Faire* (1926).

Keynes spent the years 1925–8 partly writing his *Treatise on Money*, which started as a development of the ideas of the *Tract*. His main intellectual companion at this time was Dennis Robertson, Fellow of Trinity College, a retiring man, but tenacious controversialist. Keynes had no disciples in the mid-1920s: Kurt Singer remembers him as 'a lonely figure, pathetic, rebellious and fond of dominating; but not yet in possession of the watchword that establishes leadership'. But a younger generation of those who helped make the Keynesian Revolution were starting to take root in Cambridge: the Italian *émigré* Piero Sraffa; Joan and Austin Robinson; above all Richard Kahn, whom Keynes described as his 'favourite pupil'. Keynes struck one of his students, H. M. Robertson, as 'more like a stockbroker than a don', with his City suits and City gossip.

A Treatise on Money, published in 1930, is an excellent example of Keynes's passion for generalization. In essence, Keynes built an exceedingly complicated conceptual apparatus to show how an economy on the gold standard could, under certain conditions, fall into a low-employment trap. If the monetary authority was prevented from lowering the long-term interest rate to a level consonant with investors' expectations, and if domestic costs of production prevented the achievement of an export surplus equal to what people wished to lend abroad, the result would be an 'excess' of saving over investment, a sagging price level, and a 'jammed' economy. This was Britain's fate in the 1920s. The revolutionary thought, brought out more clearly in *The General Theory*, was that there was no automatic mechanism in a modern economic system to keep intended saving in equilibrium with intended investment. As Hayek alone discerned, this was equivalent to saying that there was no automatic mechanism in the system to adjust aggregate demand to supply. It was in the notion of domestic savings unmatched by domestic or foreign investment that Keynes found his rationale for a programme of loan-financed public works to increase employment within the constraints of the gold-standard system.

Keynes's public endorsement, in April 1929, of the Lloyd George policy of loan-financed public works, in *Can Lloyd George do it?*, written jointly with Hubert Henderson, was notable for the argument that spending on public works would produce a 'cumulative' wave of prosperity. His chance to influence the policy of Ramsay MacDonald's second Labour government came with his appointment to the Macmillan Committee on Finance and Industry set up in November 1929, and to the government's Economic Advisory Council, established in January 1930. His nine-day exposition of the theory of the *Treatise* and possible remedies for unemployment to the Macmillan Committee in March 1930 marks the real start of the Keynesian revolution in economic policy. But his proposals for public works and protection made little headway at the time. The collapse of the world economy and business confidence strengthened the forces of orthodoxy. The pressure for retrenchment in the public finances brought about the replacement of the Labour government by a National government on 25 August 1931. On 21 September, the financial collapse in Central Europe, together with a burgeoning British balance of payments deficit, forced sterling off the gold standard. That autumn Keynes set out to write a new book of theory designed to emphasize the role of output changes in the adjustment to a new position of equilibrium.

IV

Although Keynes wrote one policy pamphlet, *The Means to Prosperity*, in 1933, the bulk of his 'spare time' between 1931 and 1935 was spent not advising governments, but writing his *General Theory of Employment, Interest, and Money*, published in February 1936. Two books of essays also appeared— *Essays in Persuasion* (1931) and *Essays in Biography* (1933).

The first collected what Keynes, in his introduction, called 'the croakings of twelve years—the croakings of a Cassandra who could never influence the course of events in time'. A notable feature of the second is Keynes's use of short lives of men of science to ponder and delineate the character of scientific genius.

In the period 1931–2 Keynes engaged in intermittent, but intense, correspondence on points of theory with Hawtrey, Robertson, and Hayek. He was also helped by a 'Cambridge Circus' of young economists, the chief of whom, Richard Kahn, supplied him with the theory of the multiplier. Evidence of the progress of the book is given not only by *The Means to Prosperity*, but by early drafts of chapters, fragments of lectures, and a complete set of lecture notes taken by some of Keynes's students from 1932 to 1935. One of them, A. C. Gilpin, described the Cambridge atmosphere in 1933 in a letter to his parents:

Economics lectures this year seem mainly to insist of elaborations or refutations of theories taught us last year. Shove dissects Marshall; Keynes attacks Pigou; Robertson disagrees with Keynes, and leaves it to his audience to decide who is right; an intense lady, Mrs. Joan Robinson, tries to explain why they disagree. It is interesting but confusing.

At the final proof stage in the summer of 1935, Roy Harrod made important suggestions.

Keynes was never a person to be doing one thing at a time. In addition to work on the book, he spent much of 1934–5 planning and supervising the building of the Cambridge Arts theatre, in fulfilment of a pre-war dream of endowing Cambridge with a permanent centre for the dramatic arts. As bursar of King's College, Cambridge, and as 'squire of Tilton', he became involved in ever more extensive farming operations. These are reflected in two articles he wrote in 1933 in praise of 'National Self-Sufficiency', which combined a moral attack on the international division of labour with the argument that 'most modern mass-production processes can be performed in most countries and climates with almost equal efficiency' (*CW* xxi. 233–46). There were two visits to the United States, in 1931 and 1934. On the second, Keynes met Roosevelt, and most of the architects, as well as some of the critics, of the 'New Deal'. The influence of his presence and writing on the first phase of the 'New Deal' has been underestimated.

The General Theory changed the way most economists understood the working of economies. In that sense it was explicitly, and successfully, revolutionary. It also had a revolutionary effect on policy. Not immediately, but after the Second World War, Western governments openly or implicitly committed themselves to maintaining a high level of employment. *The General Theory* itself is a profound exploration of the logic of economic behaviour under uncertainty, combined with a short-period model of income determination, which emphasized quantity, rather than price, adjustment. These two loosely linked strands gave rise to much subsequent dispute concerning the 'real meaning' of *The General Theory* between what Alan Coddington called the 'fundamentalist' and the 'hydraulic' Keynesians. It was the income-determination model, based on the multiplier, together with the consequent development of national income statistics, which made Keynesian economics acceptable to policy-makers, since it offered them a seemingly secure method of forecasting and controlling the movement of such 'real' variables as investment, consumption, and employment.

Keynes's own first attempt to apply *The General Theory* to policy came in three articles he wrote for *The Times* in January 1937 on 'How to Avoid a Slump'—a notably cautious assessment of the possibility of reducing unemployment below its then current rate of 12 per cent by injecting 'greater aggregate demand' into the economy (*CW* xxi. 384–95). Keynes had never enjoyed robust health. In May 1937, at the age of 53, he suffered a coronary thrombosis, from which he recovered only slowly. By the time war broke out, on 3 September 1939, a Hungarian physician, János Plesch, had restored him to something like his old vigour.

V

Following the publication of *The General Theory*, Keynes became the most influential figure in British economic policy. He achieved this by force of mind and personality, rather than by political position. Despite many offers, he never stood for Parliament. In June 1940 he was made a member of a Consultative Committee set up to advise the Chancellor of the Exchequer on war problems; in August he received a room at the Treasury and a part-time secretary. He had 'no routine duties and no office hours . . . but a sort of roving commission plus membership of many high up committees, which allow me to butt in in almost any direction where I think I have something to say' (KP, W/1, JMK to Sheppard, 14 Aug. 1940). Keynes used his anomalous position to intervene, often decisively, on the whole range of economic business, great and small. He became the most powerful civil servant at large Whitehall has ever had, 'less the servant and more the master of those he served'. His elevation to the peerage in 1942, as Baron Keynes of Tilton, would have given him the opportunity to enter the government, but this was never suggested, probably because he was too useful where he was. It did, however, give him the rank to represent the government on several important missions to the United States, his last as joint head (with Lord Halifax) of the British delegation to Washington in September 1945 to negotiate the American loan.

Keynes's most important service in the last period of his life was to help build the domestic and international foundations of the managed capitalism to which his theory pointed. Three of his contributions to post-war statesmanship deserve particular mention.

The first arose in the context of wartime finance. One possible implication of Keynesian theory is that the government's budget should be used to balance the accounts of the nation, not just the government, to ensure that aggregate supply and demand are equal at full employment. In wartime the problem was not to achieve full employment—which was reached in

1940—but to prevent inflation—total demand rising higher than total supply. The specific task of wartime finance was to make sure that the extra demand created by full employment was spent by the government not by the private consumer. In three articles to *The Times*, published in October 1939, and reproduced as a pamphlet, *How to Pay for the War*, Keynes put forward a scheme for compulsory saving or 'deferred pay', in which excess purchasing power would be mopped up by a progressive surcharge on all incomes (with offsets to the poor in the form of family allowances), part of which would be given back in instalments after the war in order to counteract the anticipated post-war slump. Although this scheme was adopted only in part, Keynes's analytical approach, together with the estimates of national income which he used to calculate the size of the 'inflationary gap', became the basis of the budgetary strategy for the whole war, starting with Kingsley Wood's budget in 1941. But its importance went beyond that. In 1939 Keynes had doubted whether 'capitalistic democracy' would ever be willing to make the 'grand experiment' which would prove his theory. In war the experiment was made, and the theory worked. The economy was run at full capacity with only very moderate inflation. What could be done in war could be done in peace—or so it seemed.

Keynes's second major contribution to the post-war order was his part in establishing the Bretton Woods system. This was unfinished business left over from the collapse of the old order. Even in his *Tract* period Keynes was not a currency floater. He wanted a 'managed' exchange-rate system—something consistent with *de facto* stability of exchange rates for long periods.

His famous Clearing Union plan of 1942 provided for a link between each national currency and a new reserve asset 'bancor'. Surplus countries would accumulate 'bancor' balances in the Union; overdraft facilities would be made available to deficit countries up to the total of the surpluses. The scheme was designed to discourage countries from running persistent balance of payments surpluses. If they nevertheless did so, debtors could automatically draw on the creditors' bancor balances. Despite the defeat of this plan by Harry Dexter White's alternative scheme for a gold-exchange standard backed by a small 'adjustment' facility (the International Monetary Fund), Keynes none the less worked unsparingly to achieve the Bretton Woods Agreement and to ensure support for it in Britain, taking part in two exhaustive negotiations in Washington in 1943 and 1944. In doing so, he played a decisive part in bringing Britain (and Europe) down on the liberal side of the shape of the post-war international economic order.

Keynes's third act of statesmanship was to negotiate the American loan in September–December 1945. He estimated that Britain's deficit on balance of payments would total nearly $7,000m. over the first three post-war years. Keynes went to Washington in September 1945 to seek a grant of $5,000m. 'without strings'. He returned, three months and several famous rows later, with a loan of $2,000m. conditional on a commitment to make sterling convertible into other currencies a year after the loan agreement was ratified. It was probably the most humiliating experience of his life. For someone who had started as one of the rulers of a world empire to have to go begging to the United States was a bitter pill. Yet Keynes swallowed it, and persuaded the new Labour government to swallow it, because, as he put it to Lord Halifax, the alternative was 'Nazi or Communist' methods. In the House of Lords he made an eloquent speech in defence of the agreement.

Keynes never recovered properly from the strain of the loan negotiations. There was another trip to the United States, to Savannah in March 1946, to inaugurate the International Monetary Fund. Once again Keynes was involved in a quarrel with the Americans over the question of the Fund's management. As always he pursued other business as well. During the war he had added to his Treasury duties the chairmanship of CEMA— the Council for the Encouragement of Music and the Arts. In 1945 he was appointed first chairman of the Arts Council. Stopping over in New York after the Savannah meeting, he arranged for the American ballet to come over to Covent

Garden, whose gala reopening performance of *Sleeping Beauty* he had attended on 20 February 1946. Two months later, on 21 April 1946, he was dead, of a massive coronary thrombosis. There was an imposing memorial service at Westminster Abbey, but he had chosen his own epitaph many years earlier, as an Eton schoolboy, when he quoted a passage from Bernard of Cluny's *De Contemptu Mundi*:

> Not only those
> Who hold clear echoes of the voice divine
> Are honourable—they are blest, indeed,
> Whate'er the world has held—but those who hear
> Some fair faint echoes, though the crowd be deaf,
> And see the white gods' garments on the hills,
> Which the crowd sees not, though they may not find
> Fit music for their visions; they are blest,
> Not pitiable.

2 Keynes's philosophy of practice

Keynes's economics—unlike Keynesian economics—was philosophically driven. It was informed by his vision of the 'good life'; it was permeated by his theory of probability. These philosophical foundations were laid early in his life. Philosophy came before economics; and the philosophy of ends came before the philosophy of means.

Keynes's philosophy was the product of an atheistic generation. He and his contemporaries saw themselves as replacing Christian 'hocus-pocus' by a rational system of ethics and conduct. But they used tools of thought inherited from the Christian (as well as Greek) past; and the structure of their thought was metaphysical.

Fundamental was Keynes's intuitionist epistemology. He regarded intuition, rather than sense experience, as the foundation of knowledge, including ethical knowledge—a tradition going back to Plato. His stress on intuitive reasoning in economics, as well as his hostility to econometrics, was thus philosophically based, and not just temperamental.

His ethical beliefs were derived from G. E. Moore's *Principia Ethica*, published in 1903, his second undergraduate year. 'I see no reason to shift from the fundamental intuitions of *Principia Ethica*,' Keynes said in 1938. Three things he got from Moore seem particularly important. The first was the indefinability of good. Good, Moore said, is the name of a simple, non-natural property, intuitively known. Secondly, good and bad states of mind are prior to good and bad actions: value determines duty. Finally, 'By far the most valuable things which we know or can imagine, are certain states of consciousness, which may be roughly described as the pleasures of human intercourse and the enjoyment of beautiful objects.' Moore believed this to be self-evidently true. To Moore's duo, the young Keynes added love of knowledge.

Good actions were those which brought about good states of mind. Moore said

> that it is only for the sake of these things [the pleasures of human intercourse and the enjoyment of beautiful objects]—in order that as much of them as possible may at some time exist—that anyone can be justified in performing any private or public duty; that they are the *raison d'etre* of virtue; that it is they ... that form the rational end of human action and the sole criterion of progress.

The young Keynes saw two problems with this. Moore, he said, had failed to establish a rational basis for altruistic behaviour: there is 'no necessary connection' between individual and universal goodness. 'For my goodness and the goodness of the Universe both seem to have a claim upon me and claims which I cannot easily reduce to common terms and weight against one another upon a common balance' (KP, UA/26, 'Egoism', 1906). The rival claims on Keynes, we may say, were those of Bloomsbury and Whitehall.

Secondly, because 'we never have the opportunity of direct inspection [of other people's states of mind], it is impossible to tell what kinds of action increase the goodness of the Universe as a whole' (KP, UA/21, 'Miscellanea Ethica', 1905). Moore's criterion of public action is inferior to Bentham's, because it is almost impossible, by reference to it, to establish whether ethical progress is taking place. Specifically, good states of mind do not depend, in any direct way, on good states of the world.

Moore provided a bridge to social reform with his doctrine of organic unity. The main purpose of this principle, as Keynes described it, was to limit the power to sum goodness by reference to isolated states of consciousness alone. In judging the goodness of a state of affairs, reference, had to be made to time as well as to the objects of experience (KP, UA/35, 'On the Principle of Organic Unity', 1910, 1921). Keynes decomposed Moore's 'complex wholes' into states of mind which were intrinsically good and objects which he called 'fit' or 'desirable'. Such objects need have no ethical value of their own. But, if they did not exist, the value of the experience would be less good than if they did. The social reformer could then claim that by improving the quality of the objects of experience he was increasing the ethical goodness of the universe. It follows straightforwardly from Moore that goodness is increased, *ceteris paribus*, by an increase in the amount of beauty. Keynes acted on this belief both as a philanthropist, builder of the Cambridge Arts theatre, and by accepting the job of first chairman of the Arts Council. In the depth of the depression, he also indicated that a programme of public investment, inspired by Moore's principles, would seek to endow Britain's cities 'with all the appurtenances of art and civilisation' and make them 'the greatest works of man in the world' (*CW* xxi. 242). A follower of Moore might also interest himself in raising standards of education and of comfort in so far as these improved the intelligence, sensibility, and comeliness of the population.

The snag comes with Moore's class of 'mixed goods', in which good states of mind *depend* on the existence of bad states of affairs. Feelings of pity, courage, justice, which have positive ethical value, could be said to depend on the existence of suffering, danger, injustice. To the extent that social reform rids the world of bad states of affairs, it may be decreasing the total of ethical goodness. Social reformers may regard such considerations as trivial when weighed against avoidable suffering and oppression. The fact that Keynes was alert to them shows his intellectual honesty; it also helps explain his limited passion for social reform.

It was another problem arising from Moore's discussion of duty which led Keynes to spend, as he put it, 'all the leisure of many years' on the study of probability (*CW* x. 445). We ought, Moore said, to behave in such a way as to bring about the greatest possible amount of goodness in the universe. But our knowledge of the effects of our actions is bound to be, at best, probabilistic. Since it was impossible to know the probable effects of actions stretching into a remote future, the best we could do in most cases, Moore argued, was to follow moral rules which were generally useful and generally practised, as Hume had suggested. This conclusion stuck in the young Keynes's gullet. 'Before heaven', he recalled in 1938, 'we claimed to be our own judge in our own case.' He set out to discover a rational basis for individual judgements of probability. In a paper he read to the Apostles on 23 January 1904 (KP, UA/19, 'Ethics in Relation to Conduct', 1904), he said Moore was confusing knowledge of probabilities with knowledge of relative frequencies of occurrence. He was claiming that if we do not know for certain that any good we can achieve in the near future will not be outweighed by harm in the far future we have no rational basis for individual judgement. Keynes said this was wrong. All we have to have is *no reason to believe* that any immediate good we achieve would be overturned by distant consequences. Ignorance was not a barrier to individual judgement, but a way of neutralizing the unknown. By applying the 'principle of in-difference'—assigning equiprobabilities to alternatives about which we have equal (including zero) evidence—we can extend the field of probability judgements. More generally, pro-babilistic knowledge was a kind of logical knowledge, concern-ing the 'bearing of evidence' on conclusions. It was to do with the rationality of beliefs, not the conjuncture of events. Keynes's *Treatise on Probability*, eventually published in 1921, was the working out of this audacious insight.

The question Keynes asked was: what are the principles of rational choice and action when the future is unknown or uncertain? His concern, that is, is with the rationality of means, not of ends, though the rightness of actions had to be judged by reference to both. Keynes claimed that the mind could often 'reduce' uncertainty to probability, 'intuiting' that some outcomes are more or less likely than others; in his words, 'perceiving' a probability relation between the evidence (the premiss) and the conclusion of an argument. This percep-tion sanctions a 'degree of belief' in the conclusion. The logic he proposes is that of partial entailment. The conclusion is any outcome of interest to us.

Keynes's view of probability as logical *insight* was conceived as an attack on the dominant theory of his day—the frequency theory—which said that probability was a fact of nature: if one in ten smokers dies of cancer, the probability of smokers dying of cancer is 10 per cent. The identification of frequency with probability, Keynes wrote, 'is a very grave departure from the established use of words'; moreover, it assumes the 'inductive hypothesis' which cannot itself be derived from frequencies.

The point, above all, which Keynes wanted to establish is that our knowledge of probabilities is more extensive than our knowledge of frequencies. By the same token, our knowledge of probabilities is only to a limited extent numerical knowledge—knowledge of ratios. Logical intuition, acting on evidence, can in most cases do no better than to discern that one conclusion is more likely than another, without being able to discern how much more or how much less likely. We have only a limited individual insight into the nature of the universe. Keynes allowed for unknown probabilities, as well as the impossibility in some cases of comparing probabilities based on different arguments. In deciding whether to take an umbrella on a walk, which should weigh more with us: the blackness of the clouds or the highness of the barometer? In such a case 'it will be rational to allow caprice to determine us and to waste no time on the debate' (*CW* viii. 32). Again, ignorance should not been seen as a barrier to rational judgement.

Keynes's theory of probability is both optimistic about the power of human reason and pessimistic about the ability of reason to penetrate the secrets of the universe. He quoted Locke to the effect that 'in the greatest part of our concernment, God has afforded only the Twilight, as I may so say, of Probability, suitable, I presume, to the state of Mediocrity and Probationership He has been pleased to place us in here' (*CW* viii. 356).

In deciding what is rational to do, we need to take into account two further considerations independent of probability, which Keynes called 'the weight of argument' and 'moral risk'. By the first, Keynes meant roughly the *amount* of evidence supporting a probability judgement. This does not alter the probability, but can alter the amount of confidence we have in our judgement. Keynes's distinction between the rationality of a judgement and the confidence it is rational to have in it plays a key part in the discussion of investment psychology in *The General Theory*. The principle of moral risk suggests that it is more rational to aim for a smaller good which seems more probable of attainment than to aim for a larger one which seems less, when the two courses of action have equal probable goodness. Other things being equal, 'a high weight and the absence of risk increase *pro tanto* the desirability of the action to which they refer' (*CW* viii. 348). This argument provides the philosophical basis for Keynes's rejection of revolutionary change.

In preparing his dissertation on probability for publication, Keynes added extra sections on induction and statistical inference. A thoroughgoing empiricist, he wrote, cannot make use of induction without inconsistency, for the use of the inductive method requires that a prior probability be assigned to its validity. The 100-odd pages on statistical inference are remarkable chiefly for Keynes's attempt to reduce the domain of its validity to those sets of cases for which stable as opposed to average frequencies are available. This is the root of his objection to the misuse of econometrics. There is no doubt that Keynes's philosophic objection to induction gave a strong anti-empirical bias to his economics, despite his repeated calls for better data. While he aimed to choose models capable of explaining the 'facts of experience', his models are not derived from experience, but from introspection. In this respect, his method was much closer to that of the classical economists than to that of their 'institutionalist' critics.

Students of Keynes have only recently rescued his *Treatise on Probability* from its long neglect. This is part of the growing realization of the importance of Keynes's philosophy for understanding his theory of economic behaviour. One central debate concerns the epistemological status of his theory of probability. Was it, as Roderick O'Donnell claims, a Realist construction, or was it, as Anna Carabelli argues, a 'logic of opinion'?

Keynes's insistence that probability was a 'real objective' relation, and that all rational beliefs have reference to true propositions, would seem to vindicate O'Donnell's approach, though Keynes later modified his opinion in response to criticisms by Frank Ramsey (*CW* x. 338–9). A second issue concerns the epistemological continuity between the *Treatise on Probability* and *The General Theory*. Why, asks Athol Fitzgibbons, has the 'twilight of probability' turned by 1936 into the 'dark night' of uncertainty? The watershed of the First World War gives the answer. Finally, does Keynes, in *The General Theory*, see investment behaviour as rational or irrational? Here the main division is between those who see the 'conventional' investment strategy described by Keynes in *The General Theory* as a 'weak' form of rationality, and those who argue that Keynes believed investment behaviour to be irrational. This may be a non-debate, 'conventional' judgement of probabilities being what keeps investment reasonably steady, 'animal spirits' what produces the cycle.

These discussions are not just of historic interest. Keynes was the first economist to put uncertainty at the heart of the economic problem, and thus raise the issue of the scope and meaning of rationality in economics. Is rationality possible in an uncertain world, and how it is to be specified? The question for policy concerns the conditions which would need to be satisfied for the structure of the economy not to be viewed as radically uncertain by economic agents.

Keynes's theory of politics was set in the same conceptual framework as was his ethical and economic philosophy. The nearest he got to a systematic exposition was in a 100-page undergraduate essay on Edmund Burke, which he successfully submitted for the University Members' Prize for English Essay in 1904—the same year as his earliest paper on probability (KP, UA/20, 'The Political Doctrines of Edmund Burke'). Keynes showed himself to be largely sympathetic to the views of the founder of British Conservatism. He approved of Burke's separation of ethics and politics, also his preference for present over future goods. He criticized him for excessive timidity as a reformer, and for undervaluing the claims of truth; in general for carrying reasonable propositions too far. The views he expressed in this undergraduate essay crop up time and again in his mature writings.

Burke's 'unparalleled political wisdom', according to Keynes, lay in the fact that he was the first thinker consistently to base a theory of politics on utilitarianism rather than on abstract rights, though it was a utilitarianism 'modified' by the principle of equity—governments should avoid artificial discrimination against individuals or classes. He quotes him approvingly: 'The question with me is, not whether you have a right to render your people miserable, but whether it is not in your interest to make them happy.' Keynes adds: 'This is not a very recondite doctrine, but to Burke must be given the credit of first clearly and insistently enunciating it.' The most important consequence of this approach was Burke's championship of expediency as a central political principle—one which Keynes certainly approved. There is a jotting in Keynes's papers dating from the mid-1920s: 'It is fatal for a capitalist government to have principles. It must be opportunistic in the best sense of the word, living by accommodation and good sense. If a monarchical, plutocratic or other analogous form of government has principles, it will fall' (KP, PS/6, 1925/6?). In policy-making Keynes had a pronounced, but not extreme, preference for discretion over fixed rules, for reasons which can readily be inferred from his engagement with Burke.

Keynes accepted the view he attributed to Burke that the aim of politics was not to bring about states of affairs 'good intrinsically and in isolation', but to facilitate the pursuit of ethical goods by members of the community by guaranteeing conditions of 'physical calm, material comfort, and intellectual freedom'. Up to a point the requirements of welfare and ethical goodness coincide. But Keynes never regarded politics as an arena for achieving ethical goals, and he placed limited ethical value on political passions.

Keynes endorses another key principle of Burke's: that the happiness or utility which governments should aim to maximize is short run not long run. This is a consequence of accepting the Moore–Burke criterion of 'moral risk'—'Burke ever held, and held rightly, that it can seldom be right . . . to sacrifice a present benefit for a doubtful advantage in the future.' The concept of moral risk was a guiding principle in Keynes's own statesmanship. It inoculated him equally against Communism and the sacrificial thinking implicit in much of orthodox economics.

However, Keynes thought Burke interpreted the 'moral risk' criterion too narrowly. In his essay of 1904 he criticized him for his 'preference for peace over truth, his extreme timidity in introducing present evil for the sake of future benefits, and his disbelief in men's acting rightly, except on the rarest occasions, because they have judged that it is right to act'. It was Burke's epistemological scepticism which forced him back on tradition. Burke denied the value of the pursuit of truth on the ground that it might disturb the peace of the Commonwealth (a present good) without giving any assurance of a greater benefit. This was a conclusion that Keynes wanted to resist. He argued, in the spirit of Mill, that 'whatever the immediate consequences of a new truth may be, there is a high probability that truth will in the long run lead to better results than falsehood'. This was very much in line with his attack on Moore's argument for following generally accepted rules rather than using individual judgement. However, he conceded that the 'modern prejudice in favour of truth [may be] founded on somewhat insufficient bases'. Thus the *Treatise on Probability* may be regarded as his reply both to Moore and to Burke on this matter. Rationality was an important principle in Keynes's political philosophy. In the notion of policy informed by reason is a radical potential and optimistic outlook missing from classic Conservatism. It was his belief in the power of reason, and the possibility of rulers acting according to its dictates, which led him to allow considerable economic policy discretion to rulers.

Keynes's handling of Burke's views on property and democracy in the light of his 'maxims' of statesmanship is worth particular notice. Burke defended existing property rights on the double ground that redistribution of wealth would make no real difference to the poor, since they greatly outnumbered the rich, while at the same time it would 'considerably reduce in numbers those who could enjoy the undoubted benefits of wealth and who could confer on the state the advantages which the presence of wealthy citizens always brings'. Keynes felt this argument 'undoubtedly carries great weight ... and must always be one of the most powerful rejoinders to any scheme which has equalisation as its ultimate aim'. However, it was less valid if directed against 'any attempt to influence the channels in which wealth flows', and the relief of starvation or acute poverty. It was not valid, for example, against death duties 'whose object is to mulct great masses of accumulation', nor against the expropriation of feudal estates during the French revolution. Burke was so often concerned to defend the 'outworks' of the property system, that he did not see that this might endanger the 'central' system itself.

This was a typical thought, typically expressed. In his *Tract on Monetary Reform* (1923), Keynes insisted that governments must have discretion to revise contracts between the living and the dead, since 'the powers of uninterrupted usury are too great'. It was the 'absolutists of contract', he wrote, 'who are the parents of Revolution'—a good Burkean attitude, though one Burke sometimes ignored.

In the crises of the 1930s Keynes came to think that more drastic interferences with the 'outworks' than he had contemplated in 1904 might be necessary to defend the 'central' system. Thus in *The General Theory* he proposed to bring about the 'euthanasia of the rentier' by making it impossible to take 'usury' on loans; he also defended the medieval usury laws which restricted interest to a maximum. Yet when his French correspondent Marcel Labordère pointed out to him that 'stable fortunes, the hereditary permanency of families and sets of families of various social standings are an invisible social asset on which every kind of culture is more or less dependent', Keynes readily replied: 'I fully agree with this, and I wish I had emphasised it in your words. The older I get the more convinced I am that what you say is true and important. But I must not allow you to make me too conservative.'

The issue of democracy, Keynes argued, involved two separate questions. Has the mass of people a right to direct self-government? Is it expedient and conducive to good government that there should be self-government? To both questions Burke had returned an 'uncompromising negative'. On the first, Keynes stood solidly with Burke. Government is simply a 'contrivance of human wisdom' to 'supply certain . . . wants; and that is the end of the matter'. People are entitled to good government, not self-government—a doctrine which he would apply without question at the India Office. The more difficult question is whether self-government is necessary to good government, and here Keynes was more open than Burke. He agreed with him that 'the people' are incompetent to govern themselves and that Parliament must always be prepared to resist popular prejudice in the name of equity between individuals and classes. But he criticized Burke's 'dream of a representative class', and said that he underestimated the educative value of self-government. Nevertheless, Keynes doubted whether any 'rational or unprejudiced body of men' would have dared to make the experiment in universal suffrage had they not been 'under the influence of a fallacious notion concerning natural political rights'.

So far democracy had not disgraced itself. This was because its 'full force had not yet come into operation'. The existing system was oligarchic and plutocratic, rather than democratic. The assumption that it would continue in this way, with the addition of 'technical expertise' was the Achilles' heel of Keynes's political theory.

In his political philosophy, Keynes married two key elements of Burkean conservatism—contentment as the aim and risk avoidance as the method of government—to two key elements in reforming liberalism—a commitment to truth and belief in the possibility of rational individual judgement. He rejected both unthinking Conservatism and radical Socialism. This was very much the temper of the Middle Way which he espoused between the wars.

There has been much debate about what kind of Liberal Keynes was. Peter Clarke sees him as part of the pre-1914 'progressive' movement, uniting left-wing Liberals and moderate Socialists in a common redistributive, democratic programme. Against this, Michael Freeden argues that Keynes was a tough-minded, 'centrist' Liberal, grafting technocratic solutions onto an individualist stem. By confining state intervention to spaces left vacant by private enterprise, by 'jettisoning redistribution as a major field of socio-economic policy', and by 'de-democratizing' policy-making in favour of expert control, Keynes repudiated the distinctive features of 'progressive' Liberalism.

A case can be made out for both positions. What distances Keynes most obviously from the 'progressives' is his attitude to social justice. Keynes did not object (or object strongly) to the existing social order on the ground that it unfairly or unjustly distributed life-chances; rather that *laissez-faire* did not protect existing economic and social 'norms'. Injustice to him meant arbitrary changes in settled social arrangements, such as produced by changes in the value of money. He sympathized strongly with the miners at the time of the General Strike in 1926, because he saw them as victims of the return the previous year to the gold standard at an overvalued pound. Keynes transferred the problem of justice from the microeconomy to the macroeconomy. Injustice becomes a matter of uncertainty, justice a matter of contractual predictability. Redistribution plays a minor part in his social philosophy, and then only as part of the machinery of macroeconomic stabilization, not as a means to an ideal goal such as equality.

These attitudes emerge in his essay 'The End of *Laissez-Faire*', first delivered as a lecture at Oxford in 1924 (*CW* ix. 272–94). The evils of the existing order arose largely from 'risk, uncertainty, and ignorance'. Their remedy required 'deliberate control of the currency and of credit by a central institution', the 'collection and dissemination of business facts', a 'coordinated act of intelligent judgment' concerning the aggregate volume of savings and their distribution between domestic and foreign investment, and a population policy 'which pays attention to innate quality as well as to . . . numbers'. What Keynes was after, as he later wrote in *The General Theory*, was to fill the gaps in the 'Manchester system'. As a criterion for public intervention Keynes offered the notion of a service or activity which was 'technically social' in the sense that only the State could provide it. Attached somewhat inconsistently to this set of arguments was an evolutionary perspective according to which the individualistic capitalism of family firms gave way to the 'socialized' capitalism of public utilities and large private corporations. Spontaneous industrial developments thus foreshadowed, and made possible, the conscious 'socialization of investment' Keynes was to advocate in *The General Theory*.

Despite the decline of the Liberals, Keynes refused to join either the Conservative or the Labour Parties. 'How could I bring myself to be a Conservative?' he asked himself in his essay of 1926, 'Am I a Liberal?'

They offer me neither food nor drink—neither intellectual nor spiritual consolation . . . [Conservatism] leads nowhere; it satisfies no ideal; it conforms to no intellectual standard; it is not even safe, or calculated to preserve from spoilers that degree of civilisation which we have already attained.   (*CW* ix. 296–7)

For a Liberal of Keynes's generation, the Conservative Party was the historic enemy, and remained so throughout the inter-war years, despite the 'decency' of Stanley Baldwin. It was the party of stupidity, superstition, and prejudice; the party of protectionism and jingoism. The Conservatives were also guardians of the reactionary moral code against which Keynes's generation had rebelled. As part of the agenda of Liberalism, Keynes listed 'Birth control and the use of contraceptives, marriage laws, the treatment of sexual offences and abnormalities, the economic position of women, the economic position of the family . . . drug questions'. On all these matters of special concern to Bloomsbury and Hampstead, Conservatives—at least in public—upheld positions which he habitually dubbed 'medieval'.

He attributed the stupidity of Conservatism to its attachment to the hereditary principle. This also explained the inefficiency of many British firms. British capitalism was dominated by third-generation men. His initial respect for the Conservative leader, Stanley Baldwin, rapidly waned: 'There was an attraction at first that Mr. Baldwin should not be clever. But when he forever sentimentalizes about his own stupidity, the charm is broken,' he scribbled in 1925. Yet as late as 1936 he cited Baldwin 'as a model statesman who could bring about a modified socialism if his party would let him'.

If the Conservatives were the stupid party, Labour was the silly party. But at least much of its heart was in the right place. What was needed, Keynes often suggested, was Labour's head of steam yoked to the programme of reforming Liberalism. In much of his political writing Keynes was engaged in a dialogue with the Labour movement. This sometimes involved him in a very ambiguous use of language, as he tried to distinguish his position from that of socialism and also to stress the compatibility between a range of Liberal and socialist aspirations. This ambiguity, which he seemed to see as a necessary part of his efforts at persuasion, makes it very hard to decide the question of how far Keynes would have been willing to go down the socialist road. In his lifetime he never had to make the choice which confronted many people in the 1970s.

Keynes emphatically rejected socialism as an *economic* remedy for the ills of capitalism. Both classical economists and socialists, he often said, believed in the same 'laws of economics'. But whereas the former regarded them as true and inevitable, the latter saw them as true and intolerable. Keynes proposed to show they were not true. He added that the very fact that capitalism was 'socializing' itself made public ownership unnecessary.

Keynes objected to socialism's revolutionary strain. He understood that the bulk of the Labour Party were not 'Jacobins, Communists, Bolshevists', but he thought the malignity and envy of these groups affected the whole party, consorting ill 'with ideals to build up a true social republic'. In a debate with the Scottish Socialist Thomas Johnston in 1929, he argued that Labour had to 'put on an appearance of being against anyone who is more successful, more skilful, more industrious, more thrifty than the average . . . This is most unjust and most unwise. It disturbs what is and always must be the strongest section of the community and throws them into the reactionary camp' (KP, PS/4).

Keynes explicitly rejected the class basis of socialist politics. A much quoted remark of his is: '[The Labour Party] is a class party, and the class is not my class. If I am going to pursue sectional interests at all, I shall pursue my own . . . I can be influenced by what seems to be justice and good sense; but the *class* war will find me on the side of the *educated* bourgeoisie' (*CW* ix. 297). He was a leveller who wanted to level upwards not downwards. 'I want to give encouragement to all exceptional effort, ability, courage, character. I do not want to antagonize the successful, the exceptional' (KP, PS/4).

Finally, Keynes rejected Labour's anti-élitism. He felt that the intellectual elements in the Labour party will '[n]ever exercise adequate control; too much will always be decided by those who do not know *at all* what they are talking about'. The Conservatives were much better off in this respect, since 'the inner ring of the party can almost dictate the details and the technique of policy' (*CW* ix. 295–6). As his earliest writings show, Keynes believed in rule by a Platonic guardian class, constrained, but not dominated, by democracy.

Keynes admired three things about socialism: its passion for justice, the Fabian ideal of public service; and its utopianism, based on the elimination of the profit motive. Keynes had his own Utopia which inspired his work as an economist, expressed notably in his essay, 'Economic Possibilities for our Grandchildren', published in 1930 (*CW* ix. 321–32). Here he outlines his vision of a society which is a paradise of abundance, leisure, beauty, grace, and variety, and in which 'love of money' comes to be regarded as a mental disease. But this Utopia owed more to Cambridge than to socialist philosophy (there is no obvious place in it for equality, fraternity, or democracy). Besides, it was to come about only after the economic problem was solved. Meanwhile, as Keynes put it, 'we must go on pretending that fair is foul and foul is fair; for foul is useful and fair is not'. In short, Keynes rejected socialism as a means; and as an end endorsed it only in his own idiosyncratic sense.

That occasionally penetrating observer of inter-war British culture, Dmitri Mirsky, gave a Marxist interpretation of Keynes's philosophy of practice in his book *The Intelligentsia of Great Britain*. The intellectual aristocracy, he said, not being directly involved in the production process, could consider itself outside or above class. In economics, it demanded organization, which it called socialism, but in individual life it wanted more freedom, which chained it to capitalism.

Today such antitheses seem less compelling. Few people now believe that socialism, in the sense which Keynes rejected it, is relevant to our economic problems. The question is whether Keynes's Middle Way is still relevant. He believed that there would be a growing deficiency of aggregate demand in mature capitalist economies, as investment opportunities flag, but savings habits appropriate to the individualistic era persist. Public intervention would be needed to maintain investment demand, redistribute income to high consuming groups, and rearrange conditions of work and pay in order gradually to increase the attractions of leisure as science increased the power to produce. Otherwise, he warned, the Great Depression of 1929–32 would be the foretaste of permanent semi-slump. His political ideas were embedded in his economic response to British mass unemployment in the 1920s, which we must now examine.

3 The monetary reformer

Keynes's discussion of the British unemployment problem in the 1920s took place within the framework of the quantity theory of money. He had no doubt that fluctuations in business activity could be prevented by appropriate monetary policy. The quantity theorists of Keynes's day were monetary reformers who wanted to use the theory of money to stabilize economic activity. The quantity theory of money was the first theory of short-run macroeconomic stabilization.

On the face of it this is curious, because the quantity theory of money is a theory relating the supply of money to the *price level* at which goods are bought, not to the *quantity* of goods produced. Yet, as a matter of observed fact, changes in money and prices *were* associated with fluctuations in quantity of output and employment, and this needed to be explained. For the first thirty years or so of this century, economists, including Keynes, tried to use what they called the quantity theory of money to explain fluctuations in output. They did so, partly because of the observed correlation between monetary events and fluctuations in business activity, and partly because monetary policy offered the most promising parameter of action for those who wanted to manage, but not destroy, the capitalist system. In the 1930s Keynes abandoned the quantity theory approach to the explanation of short-run fluctuations in output. In *The General Theory* money still retains its power to disturb the real economy. But its disturbing power arises from its function as a store of value rather than as a means of exchange. This had the further consequence of calling into question the reliability of monetary policy as an instrument of economic management.

The quantity theory was based on the transactions view of money. Money was a medium of exchange, a means of effecting purchases and sales of goods and services. It has no other purpose, at least in a 'modern' economy with a stable legal and political order and a developed banking system. This being so, a change in the quantity (or value) of money could disturb a previous equilibrium only if it produced non-proportionate changes in agents' money stocks. This indeed was the assumption of those who used the quantity theory to analyse economic fluctuations. Rising prices, it was typically said, benefit investors and entrepreneurs at the expense of savers and wage-earners; falling prices, the reverse. This argument hinged on the distinction between flexible and non-flexible prices. Thus wage rates were assumed to be 'fixed' or at least 'sticky' in the short run, selling prices 'flexible'. At the same time, the transactions view of money made stabilizing the price level seem deceptively easy. Money had no utility other than as a means of effecting transactions. People 'demanded' it, Keynes used to say before 1914, only to get rid of it as quickly as possible. All the central authority had to do was to ensure an appropriate supply of money and all would be well. From before the First World War up to and including his *Treatise on Money*, Keynes's work was in this tradition, though by the end it was becoming increasingly problematic for him.

Two forms of the quantity theory were available when Keynes started work as an economist—Irving Fisher's 'transactions' version, and the Cambridge 'cash balances' approach, developed by Alfred Marshall, who taught Keynes his economics. Keynes used both in his pre-1914 lectures, saying they come to 'practically the same thing'. Fisher's equation of exchange, $MV = PT$, states that, in any period, the quantity of money (M) times its velocity of circulation—the average number of times per period which a pound or dollar is spent (V)—equals the average price of each transaction (P) multiplied by the total number of transactions (T). All this means is that the value of what is spent is equal to the value of what is bought, hardly a surprising conclusion. Three further propositions are needed to convert the equation of exchange into a theory of the price level. First, causation runs from money to prices. Secondly, the velocity of circulation is determined independently of the money supply by the community's level of income and payments habits. These change only slowly. Thirdly, the volume of transactions is determined independently of the quantity of money by 'real' forces. If these propositions are true, any change in the quantity of money will lead to a proportional change in the price level.

In the Marshallian 'cash balances' version of the quantity theory, $M = k\,PT$, M, P, and T have the same meaning as before, and k—the fraction of the community's wealth or income (Marshall tended to use the terms interchangeably) which on average is held as cash during the period—is the reciprocal of V, the velocity of circulation. The Cambridge equation emphasized not the spending of money, but the role of money as a temporary abode of purchasing power between selling and buying. It was a bridge to the 'store of value' function of money by pointing to individual motives for holding liquid assets and suggesting that they could be further analysed.

It did not point too far in this direction to the pre-war Keynes. He regarded the quantity theory of money not just as a logical exercise—as a statement of the conditions necessary for it to be true—but as a realistic set of assumptions about the real world. He certainly believed that the causation ran from money to prices, castigating 'businessmen' and 'popular opinion' for holding the contrary view (*CW* xii. 701–2, 730–1). He believed that the 'rapidity of circulation' or 'demand for money balances to hold' is institutionally determined and not subject to erratic shifts (*CW* xii. 760). He also accepted the third proposition—that the volume of transactions is determined by 'real' forces (*CW* xii. 696). All this being so, he accepted the quantity theory in both its versions. At the same time he recognized that fluctuations in prices can have temporary effects on the velocity of circulation and the state of trade, though his discussion was distinctly perfunctory (*CW* xii. 715–17, 730–1, 761).

Keynes's account of the 'transmission mechanism' from money to prices is strictly Marshallian; indeed he accused Fisher of failing to specify a mechanism (*CW* xi. 377). An increase in the central bank's gold reserves leads to lower interest rates. Entrepreneurs increase their borrowing; it is the spending of their new deposits which first causes prices to rise, and this stimulus 'gradually spreads to all parts of the community, until the new gold is needed to finance a volume of real trade no larger . . . than before' (*CW* xii. 706–7). The price level is what equilibrates the 'demand for cash' with the 'supply of cash'. The important point, though, is that it takes *time* for an injection of money to have its final effect on prices, and it is while prices are adjusting to changes in the money supply that trade may be boosted or depressed. It follows also that under the gold standard 'the supply of purchasing power depends upon banking and gold jointly' (*CW* xii. 764).

The pre-1914 monetary reformers aimed to reduce the influence of gold on the 'supply of purchasing power'. Stabilization of the price level required the quantity of money to be under the control of the central monetary authority. But where legal tender money consisted of gold coins, the long-run value of money was determined by unregulated conditions of supply and demand in the gold market. The late nineteenth-century fall in the price level was widely attributed to the increased cost of extracting gold from the depleted Californian and Australian mines, as well as to increased gold hoarding in India. Technically, the quantity of gold money was not an exogenous variable. Reformers devised schemes to vary the quantity of gold in money—the tabular standard of Marshall, the compensated dollar of Fisher were examples—so as to achieve a more stable price level. The Swedish economist Knut Wicksell took the bull by the horns: the ideal international standard would be a paper standard, giving central banks complete control over the money supply. In his *Interest and Prices*, published in German in 1898, Wicksell argued that 'there is a certain rate of interest on loans which is neutral in respect to commodity prices, and tends neither to raise them nor lower them'. He called this the 'natural' (or profit) rate. The crux of Wicksell's argument against the gold standard was that it prevented the central bank from adjusting the market rate of interest to changes in the 'natural' rate. Keynes did not pick up this thread till 1930. But even before 1914 he echoed Irving Fisher in advocating a 'more rational and stable' standard than the gold standard. In his *Indian Currency and Finance* (1913) he proposed a reform of the Indian banking system to increase the seasonal elasticity of the stock of rupees, and looked forward to the day when gold-based currencies would be restricted to one or two countries, whose central banks would 'manage' what was, in effect, a fiduciary international standard. 'It is not likely', he wrote, 'that we shall leave permanently the most intimate adjustments of our economic organism at the mercy of a lucky prospector, a new chemical process, or a change of ideas in Asia,' and 'A preference for a tangible reserve currency is . . . a relic of a time when governments were less trustworthy in these matters than they now are' (*CW* i. 71, 51). His successive plans for managed currencies up to Bretton Woods none the less retained a 'constitutional monarch' role for gold as the foundation of a pegged exchange-rate system and ultimate safeguard against inflation.

Though 'constitutional' schemes for reforming the gold standard failed before the First World War, it was becoming an increasingly 'managed' standard as central banks used a variety of devices to offset or neutralize gold flows in the interests of domestic price stability. The effect of an inflow or outflow of gold was seen to depend within wide limits on the action of the central bank. This led pre-war monetary theory to give increasing emphasis to the role of banking policy in determining the money supply. Attention switched from the influence of gold movements on prices to that of credit flows. The quantity theory of money was becoming a quantity theory of credit. In a paper 'How Far are Bankers Responsible for the Alternations of

Crisis and Depression?', read to the Political Economy Club in December 1913, Keynes argued that banks can lend to entrepreneurs without borrowing the equivalent amount from savers; credit creation can be an independent source of inflation. However, when investment 'runs ahead' of saving, there has to be a depression to enable saving to 'catch up' (*CW* xiii. 2–14). These ideas were to be taken up again in the mid-1920s. However, as long as it could be assumed that the central bank had the means to regulate the rate of credit creation by the commercial banks, the existence of credit money posed no danger to its ability to 'control the money supply'.

Much of the theory and practice of monetary reform was in place before 1914; but Keynes's war experience and its monetary consequences enriched his theory and gave his policy discussion an urgency it never had before the war. He had advised the Treasury during the banking crisis of July–August 1914, explaining the crisis in terms of an 'unusual demand for money' by the banking system, following the failure of foreign remittances and the stock-market collapse. The crisis was averted by the Bank of England purchasing bills from the market. The duty of the central bank to act as 'lender of the last resort' to the banking system had been part of central banking theory since the time of Walter Bagehot, who enunciated the doctrine in his classic, *Lombard Street* (1870), and Keynes accepted it without question. His wartime Treasury experience also led him to identify inflation as the mechanism by which a needy government, too weak to tax honestly, can transfer real resources to itself. In a wartime correspondence with the economist Edwin Cannan of the London School of Economics Keynes denied that inflation could be overcome simply by limiting the note issue. He wrote to Cannan on 28 January 1918:

The excessive issue of currency notes and the degree of inflation which exists, connected partly with this note issue, and partly with the increase in bank credits, seems to me due to national expenditure being on a scale beyond what the government can pay for by taxes and loans . . . As long as this is the case, regulation of the note issue is impossible. . . . It is more scientific I think to attribute the inflation to the excess expenditure by Government and to hold that it can only be cured by the diminution of expenditure public and private.

More generally, the topics which gained in prominence as compared to pre-war were those arising from wartime inflation, post-war currency disorders, and the overhang of wartime debt. The war and post-war inflations were explained along quantity theory lines by inflationary government finance. The 'purchasing power parity' theory of the exchanges was developed by the Swedish economist Gustav Cassel to explain the link between domestic price inflation and exchange depreciation. The issue of Germany's capacity to pay reparations generated a technical discussion on the nature of the 'transfer problem'. Keynes took an active part in all these discussions. Of particular note is his warning against inflation. In his *Economic Consequences of the Peace* he quoted with approval a remark attributed to Lenin that 'there is no subtler, no surer means of overturning the existing basis of society than to debauch the currency' (*CW* ii. 148). The immense volatility of prices and exchange rates in the immediate post-war period, as well as the change in the balance of power between the United States and Europe, formed the historical raw material of his *Tract on Monetary Reform* (1923).

II

The explicit goal of *A Tract on Monetary Reform* was domestic price stability. Only stable prices could produce stable or normal business activity. 'I regard the stability of prices, credit and employment as of paramount importance,' Keynes wrote. His argument was that fluctuations in the value of money trigger short-run fluctuations in business activity, because they change class income shares and disturb settled expectations. Falling prices are said to injure employment, both because money-wages are fixed in the short run, and because falling prices depress expectations of sales proceeds. 'It is worse, in an impoverished world', Keynes wrote, 'to provoke unemploy-ment than to disappoint the *rentier*' (*CW* iv. 36). This combina-tion of institutional and theoretical arguments was typical of Keynes. It is one of the sources of the many disputes about what he 'really' meant. The important point being made was that price stability was necessary for contractual predictability, which was related to economic stability. Monetary reform was an antidote to social revolution.

Four particular points of interest stand out from the *Tract*. First, Keynes attacked the policy of restoring the gold standard. In this he took to its logical conclusion the argument of the monetary reformers that stable domestic prices might be incon-sistent with stable exchange rates. Instead of domestic prices being required to adjust to the exchange rate, the exchange rate should be adjusted to a domestic price level consistent with a 'normal' (that is, reasonably full) level of employment. A scin-tillating section on the forward market in exchanges is designed to show that traders can 'hedge' much more easily against exchange-rate fluctuations than can producers against domestic price fluctuations. Thus 'contracts and business expectations, which presume a stable exchange, may be far fewer, even in a trading country such as England, than those which presume a stable level of internal prices' (*CW* iv. 126).

The crucial context of the argument was the new dominance of the United States. 'With the existing distribution of the world's gold, the reinstatement of the gold standard means, inevitably, that we surrender the regulation of our price level and the handling of the credit cycle to the Federal Reserve Board of the United States.' The American monetary authori-ties would determine their monetary policy by reference to domestic conditions, not to the requirements of other countries like Britain (*CW* iv. 139–40). The best solution was to divide the world into 'managed' sterling and dollar currency blocs. 'So long as the Federal Reserve Board was successful in keeping dollar prices steady the objective of keeping sterling prices steady would be identical with the objective of keeping the dollar–sterling exchange steady' (*CW* iv. 147). Gold would be retained as the ultimate means of settling international debts (*CW* iv. 158–60).

Secondly, Keynes thought that stable prices could be achieved by monetary policy alone. He did not see wage pressure as a complicating factor. Nor did he query the interest-elasticity of investment, though he did understand that there were expectational limits to real interest-rate changes—an insight he did not exploit till *The General Theory*. Controlling inflation was mainly a matter of stopping inflationary government finance.

Thirdly, Keynes was a broad, not narrow, money man. The right policy was 'to watch and to control the creation of credit and to let the creation of currency follow suit'. This was because the quantity of cash was a backward-looking indicator. It was not the past rise in prices but the future rise which had to be counteracted (*CW* iv. 146, 148). The wartime debate between Keynes and Edwin Cannan foreshadows the debates between the 'broad' and 'narrow' money versions of monetarism in the 1980s. The problem of which kind of money to track or monitor was posed for the first time.

Finally, Keynes favoured discretionary management, rejecting a money-supply rule as unsuitable for controlling the credit cycle. He wrote down a simplified form of Pigou's monetary equation, $n = p(k + rk')$, where n is currency notes and other forms of cash in circulation, p is the index number of the cost of living, k is the real value of cash in hand, k' the real value of bank deposits including overdrafts, and r the ratio of the banking system's reserves to liabilities. The quantity theory, he said, was based on the assumption that 'a *mere* change in the quantity of the currency cannot affect k, r, and k''—that is to say, that these variables are determined independently of n. Consequently a change in n will cause an equiproportionate movement in p. Double the quantity of money, and you double the price level.

Now, 'in the long run' this is probably true. . . . But this *long run* is a misleading guide to current affairs. *In the long run* we are all dead. Economists set themselves too easy, too useless a task if in tempestuous seasons they can only tell us that when the storm is long past the ocean is flat again.   (*CW* iv. 65)

When prices are rising, people reduce their 'real balances' (k and k'); when prices are falling they increase them. Central banks vary their reserve requirements to offset gold flows.

Given the short-run instability of what would now be called the 'demand for money' function, there was no stable short-run relationship between the money stock and money national income. Keynes saw that 'the mood of the public and the business world' could exert an independent influence on the price level. In trying to stabilize prices the monetary authority had to be prepared to act on both the supply of money *and* the demand for money; in Keynes's language, its duty consisted in 'exercising a stabilising influence over k and k', and, in so far as this fails or is impracticable, in deliberately varying n and r so as to *counterbalance* the movement of k and k'' (*CW* iv. 68). The algebraic symbolism made the task of monetary management seem all too easy. Any tendency for real balances to increase can be counteracted by lowering bank rate 'because easy lending diminishes the advantages of keeping a margin for contingencies in cash' (*CW* iv. 68). The central bank can vary the amount of cash it makes available to the banking system by buying and selling securities (*CW* iv. 144). As long 'as we refrain from inflationary finance on the one hand and a return to an unregulated gold standard on the other', the control of the money supply and thus of the price level will be in the hands of the central bank (*CW* iv. 69).

The *Tract on Monetary Reform* recognizes that monetary shocks can affect business activity because of uncertainty about the future course of prices. Quantity theorists had tended to argue that it was only *unanticipated* changes in the price level which produced disturbances to proportionality. Keynes argued, more realistically, that even if price rises or falls are *expected*, uncertainty about the extent of the movement can affect business behaviour. Keynes has identified the central importance of uncertainty: but to what price, or particular set of prices, to attach it in order to explain the rhythms of trade was a problem which was to occupy him over his next two books.

These deeper questions were hardly tested by Winston Churchill's decision to return sterling to the gold standard in April 1925. In his pamphlet *The Economic Consequences of Mr. Churchill*, published in July, Keynes treated the decision straightforwardly as a monetary shock inflicted by the government on the industry of the country. His argument was that returning the pound to its pre-war parity with the dollar—£1 = \$4.86—overvalued sterling by 10 per cent, requiring a 10 per cent fall in the money costs of production if the existing volume of British exports was to be maintained. This would meet with intense worker resistance, which could only be overcome, Keynes argued, by 'intensifying unemployment' without limit. Keynes said that these economics of the 'juggernaut' could be short-circuited by means of a 'national treaty' to reduce wages and other incomes by agreement. He suspected, though, that government policy would actually produce a 'jammed' low-employment economy. The government would carry deflation far enough to provoke, but not cure, unemployment, and borrow from abroad to plug the export shortfall.

This is roughly what happened. By 1928 Keynes was producing what was to be his standard summary of the whole episode:

we have deflated prices by raising the exchange value of sterling and by controlling the volume of credit; *but we have not deflated costs* ... The fundamental blunder of the Treasury and Bank of England has been due, from the beginning, to their belief that if they looked after the deflation of prices the deflation of costs would look after itself. (*CW* xix. 762)

III

Less than a year after the *Tract* was published, Keynes started a new book which he first called 'The Theory of Money and Credit'. It was to be a study of the theory of money in relation to the 'credit cycle'. In the *Tract* Keynes had given the monetary authority the duty of offsetting fluctuations in 'cash balances'. But the composition of these balances, and causes of their fluctuations, had not been analysed. In tackling the problem Keynes reverted to the ideas of his paper of 1913 (see above p. 283). Banks can lend more or less than the public want to save. The task of monetary policy is to keep bank-lending equal to saving intentions.

In analysing the relationship between 'bank money' and saving, Keynes was greatly influenced by his Cambridge colleague Dennis Robertson, who was then writing his *Banking Policy and the Price Level*, published in 1926. His intellectual engagement with Robertson at this point was decisive for the development of his own ideas. Robertson was, above all, a business-cycle theorist, drawing on a rich Continental literature to explain why the growth of wealth was spasmodic. Keynes was permanently influenced by two features of business-cycle theory: first, the view that the business cycle is an investment cycle, caused by fluctuations in the expected profitability of capital goods; secondly, that this 'real' cycle is amplified to boom and slump by monetary factors—particularly by the failure of monetary policy to keep investment equal to saving. Robertson thought that 'real' business fluctuations were inseparable from progress. He wanted to use monetary policy, though, to eliminate 'inappropriate' fluctuations in real activity. This might entail abandoning the goal of price stability.

Keynes and Robertson started out by agreeing that only credit inflation or deflation could make investment diverge from voluntary saving. Much of Robertson's *Banking Policy and the Price Level*, including its array of peculiar terms, was devoted to showing how different forms of non-voluntary spending and saving could be brought about by credit operations. This included the idea that temporary inflation creates an investment fund by 'forcing' people to consume less and therefore 'save' more. The famous doctrine of 'forced saving', first stated by Thomas Joplin after the Napoleonic wars, was rediscovered from observation of how the government 'confiscated' its citizens' incomes without taxing them in the First World War. Basically, the government pre-empts a slice of national output by spending an additional amount of new money created at its behest through the banking system. The additional spending raises the general level of prices (having generated excess demand at the previous level of prices) and private economic actors find themselves needing (or wishing) to *hold* rather than to respend the additional money created, because the increase in the price level has raised their requirements for nominal cash holdings relative to the physical volume of transactions. Attempts by the government to repeat the process will eventually bring an accelerating inflationary spiral, as private actors anticipate and try to thwart the government's purposes by adjusting their own spending.

Keynes's new book started along this track, but eventually left it. He explained to Robertson in 1931:

> When you were writing your *Banking Policy and the Price Level*, and we were discussing it, we both believed that inequalities between saving and investment—using those terms with the degree of vagueness with which we used them at that date—only arose as a result of what one might call an act of inflation or deflation on the part of the banking system. I worked on this basis for quite a time, but in the end I came to the conclusion that this would not do. As a result of getting what were, in my opinion, more clear definitions of saving and investment, I found that the salient phenomena could come about without any overt act on the part of the banking system. (*CW* xiii. 273)

Robertson had talked about savings being either invested or hoarded. Keynes emphasized a third alternative: savings neither invested nor hoarded but used to buy existing assets. Thus saving can 'run ahead' of investment (defined as buying *new* capital equipment), without any slowdown in the overall velocity of circulation. This line of thought was influenced by the speculative Wall Street bull market of 1927–9. Keynes lost faith in the ability of the 'transactions' version of the quantity theory of money to explain short-term business fluctuations. What was important for employment was not the total of transactions in a period, but whether or not money income was being spent on current output.

Another crucial distinction in the *Treatise*, between 'foreign investment' and 'foreign lending', was influenced by Keynes's involvement in the debate on German reparation payments. The fact that British savings, uninvested at home, were being lent abroad, did not mean that all savings were being invested, because, with a fixed exchange rate, any attempt to lend more abroad than Britain's export surplus allowed would cause a drain of gold and force a rise in bank rate at home. This would cause domestic investment to fall by the amount of the excess of foreign lending over the current account surplus.

What Keynes and Robertson were both trying to do, not yet very successfully, was to integrate saving-investment analysis with the theory of money, rather than maintain the rigid separation between them which was a feature of the classical or quantity theory approach.

In his *The Keynesian Revolution in the Making* (1988), Peter Clarke has persuasively argued that the publication of the *Treatise* was held up, and its analysis altered, by Keynes's need to confront the 'Treasury View' developed in 1928–9 to refute Lloyd George's plan to cure unemployment by a programme of loan-financed public works. The author of this notorious 'View' was Ralph Hawtrey. In an article in *Economica* in March 1925, Hawtrey had argued that, with a fixed money supply, any loan raised by the government for public works would 'crowd out' (in today's parlance) an equivalent amount of private spending. Employment could be increased only by credit expansion—borrowing from the banks. But it was the credit expansion which was important, not the public works, which Hawtrey condemned as a 'piece of ritual'. From late 1928, the Treasury, primed by Hawtrey, started to argue that 'What Keynes is after, of course, is a definite inflation of credit'—which was inconsistent with the maintenance of the gold standard. The prime minister, Stanley Baldwin, was fed the lines: 'we must *either* take existing money *or* create new money.' Since the latter was ruled out by the gold standard, the crowding-out argument seemed to hold. Keynes as yet had not developed his consumption function/multiplier analysis to refute it; and even if he had developed it, its applicability in the absence of cheap money would have been open to question.

He took a stride towards developing it in *Can Lloyd George Do It?*, a pamphlet he wrote with Hubert Henderson in May 1929 (*CW* ix. 115–25). To the Treasury argument that no savings were available to finance *additional* investment Keynes replied that this assumed full employment of all resources. The unemployed resources included savings which had not 'materialized' owing to the 'want of prosperity'. This was an odd way of putting it. But the thought Keynes was expressing—in the language of the *Treatise*—was that business losses caused by recession made the national savings less than they would have been had entrepreneurs been earning 'normal' profits. The implication of this was that any policy (including a loan-financed public works' programme) which succeeded in restoring a 'normal' level of income would create the saving needed to finance the investment.

Corresponding to this, the employment-creating effects of additional government spending would not be limited to those directly employed on government projects. For every man put to work building a road or a house, at least another would find a job supplying the inputs required. Furthermore, the additional purchasing power thus created would exert a 'cumulative force' on trade activity, making the employment effects of a given capital expenditure far larger than the direct and indirect effects indicated above, though 'it is not possible to measure effects of this character with any sort of precision'. The 'employment multiplier', worked out by Richard Kahn in 1931, was an attempt to measure these 'cumulative' effects.

The more direct approach to the analysis of output and employment opened up by Keynes's confrontation with the Treasury View in 1929 had, in a sense, made much of the *Treatise on Money* redundant, from his point of view, when it was finally published in October 1930. Nevertheless it is a book with a wealth of institutional understanding of financial and money markets, some fundamental theory, and some theoretical loose ends on which Keynes soon started to work.

It is a difficult book to summarize. Its central theoretical proposition is that saving and investment are done by two different sets of people for different motives and there is no automatic mechanism in a credit money economy to keep them equal. There is a rate of profit on capital (which Keynes, following Wicksell, called the 'natural' rate) and there is a rate of interest on loans—the 'market' rate. But the market rate demanded by lenders may be higher or lower than the profit rate available to or expected by investors. Thus the possibility arises that not all income earned will get spent by consumers or investors.

The practical import of all this is that the only balancer a credit-money economy has is banking *policy*. Under the gold standard the Bank of England was prevented from setting bank rate low enough to allow a level of investment equal to what the community wanted to save: hence mass unemployment. Crucial to this demonstration is Keynes's switch in emphasis from the stock of money to the flow of spending. It was insufficiency of spending on investment relative to the rate of saving which caused both the price level to fall *and* people to be unemployed.

Fundamental in terms of economic psychology is Keynes's break from the classical view of saving as providing an automatic route to investment. He dismissed the 'abstinence' theory of economic progress in a couple of superb paragraphs:

It has been usual to think of the accumulated wealth of the world as having been painfully built up out of the voluntary abstinence of individuals from the immediate enjoyment of consumption which we call thrift. But it should be obvious that mere abstinence is not enough by itself to build cities or drain fens. . . . It is enterprise which builds and improves the world's possessions . . . If enterprise is afoot, wealth accumulates whatever may be happening to thrift; and if enterprise is asleep, wealth decays whatever thrift may be doing.

Thus, thrift may be the handmaid and nurse of enterprise. But equally she may not be. And, perhaps, even usually she is not. For enterprise is connected with thrift not directly, but at one remove; and the link which should join them is frequently missing. For the engine which drives enterprise is not thrift, but profit. (*CW* vi. 132)

Unfortunately Keynes tried to formalize these pathbreaking ideas in 'Fundamental Equations', whose origins lie in an earlier phase of the book, when he was still trying to use the quantity theory of money to explain business fluctuations. Throughout the *Treatise* the reader is being tripped up by dead skins which Keynes had sloughed off while writing it. To adapt the new ideas to the older ones critical terms like 'income', 'profits', and 'saving' are used in special ways. Though Keynes is trying to explain how, if interest rates are prevented from falling, a slump can develop and persist, the spotlight is on changing price levels, not on changes in output and employment.

The three sets of relevant definitions are: (*a*) the community's money income (otherwise the 'normal' or equilibrium earnings of the factors of production, or costs of production); (*b*) profits, which are defined as the difference between costs of production and selling prices, and exclude entrepreneurs' 'normal' earnings; and (*c*) saving, defined as that part of the community's 'normal' income withheld from consumption. The purpose of excluding profits and losses (which Keynes also calls 'windfalls') from income is to segregate the variable causing output to expand or contract. But the attempt results in non-operational definitions of income and saving which were the cause of much misunderstanding. We have the illusion that they stay constant even though profits are positive or negative. The idea that aggregate saving can 'run ahead' or 'fall behind' investment depended entirely on the way income and saving are defined.

Formally, the *Treatise* is an attempt to capture, in a set of equations, the dynamics of an economy in transition from one (consumer) price level to another. We are presented, on the one side, with the flow of money earned by the factors of production in producing consumption and investment goods, and, on the other, its division into the parts which are spent on buying consumption goods and those which are saved. The price level of consumption goods is stable if the proportions of money earned in producing consumption and investment goods are the same as the division of spending between current consumption and saving.

In this situation costs of production equal the selling prices of consumption goods; profits are zero; saving equals the cost of investment: all true by definition. If, on the other hand, people spend less on buying consumption goods than they have earned producing them, consumer prices fall. In this situation, by definition, costs exceed prices; profits are negative by the same amount; and saving 'runs ahead' of the cost of investment.

This tortured approach was designed to emphasize one key point. If what people want to save exceeds the cost of investment the economy as a whole becomes depressed unless something is happening simultaneously to raise the *value* or profitability of investment. The required transfer of spending from consumption to investment does not happen automatically. Whether it happens depends on 'a different set of considerations' (*CW* v. 121): whether the anticipated profitability of investment is going up, or the rate of interest falling, or a mixture of both, at the same time.

Depression arises if the incentive to buy *new* pieces of capital equipment is insufficient to absorb the rate of saving out of 'normal' income—in other words if the expected rate of profit falls below the market rate set by the banking system. Keynes applies the uncertainty analysis started in the *Tract* to a specific set of prices—those of capital goods. It is the oscillations of the 'natural' rate of interest, driven by volatile expectations, around the market rate set by banking practices which explains the business cycle.

The *Treatise* contains the first of Keynes's two famous discussions of the pyschology of the stock exchange, much influenced by the collapse of the long 'bull' market on Wall Street in

1929. The key idea is that part of savings is 'held' for speculative purposes, because of uncertainty about the future value of capital assets. If the price of shares on the stock-market is expected to go up, savings will be redistributed from 'hoards' to 'securities', and vice versa if the price of shares is expected to fall. When most investors are 'bulls' you get a stock-market boom; when most of them are 'bears' you have a stock-market slump. Thus a 'speculative' motive for money balances to hold is identified in the *Treatise*, but it does not become Keynes's liquidity-preference theory till *The General Theory*.

Keynes does not doubt that the 'gap' between investment and 'saving' can be cured by lowering the market rate of interest. But this was prevented by the gold standard. In an open economy under a fixed exchange-rate system, the rate of interest has two jobs to do which may be incompatible: to regulate investment and to manage the balance of payments. If a community's desire to lend savings abroad exceeded its net export surplus, gold would be exported, which the monetary authority would have to offset by raising the rate of interest, thus increasing the cost of capital at home. The ultimate effect of a high bank rate would be a decline in 'efficiency wages' (national income), making possible an enlargement of the export surplus. This restates the inconsistency of policy thesis expounded in the *Tract*. Keynes's exposition of the *modus operandi* of bank rate remains a classic of its kind; but it is a price-level, rather than output, adjustment model that he has in mind.

Did Keynes see flexible wages as a complete cure for any shift in the consumption or investment function? One part of the *Treatise* suggests he did. In Book IV, we get a classical credit-cycle story depending on lagged wage adjustment. In the upswing there is a sequence of commodity (price) inflation, profit inflation, and income inflation, which then reverses itself in the downswing: prices fall, profits fall, and finally money-wages fall as the final act in the adjustment process (*CW* v, ch. 18; more vividly, *CW* vi, 'Historical Illustrations'). Yet in Book III, Keynes tells the famous 'banana parable', in which flexible wages do not cure the initial disturbance because, if intended saving goes up in response to a thrift campaign, while employers reduce wages, 'the spending power of the public will be reduced by just as much as the aggregate costs of production' (*CW* v. 158–60). If interest rates are fixed, there will be no position of equilibrium till either all production ceases and the community starves to death, or till growing impoverishment causes the community to save less, or unless 'investment is stimulated by some means or another', for example, by loan-financed public works.

If both interest-rate adjustment and public works are ruled out, then the only realistic adjustment mechanism left is impoverishment. Keynes called this 'nature's cure'. He did not make sufficiently clear that the first story (Book IV) related to an open economy in which cost reductions can lead to an increased export demand, and the second to a closed economy in which there is no export sector. He also failed to explain how 'saving' could continue to exceed investment in banana-land in face of cumulative business losses and income decline. This was the main technical business left over from the *Treatise*, largely the result of his non-operational definition of 'saving'.

The main object of national monetary policy should be to maintain a rate of interest consistent with full employment at a price level given, in the long run, by the behaviour of 'efficiency wages'. Such interest-rate autonomy could only be guaranteed by periodic adjustment of the exchange rate. The existence of downward wage rigidity, Keynes argued, was incompatible with a 'laissez-faire attitude to foreign lending'. Hence he doubted whether 'it is wise to have a currency system with a much wider ambit than our banking system, our tariff system and our wage system' (*CW* vi. 299). This somewhat extreme statement of monetary nationalism was not entirely inconsistent with the idea of a more flexible international currency system.

Keynes rightly regarded the Fundamental Equations of the *Treatise* as variations on the Fisher and Cambridge equations of exchange. But the causal sequence had been reversed. It was the forces affecting the demand for money balances, not the actions of the monetary authority in supplying those balances, which triggered off changes in the price level. However, he still expected the monetary authority to be able to neutralize the effect of those forces by supplying an appropriate quantity of money. 'Those who attribute sovereign power to the monetary authority in the governance of prices', he wrote,

do not, of course, claim that the terms on which money is supplied is the *only* influence affecting the price-level. To maintain that the supplies in a reservoir can be maintained at any required level by pouring enough water into it is not inconsistent with admitting that the level of the reservoir depends on many other factors besides how much water is poured in. (*CW* vi. 304)

IV

Between 1929 and 1931 Keynes used the *Treatise*'s saving-investment disequilibrium model as the basis of his policy advice to Ramsay MacDonald's Labour government, caught up in the first stages of the world depression. On the Macmillan Committee, set up by Philip Snowden, Labour's Chancellor of the Exchequer, to advise him on currency and credit matters, Keynes put forward six possible remedies for the slump, applicable to Britain's existing position. He ruled out devaluation except as a last resort. There were a number of suggestions for lowering domestic costs of production. One of them, 'an agreed reduction of the level of money incomes', reverted to his suggestion of 1925. Export industries might be relieved of taxes like national insurance contributions; or they might be rationalized. Three further remedies were directed to increasing employment at existing costs of production. The first was Protection, which 'does the trick, whereas in present conditions free trade does not'. The second was his old policy of mobilizing savings running to waste abroad in a loan-financed public works programme. His final remedy was for concerted international action to raise the world price level (*CW* xx. 99–132).

This litany of suggestions was put forward in February–March 1930. Protection became increasingly appealing as the world slump deepened. Keynes had been appointed to the prime minister's new Economic Advisory Council in January 1930; in July he was made chairman of a subcommittee of economists to produce 'an agreed diagnosis . . . and a reasoned list of possible remedies'. In his own memorandum to the committee, dated 21 September 1930, Keynes invented an elegant language for talking about the relationship between Britain's rigid economic structure and its declining international position. He defined the 'equilibrium terms of trade' as those which prevail 'when the level of money wages at home relatively to money wages abroad is such that the amount of the foreign balance (i.e. of foreign investment) *plus* the amount of home investment at the rate of interest set by world conditions . . . is . . . equal to the amount of home savings' (*CW* xiii. 178). British unemployment was largely due to the equilibrium terms of trade having been worsened by the return to gold in 1925 without any corresponding reduction in the money costs of production. Sterling's overvaluation had narrowed the export surplus available for foreign investment while imposing a high bank rate, which lowered domestic investment. Thus total investment was falling short of full-employment saving—whence business losses and unemployment.

The policy alternatives suggested by this analysis were to *meet* the worsened equilibrium terms of trade by cutting costs of production (particularly money-wages) or to *improve* them by reducing the pressure to lend abroad and/or enlarging the foreign balance at given terms of trade—pointing to a mixture of loan-financed public investment and protection. Keynes accepted that Britain's standard of living had to fall, but argued that raising prices was a better method for achieving this than lowering money-wages: there would be less social resistance, and the burden would fall on the whole community, including the *rentier* class.

In arguing the case for loan-financed public investment Keynes made use, for the first time, of a primitive version of

Richard Kahn's multiplier theory. Tariff protection was put forward as a way of increasing the foreign balance as well as business confidence, but also because 'any manufacturing country is probably just about as well fitted as any other to manufacture the great majority of articles'. The last sentiment was a fundamental breach with free-trade thinking. If the government rejected such policies, it would logically be forced to meet the equilibrium terms of trade by making deflation effective. The worst policy of all was wobbling between the two.

The exclusion of devaluation and the importance of business 'confidence' thus led Keynes to a theoretically based argument for protection as his favourite 'remedy' for the slump in the period leading up to Britain's abandonment of the gold standard in September 1931. In reaching this politically conservative, if theoretically radical, conclusion Keynes had been shaken by the evidence of both the Bank of England and the Treasury to the Macmillan Committee earlier that year. The Bank of England had cast doubts on Keynes's belief in the sovereign efficacy of monetary policy. Low interest rates, the Bank's spokesmen had argued, were not enough to make businessmen borrow if investment prospects were gloomy: one could lead the horse to the water, but not make it drink. A loan-financed public works programme, argued Sir Richard Hopkins of the Treasury, would produce 'psychological' crowding out of private investment if there was widespread mistrust of the schemes on which the proceeds of the loan were to be spent—or, he might have added, of the government doing the spending. Protection was the only policy which promised to meet the theoretical *and* confidence requirements of success in the given conditions.

These considerations influenced the subsequent development of Keynes's theory, and indeed of the Keynesian revolution in policy-making. Inventing theoretical models 'relevant' to the real world implied the development of policy instruments appropriate to a wide variety of realistic circumstances. Keynes the theoretician and Keynes the policy adviser were never far apart.

4 The General Theory

A strong common core of ideas links the *Treatise on Money* with *The General Theory of Employment, Interest, and Money*. The separation of saving and investment plans; the lack of any 'internal efficacious economic process' (in Samuelson's words) to equilibrate them; the stability of consumption and the volatility of investment; the store of value function of money—all these are present in the earlier book. *The General Theory* added a unifying mechanism in the shape of the 'principle of effective demand'. Keynes offered his profession, for the first time, a theory of demand and supply for output as a whole; he showed that if demand falls short of supply, output may have to run down to bring them back into balance; hence the possibility that 'the economic system may find itself in stable equilibrium ... at a level below full employment' (*CW* vii. 30). For economists who wanted to make the world better this was *the* crucial breakthrough. It explained the slump and showed how an escape from it might be consciously organized.

As Keynes put it, the new book switched attention from the analysis of the *causes* of a change in the level of output to the analysis of the *effects* of a change in the level of output—something which had been left 'incomplete and extremely confused' in the earlier book (*CW* vi, p. xxii). This is the nearest Keynes got to saying that both books are needed to understand the *Gestalt* of modern economies. In practice, the *Treatise* was forgotten and *The General Theory* became the bible of the economics profession and the politicians they advised.

Whether, but for the collapse of the world economy, Keynes, or anyone else, would have been thus interested in switching the spotlight from causes to effects is doubtful. What people wanted analysed in the 1930s was not institutional obstacles to the adjustment from one position of satisfactory equilibrium to another, but factors capable of keeping economic activity at a low level. Equally policy was now required not to dampen oscillations round a full-employment equilibrium—the traditional aim of the monetary reformers—but to raise the equilibrium level of employment. Keynes provided both theory and policy for the new conditions. Psychology and expectations move to the centre of his analytical picture; and he provided new concepts, terms, and tools directly useful to the policymaker.

Keynes's thinking was directly affected by the world depression in two ways. First, the depression undermined his faith in monetary policy—a radical break from his personal past. Despite the cheap money which followed sterling's depreciation in 1931, recovery was very weak. Keynes concluded that 'direct state intervention to promote and subsidise new investment' might offer the only 'means of escape from prolonged and perhaps interminable depression' (*CW* xxi. 59–60).

Secondly, it shifted his attention, more than ever before, from Britain to the United States. The problematic of the *Treatise on Money* was that of a sclerotic economy with an overvalued exchange rate. American wages and prices were much more flexible than those in Britain, its foreign sector much smaller, yet its output collapse was much more dramatic. American events spurred Keynes to think more generally about the predicament of wealthy economies. Moreover, the fact that the slump was world-wide made the search for remedies involving devaluation, protection, or other 'external' elements irrelevant. *The General Theory* would try to explain how the closing of the investment frontier, combined with a high propensity to save and hoard, could make 'involuntary' unemployment endemic in rich Western societies at large. The 'closed economy' model of *The General Theory* and 'fiscal' Keynesianism can both be seen as products of the world slump.

One early technical debate provoked by the *Treatise* was directly influenced by the state of the world. The Fundamental

Equations are price-level equations. Changes in output and employment are merely incidents—even if potentially protracted and painful ones—in the adjustment of the cost of producing output to the price at which it can be profitably sold. This analytic picture, taken over from Keynes's earlier *Tract on Monetary Reform*, seemed to fit the slump of 1920–1, when the fall in output and employment appeared to be an induced effect of falling prices. But it was at odds with the slump of 1930–1, whose earliest, most dramatic, and enduring effects in industrial countries were felt on output and employment, not prices.

Even before the *Treatise* was published Ralph Hawtrey tried to convince Keynes that the causation ran directly from changes in spending to changes in output. 'If anything occurs to affect the demand for goods,' Hawtrey wrote to Keynes in 1930, 'the first result is an increase or decrease in sales *at existing prices*. . . . There is always some interval of time before prices are adjusted, and the interval may be considerable.' On 28 November 1930 Keynes conceded that price and output changes might both play a part in adjusting an economy to a demand shock, and that 'it will probably be difficult in the future to prevent monetary theory and the theory of short-period supply from running together' (*CW* xiii. 146). In Keynes's mind the direct effects of a change in spending on quantities start to overshadow its effects on costs and prices.

The disequilibrium analysis of the *Treatise* posed a different technical problem. How did Keynes suppose the 'excess of saving over investment' to be eliminated if, for some reason or other, the rate of interest was not free to fall? In the banana parable he suggested that the growing impoverishment of the community would eventually restore equilibrium by reducing the amount it saved. But this shadowy sketch of an income-adjustment mechanism was hampered by the *Treatise* definitions which made the 'excess of saving over investment' identical to business losses. This meant that saving would always 'run ahead' of investment as the economy ran down. Dennis Robertson's criticism of September 1931 was decisive:

How many of those . . . who have taken up the cry that a slump is due to an excess of Saving over Investment realise that the savings which are so deplorably abundant during a slump consist largely of entrepreneurs' incomes which are not being spent, for the simple reason that they have not been earned?

If businessmen's losses were counted as deductions from the national income, the 'excess savings' disappeared.

In a note of 22 March 1932 Keynes 'bowed the knee' to Robertson (as well as to Hawtrey and Hayek) by proposing a definition of 'total income' to include 'abnormal' profits and losses, so that 'savings and investment are, necessarily and at all times, equal'. Further 'S[aving out of total income] always and necessarily accommodates itself to I[nvestment] . . . [It] is no longer the dog . . . but the tail' (*CW* xiii. 275–6). Thus by 2 May 1932 Keynes can say that 'the volume of employment depends on the amount of investment, and . . . anything which increases or decreases the latter will increase or decrease the former' (*CW* xxix. 40).

From the wreck of the *Treatise*'s special definitions the fundamental units of Keynes's *General Theory*—consumption, investment, income, output—are starting to emerge. These would lend themselves to statistical measurement, hence to national income accounting, hence to precise policy targets.

'Gentlemen, the change in title of these lectures'—from 'The Pure Theory of Money' to 'The Monetary Theory of Production'—'is significant'. With these words on 10 October 1932, recalled Lorie Tarshis, 'Keynes began the first of his eight lectures and in effect announced the beginning of the Keynesian Revolution'. The subject of Keynes's enquiry was: what determines the volume of output in a monetary economy? The question is *The General Theory*'s, but much of the answer is still wrapped up in the language and concepts of the *Treatise on Money*. Nevertheless, many of the familiar building-blocks of *The General Theory* are in view. They are even clearer in the repeat set of lectures he delivered in the autumn of 1933.

The volume of output is determined by aggregate 'disbursement', or expenditure. If spending on current output falls short of current income—if, in the language of the *Treatise*, the sales proceeds from current output fall short of the costs of producing it—income has to fall to the level of expenditure, via a reduction in output and employment. In explaining why the costs of production can be reduced only by cutting employment rather than by cutting money-wages, Keynes offers a first sketch of chapter 2 of *The General Theory*. The argument is sharpened in 1933 by the proposition that the real wage depends on the state of effective demand, not on the money-wage bargain ('there may be no escape for labour from high real wages in a slump') and by the corresponding concept of 'involuntary unemployment'. In the absence of the possibility of real wage adjustment, the classical theory's reliance on Say's Law—'supply creates its own demand'—for the continuous maintenance of full employment is also asserted (Rymes, 50–3, 85–93).

Expenditure is determined, in a *laissez-faire* economy, by the 'factors of market psychology': the state of time preference (later the consumption function) relating saving to income; expected 'quasi-rents' or the expected profitability of investment (later the marginal efficiency of capital); and the state of liquidity preference, which, together with the quantity of money, determines the rate of interest. These 'parameters' of a monetary economy, together with the aggregate supply schedule and 'earnings response' (of costs to prices) tell us 'what state of output would ensue . . . and how the parameters would have to be influenced to get the desired output'. This is put more sharply in 1933: 'the fundamental forces determining the volume of employment are the state of confidence, the propensity to consume, liquidity preference and the quantity of money. We may call this the General Law of Employment' (Rymes, 126). The role of expectations and uncertainty are now much more prominently highlighted.

That the amount of aggregate disbursement determined by the 'factors of psychology' may be insufficient to maintain a full employment volume of output is clear to Keynes but the reason is not precisely stated in 1932. Keynes has already decided that the rate of interest is determined by the demand for money, rather than by the demand for loans. So decided, the interest rate 'fixes the present value of the prospective quasi-rents' (Rymes, 66–7, 70). But there is no clear statement of his later doctrine that the validity of Say's Law depends on the efficacy of the classical interest-rate adjustment mechanism. Rather, he sticks to the *Treatise* doctrine that the monetary authority has complete control over the short and long rates, its duty being to 'maintain a rate of interest which leads to an optimum level of investment' (*CW* xiii. 405). The proposition that the 'speculative' motive for holding money may set a floor to the fall in the interest rate is not clearly stated till 1933 (Rymes, 123–7).

Keynes asks: what, in the absence of stabilization policy, is to stop income and output running down 'until production was at a total standstill?' The short answer is that, following a shock to investment, expenditure (consumption) falls less than income. It is this which makes possible 'stable equilibrium' (Rymes, 78; see also *CW* xiii. 401). This, too, is said more sharply in 1933: 'Saving must equal Investment, income will adjust itself to meet this condition' (Rymes, 122). From any low level, income cannot be increased unless the 'propensity to save' is reduced or the amount of investment is increased (Rymes, 112–13). The advantage of Keynes's less precise formulation of 1932 is that it retains the cyclical analysis of the *Treatise*. The slump in income will tend to bring about a fall in interest rates as the ratio of money stock to income rises, allowing increased investment. But unless the interest rate is deliberately lowered further by banking policy, the 'increase in investment . . . may not be as rapid as the increase in savings as output begins to rise again', leaving the recovery to peter out before full employment is reached (*CW* xxix. 57, 395–6). This gives a more complete idea of Keynes's notion of subnormal 'equilibrium' than he managed in *The General Theory*, whose static analysis was designed to fix the economy at a point in time in order to give policy a precise target to aim at.

One reason for the relative imprecision of the 1932 lectures is that Keynes made no use of Kahn's multiplier theory. Like

Kahn himself, he failed to see its logical connection with monetary equilibrium analysis.

Richard Kahn's article, 'The Relation of Home Investment to Unemployment', published in the *Economic Journal* in June 1931, was designed to combat the British Treasury's objections to loan-financed public works programmes as a remedy for unemployment. These were based on the meagreness of the employment afforded by a given expenditure of money, the budgetary burden entailed, and the 'crowding out' of private investment. In their pamphlet of 1929, *Can Lloyd George Do It?* Keynes and Henderson had asserted that a public works programme would provide, in addition to a calculable amount of primary employment, 'secondary' employment resulting from the newly employed spending their wages, but that these secondary effects were incalculable. The question Kahn asked was: what was to stop an extra £1 of income in one person's hands from raising the community's income to infinity? The intuitive answer is that some fraction of the extra income will be 'saved' each time it is spent until the stimulus exhausts itself. Provided this fraction is known, the total of increased income or secondary employment can be summed to a finite number, which can be expressed as a ratio or multiple either of the initial investment or of primary employment. Moreover, the additional investment would, by raising aggregate incomes, create an equivalent amount of saving, thus exemplifying Keynes's assertion that 'investment always drags saving along with it at an equal pace', and countering the Treasury argument that loan-financed public investment would take savings from existing uses. This in essence is the multiplier theory.

It was not how Kahn set it out. He achieved his 'leakages' from the enlarged expenditure stream by deducting unemployment benefit (what the unemployed were already spending) and extra spending on imports (which did not directly increase domestic employment); and he failed to realize that his formula had established the necessary equality between saving and investment. (In an 'open' economy the necessary equality is not between saving and investment but between saving and imports and investment and exports.) The *personal* saving leak-age first entered the multiplier literature with an article by the Danish statistician Jens Warming in the *Economic Journal* of June 1932. Warming 'combined an exclusively income-related personal saving function with Kahn's own multiplier algebra to render neatly the income adjustment mechanism by which saving is equilibrated with an initiating change in investment'. Keynes almost certainly saw Warming's article when it was first submitted to the *Economic Journal*. So the theoretical influence may have run more directly from Warming to Keynes than from Kahn to Keynes at this point. Kahn, influenced in turn by Warming, presented a multiplier derived from the mar-ginal propensities to save and import in a paper in Cincinatti, USA, in December 1932. Keynes's *The Means to Prosperity*, published three months later, presented this revised version of Kahn's theory in support of his argument for a loan-financed public works programme (*CW* ix. 347).

The multiplier is the most notorious piece of Keynesian magic. It abstracted from the confidence ('crowding out') issue and from the budget-funding problem. The precision of the employment, as opposed to the income, multiplier was always something of a confidence trick, depending on an arbitrary assumption as to how the increased spending would be split between higher production and higher prices. This did not mat-ter much in the early 1930s when prices were falling, but it was to have baleful effects after the war. Many Keynesians would assert baldly that 'quantities adjust, not prices'. Keynes's own famous mistrust of the notion of a 'calculable future' fell victim in this case to his passionate urge to give governments tools of action.

Much ink has been spilt over the question of when exactly Keynes came to understand his new theory of effective demand. That it was some time between 1932 and 1933 is indisputable. Beyond that it depends on the test of understanding being used. Perhaps Keynes himself should have the last word, though this is too much to be hoped for. Original thinking, he remarked in his lecture of 6 November 1933, starts as a 'grey, fuzzy, woolly monster' in one's head. 'The precise use of language comes at a late stage in the development of one's thoughts. You can think accurately and effectively long before you can, so to speak, photograph your thought' (Rymes, 102). Keynes knew more than he could say in the autumn of 1932, but he was more confident about what he knew a year later, and therefore could say it better.

II

The General Theory of Employment, Interest, and Money, published on 4 February 1936, is a work of enduring fascination. It is simple and subtle, obscure and profound. It offered a systematic way of thinking not just about behaviour of contemporary economies, but about the pitfalls in the quest for greater wealth at all times. It combined a vision of how economies behave with a rigorous demonstration of the possibility of underemployment equilibrium. Although young economists of speculative bent were drawn to it as a storehouse of suggestive ideas, it was its practical usefulness which chiefly attracted them in a world poised between a decaying democracy and rampaging totalitarianism.

It is by no means as badly organized as it is often held to be. The reader who starts with chapter 3 and then reads chapters 8–13, and chapter 18 can get an accurate idea of the core of Keynes's theory. The main problems arise when Keynes tries to relate his own theory to what he calls 'classical theory', by way of comment, attempted reconciliation, or, more usually, destructive criticism. The difficulties are particularly acute in chapter 2, 'Postulates of Classical Economics', chapters 14 and 15, which deal with the classical theory of the rate of interest and the more complete statement of his own theory of interest, and in Book V on 'Money-Wages and Prices'. Chapter 16, 'Sundry Observations on the Nature of Capital', and chapter 17, 'The Essential Properties of Interest and Money', as well as Book VI (chapters 22–4), are best read as general thoughts, speculative and visionary, arising from the core theory. Book II, 'Definitions and Ideas' (chapters 4–7), can be, and usually is, skipped.

In *The General Theory* Keynes used a Marshallian 'short-period' analysis. The capital stock is fixed, so that the only way the economy can adjust to a demand shock is by a more or less intensive use of existing plant. This seemed a reasonable analytic device in the circumstances of the Great Depression. But it excluded changes in the 'structure of production' which the Austrian and Swedish economists regarded as central to the adjustment process, whether or not it was accompanied by unemployment.

Another characteristic of Keynes's analytical method should be noted. He abjures Walrasian-type general equilibrium reasoning in favour of a logical chain of causation. Typical from *The General Theory* is the following sequence: given the propensity to consume, the amount of employment is determined by the amount of investment; given the expected profitability of investment, the amount of investment is determined by the rate of interest; given the quantity of money, the rate of interest is determined by liquidity preference. This causal chain, as we shall see, is used to demonstrate that if the income (sales proceeds) which entrepreneurs expect from employing *n* people is expected to fall below the costs of employing that number, then output and employment will fall till the costs of employment equal expected sales proceeds.

Keynes rearranges the 'classical' view that 'involuntary' unemployment is impossible into the same kind of chain logic in order to emphasize its dependence on the classical theory of the rate of interest. Given the real wage, the level of employment depends on Say's Law that 'supply creates its own demand'; given the expected profitability of investment, Say's Law depends on the rate of interest being wholly determined in the market for loans. If this is untrue, the classical theory falls to the ground.

Three points need to be made about Keynes's definitions (Book II) before we get into the main argument. First, saving and investment are equal by definition, according to the equations: Income = Consumption + Investment; Saving = Income − Consumption; therefore Saving = Investment. This raises the question: what has to adjust in the economy to validate the last equation? Secondly, Keynes proposed to deflate changes in nominal income by wage rates—money payments per hour worked—in order to measure the employment impact of a change in demand. Given the average wage rate, employment will change by the same amount as nominal income. This seemed a reasonable short-period simplification, but it begged the question how adjustment is shared between employment and wages in actual situations. Finally, by making short-period employment depend mainly on expectations of long-period profit, Keynes introduced the 'method of expectations' into the determination of short-period equilibrium.

The General Theory makes explicit an idea that is only implicit in Keynes's previous two books: that money is not just a medium of exchange but a store of wealth. The necessary condition for this function of money is uncertainty: holding it reduces exposure to risk and thus alleviates anxiety. It is rather unfortunate that it was not till p. 168 that Keynes introduced the 'demand for money' into his 'causal nexus', since all his conclusions, indeed the *raison d'être* of *The General Theory*, flow from his perception that, when uncertainty becomes too great, liquidity provides a retreat from activity. The entrepreneur always faces a choice between using money in this way or in some other way *or not using it at all*. People's freedom not to spend in a monetary economy is thus the logical crux of Keynes's denial that 'supply creates its own demand'. Instead 'expenditure creates its own income' (*CW* xxix. 82; Rymes, 92). These thoughts underlie his 'vision'.

Books III and IV, dealing with consumption demand, investment demand, and the rate of interest, are the analytical kernel of Keynes's book, because these variables are what determine the volume of output and the level of employment. In the short run, the 'propensity to consume' (and therefore to save) is a 'fairly stable' proportion of current income (*CW* vii. 27). The shape of the function (what fraction of increasing or decreasing income is saved) enables one to sum (via the multiplier) to a finite number the amount of income adjustment needed to equilibrate saving and investment plans. The consumption function enables Keynes to explain why, following a demand shock, income and output do not run down forever (as in banana-land) but issue in a position of 'underemployment equilibrium', and tells governments how much extra they need to spend to eliminate the 'output gap'. Together with the investment multiplier it is the most useful policy tool bequeathed by *The General Theory*.

It is important to notice that, while *realized* saving and investment are equal by definition, *planned* saving and investment need not be. When they are not, some plans at least will be either exceeded or disappointed. An excess of planned saving over planned investment sets up contractionary forces; an excess of planned investment over planned saving sets up expansionary ones.

In all this, Keynes stands the classical psychology on its head. The classical economists praised 'parsimony' or 'thrift' as increasing the supply of capital. Keynes's 'paradox of thrift' was that an increase in intended saving was liable to lead to a reduction in actual saving, via a fall in income, unless the expected profitability of investment was going up independently. But an increased propensity to save was liable to have exactly the opposite effect on investment by reducing entrepreneurs' expectation of future consumption on which the profitability of investment depends (*CW* vii. 210). Moreover, in so far as the marginal propensity to save was likely to rise with income, the problem of securing an adequate amount of investment tended to worsen over time. To maintain full employment a rich society will need to invest an increasing proportion of its income even as the expected profitability of investment declines, as the gap between income and consumption widens.

Given the 'propensity to consume', the amount of employment depends on the rate of investment, or additions to capital stock. There is an 'inducement to invest' when the expected return on the investment is higher than the cost of borrowing money: when what Keynes calls the 'marginal efficiency of capital' is positive. In chapter 12, 'The State of Long-Term Expectations', the instability of investment demand emerges as the crucial cause of economic fluctuations. The reason is the volatility attaching to expectations of the future yield of investment.

Keynes's starting-point is the 'extreme precariousness of the basis of knowledge on which our estimates of prospective yield have to be made' (*CW* vii. 149). The stock exchange reduces the riskiness of investments by making them 'liquid' for individuals, but this makes investment as a whole much more volatile, since investors can buy and sell at a moment's notice. Share prices depend not on real investment prospects, which are largely unknowable, but on prevailing sentiment, which can fluctuate violently with the day's news. It is the flimsiness of knowledge supporting conventional share valuations which makes the investment function peculiarly dependent on 'animal spirits', defined as 'a spontaneous urge to action rather than inaction' (*CW* vii. 150, 161–3).

Many Keynesians have seen chapter 12 as containing the 'vision' of *The General Theory*, and indeed of the Keynesian revolution, both in its attack on the ethics of capitalism— 'when the capital development of a country becomes a by-product of the activities of a casino, the job is likely to be ill-done'—and in its rejection of calculability in human affairs. The discussion leads naturally to the conclusion that the state should take 'an ever greater responsibility for directly organizing investment . . . on long views' (*CW* vii. 163–4). It also establishes the rationality of liquidity preference—a preference for holding cash rather than investing it—which plays a central part in Keynes's theory of the rate of interest.

Given the state of expectations, the amount of investment is determined by the rate of interest. Keynes's belief is that the rate of interest is determined in the market for money. He takes interest to be the price for giving up liquidity—instant command over sums of money. It is, he was to say in 1937, 'the measure of the degree of our disquietude' (*CW* xiv. 116). The greater people's preference for holding their savings in money, the greater the rate of interest people will demand for parting with money. The chain of logic of *The General Theory* is thus completed by showing that the rate of interest can remain above the 'rate of return to capital' necessary to secure full employment.

The 'necessary condition', indeed the 'sole intelligible explanation' of the existence of liquidity preference is 'the existence of *uncertainty* as to the future of the rate of interest' (*CW* vii. 168, 201). Keynes reasons that, if this were not so, investors who wanted to get out of equities would buy government debt. This would drive up the price of bonds and lower their yield, making it more profitable for businessmen to borrow for investment. But if speculators think the interest rate is 'too low'—has fallen below its 'conventional' or expected level—they will sell bonds for cash, thus aborting, or reversing, the fall in the rate. Keynes does not enquire into what causes the expected rate of interest to be what it is—a point which Dennis Robertson was to pick up.

The monetary authority can step in by buying bonds itself (open-market operations). But this can generate offsetting bond sales by the private sector if monetary policy is regarded as 'unsound'. One can then get a 'liquidity trap', a situation when monetary policy cannot push the interest rate beneath a floor set by the fear of inflation or default. The lower the rate of interest the smaller the 'earnings from illiquidity' available to insure against risk of loss on capital account. This, says Keynes, is the main obstacle to the fall of the interest rate to a very low figure. A long-term interest rate of 2 per cent 'leaves more to fear than to hope, and offers, at the same time, a running yield which is only sufficient to offset a very small measure of fear'. Liquidity preference may then become 'virtually absolute' in that almost everyone prefers holding cash to holding a debt. However, the flight into cash might occur at a higher rate of interest, as in the United States in 1932. In this event the monetary authority will have lost effective control over the long rate. However, a monetary policy in which the public has confidence may succeed where one judged 'experimental in character or easily liable to change' will fail (*CW* vii. 202, 203, 207–8).

Keynes's discussion of the interest-rate problem goes to the heart of his theory. His assertion that liquidity preference may keep the interest rate too high for a full-employment level of investment clinches, in his view, his theoretical assault on the doctrine that 'supply creates its own demand'. The rejection of the idea that interest is a reward for saving undermines the classical idea that thriftiness is a virtue in a depression, since it does not lower the interest rate and thus encourage investment. The possible inefficacy of monetary policy to assure the same result reinforces the case for fiscal policy in combating depression.

This concludes the positive part of Keynes's 'general theory'. The basic ideas are 'extremely simple', as he said in his preface. The real difficulties arise in understanding not so much his own theory but its relationship to what he called 'classical' theory. To what extent was it inconsistent with received doctrine? And if inconsistent, to what extent was it a 'truer', or as Keynes put it, a more 'general' theory? To neither of these questions is a conclusive answer possible. Keynes set up his own theory against his own version of 'classical' theory, which many of his opponents denied holding. Also it is not very clear what he meant by 'general'. In the book's first chapter he contrasted it with the 'special case assumed by the classical theory'; elsewhere he contrasted it with 'partial', as when he attacks the classical theory for ignoring the interdependencies between the labour and goods markets.

Keynes opened his account by attacking the 'classical' view that employment is determined in the labour market. Basing himself on Pigou's *Theory of Unemployment* (1933), he argued in chapter 2 that the classical theorists believed that, with perfect money-wage flexibility, there was no obstacle to full employment, whatever the state of nominal demand.

In the 'classical' account, as Keynes depicted it, the amount of employment depends on two 'real' wage 'postulates': that, in equilibrium, the wage equals the marginal product of labour, and that it is equal to the marginal disutility of labour. The first gives a downward-sloping demand curve for labour, which reflects the decreasing marginal efficiency of work; the second gives an upward-sloping supply curve, reflecting the increasing marginal disutility or 'pain' of work. With perfectly flexible wages, the amount of employment is determined at the point where the real disutility suffered (and wage paid) for the last hour worked just equals the value of what it is worth in revenue to the employer, i.e. there is no obstacle to continuous full employment. In such a world, there can be no involuntary unemployment, only voluntarily chosen leisure together with some 'frictional' unemployment. The leisure was voluntary because workers could always escape from it by revising their psychic computations of pain and pleasure, and accepting whatever was available to them for additional work. (It was never obvious how notions of diminishing efficiency and pleasure attached to 'hours' of work could be translated into quantities of employment in a weekly waged system. The usual solution was to assume that increasing employment absorbed workers of decreasing quality and increasing leisure-preference.)

Keynes accepted the first, but rejected the second classical postulate. He thought that circumstances could arise in which more workers were willing to work at whatever *money*-wage was 'going' than the amount of jobs being offered. Labour as a whole would be off its supply curve: hence 'involuntary unemployment'. The reason was that wage bargains were made in money. If, following a negative shock to demand, wages and prices immediately fell together, the real wage would remain the same. Nothing would have happened to improve business prospects, so unemployment would still develop. Pigou argued that, with perfect wage flexibility, wages would fall more than employers' incomes (profits)—costs more than prices—reducing the real wage and allowing more employment. Keynes turned this argument neatly round by putting 'expected' in front of 'incomes'. The effect of a fall in money-wages on employment would depend on what it did for profit expectations. As he had put it neatly in 1933: 'Income is the expectation that induces [entrepreneurs] to do what [they] are doing.'

Here the argument in chapter 2 was broken off to be resumed in Book V, after Keynes had explained his own theory. In chapter 19, 'Changes in Money-Wages', Keynes considers the effect of money-wage reductions on the determinants of aggregate demand: investment, saving, and liquidity preference. His main conclusion is that an all-round reduction in money-wages *can* indirectly improve employment in a closed system, on two conditions: (a) if falling wages improve business confidence, and (b) by leading to a reduction in the price level and hence in the demand for transaction balances relative to the stock of money, allowing a fall in the interest rate. But a surer policy for achieving (b) would be to increase the nominal stock of money: 'only . . . a foolish person . . . would prefer a flexible wage policy to a flexible money policy' (*CW* vii. 268). As he had put it in chapter 2: involuntary unemployment exists when a rise in prices relative to wage rates would increase the quantity of employment (*CW* vii. 15).

In his review of *The General Theory*, David Champernowne attached a condition to Keynes's employment-raising policy: it would work only if employed workers refrained from demanding a higher money-wage in response to a rise in prices. He predicted that their acceptance of a real wage reduction would be undermined by inflation, as unfortunately turned out in the end to be the case. This has led to the frequent charge that Keynes's methods of increasing employment depend on 'money illusion'—lowering the value of money and hoping that workers would not notice that their real wage had gone down. The charge is unfair. Keynes was merely echoing the prevalent belief that a recovery from depression required the *recovery* of prices to their pre-depression or 'normal' level. He assumed, that is, a continuation of a stationary cost of living, with wage-earners not adjusting their contracts to hold on to temporary windfalls. He was not suggesting pumping more money into an economy already subject to inflationary pressure.

In chapter 21, 'The Theory of Prices', Keynes acknowledges that rising employment will be accompanied by moderately rising prices, apart from any change in average wage rates, because labour is not homogeneous, because there are likely to be supply 'bottlenecks', and because the cost of capital might rise faster than the cost of labour. Indeed, such a rise in the price level relative to wage rates was accepted by Keynes as a necessary condition of increased employment, as we have seen. But, in addition, recovery is likely to put upward pressure on money-wages. Thus there are likely to be positions of 'semi-inflation' short of full employment. At full employment, the quantity theory of money comes into its own, any further increase in money demand going wholly into raising prices. Chapter 21 makes it clear that the conventional summary of *The General Theory*'s message, 'quantities adjust, not prices', is seriously incomplete. Indeed chapter 21 leaves indeterminate how the increase (or for that matter decrease) in money demand is divided between prices, wages, and output, though Keynes thinks it reasonable to assume that 'a moderate [increase] in effective demand, coming on a situation where there is wide-spread unemployment, may spend itself very little in raising prices and mainly in increasing employment' (*CW* vii. 300). In 1939 he was half-persuaded by J. G. Dunlop and L. Tarshis that increasing returns and imperfect competition would lower average unit costs as employment increased, obviating the need for prices to rise and real wages to fall (*CW* vii. 394–412); and many post-war Keynesians thought that this factor would be sufficient to rob full-employment policies of any inflationary danger. That was the real illusion.

The upshot of Keynes's discussion of the wages problem was to knock on the head the 'classical' contention, that, with money-wage rates perfectly flexible, there is no obstacle to full employment at any level of money income. Rather Keynes showed that only one level of money income (or aggregate demand) will bring about a real wage consistent with full employment, i.e. that over a wide range of actual circumstances the real wage was determined not in the labour market but by the whole range of factors influencing the level of demand for goods in the economy.

How important is Keynes's rate-of-interest theory in his denial of Say's Law? The consumption function/multiplier mechanism seems sufficient to explain the process of income adjustment. Consumption is strictly a function of income; the multiplier tells you how much income will have to change to equilibrate saving and investment plans. If the further assumption is made that investment is not sensitive to small interest changes, then the interest rate is not actually needed to explain anything: as Keynes said, it was left 'hanging in the air'. But, as a concession to Roy Harrod, Keynes had agreed to include a diagram (*CW* vii. 180—the only diagram in *The General Theory*), which showed saving as a function of interest as well as income. Thus the rate of interest was needed to establish a 'determinate equilibrium' (*CW* vii. 181). Consumption-function Keynesians have always regretted this concession to Harrod, because it seems to make the theoretical relevance of *The General Theory* depend on the existence of liquidity preference. If one could then show that Keynes had exaggerated the pervasiveness of liquidity preference, or that it did not provide a complete theory of interest, the way was open to make some damaging attacks on Keynes's theoretical structure.

Keynes's erstwhile collaborator, Dennis Robertson, concentrated on the second of these points. He pointed out that to say that the rate of interest is a function of the 'speculative' demand for money does not provide a complete theory of interest, because a fall in the transactions demand for money relative to the money stock will reduce the rate of interest and promote investment (something Keynes had admitted, *CW* vii. 263). Robertson claimed that this re-established the classical loanable-funds theory of the rate of interest, related to the underlying forces of 'productivity and thrift'. It explained the observed fact that interest rates fell in a slump and rose in a boom. A testy series of articles and rejoinders in the *Economic Journal* followed, which ended with Keynes proposing to print a note which contained the words, 'I hear with surprise [from

Robertson] that our forebears believed that ... an increase in the desire to save would lead to a recession in employment and income and would only result in a fall in the rate of interest in so far as this was the case.' He wrote to Robertson on 25 July 1938: 'Our forebears believed that ... the rate of interest depends on the supply of saving. My theory is that it depends on the supply of inactive money. There is no possible reconciliation between these views' (*CW* xxix. 179, 180).

Keynes's other eminent Cambridge colleague and principal stalking-horse of *The General Theory*, Arthur Pigou, attacked Keynes from a different standpoint. Pigou claimed, in the *Economic Journal* of December 1943, that a deficiency in aggregate demand would lead to lower prices, thus increasing the real value of cash balances and hence net wealth in so far as such balances were unmatched by debts. This 'Pigou effect' increases consumption, raising aggregate demand back eventually to its long-run full-employment level.

Robertson and Pigou were fighting a rearguard action to show not that the classical scheme of thought denied the possibility of 'involuntary unemployment', but that such unemployment could not be part of an equilibrium state. The decline in the economy set in motion forces of recovery, irrespective of the policy of the monetary authority. However, though the existence of these forces was later admitted, and Keynes's assault on the classical theory judged to be logically flawed, orthodox theory was not thereby rehabilitated. Keynes's critics were forced to concede that recovery forces came into play uncertainly and feebly after a long period of subnormal activity; and they were thus of little interest to economists or governments who believed that Keynes had given them the tools to prevent large-scale fluctuations in demand from occurring in the first place, or reversing them quickly when they did occur.

Much of the rest of *The General Theory* is intended to be suggestive rather than conclusive. It contains a theory of economic history, in which the weakness of the 'inducement to invest', owing to uncertainty, is presented as a permanent problem, and in which the nineteenth century is seen as a 'special case' in which the psychological propensities are in such a relation as to establish 'a reasonably satisfactory average level of employment' (*CW* vii. 307). There are the 'Notes on Mercantilism' in chapter 23 in which Keynes tries to establish a historical lineage for his concern with effective demand, in contrast to mainstream economic thinking based on Ricardo, which supposes that economics is the study of how given resources are allocated among different uses. There are what Pigou called his 'Day of Judgment' reflections on the fate of mature capitalist economies if the state is not brought in to supplement failing private investment demand. One version of the 'secular stagnation' thesis, in chapter 17, 'The Essential Properties of Interest and Money', has particularly fascinated some economists. In this superb crystallization of his deflationary vision Keynes suggests that the desire to accumulate money can knock out all other forms of production, so that wealthy societies, like King Midas, drown in a sea of gold. After the war, governments succeeded in making money 'go bad', with consequences that Keynes—in another frame of mind—predicted in 1933: 'an entrepreneurial system which would be as prone to excessive demand and over-employment, as our actual system is to deficient demand and under-employment' (*CW* xxix. 87).

Keynes's last chapter, 'Concluding Notes on Social Philosophy', may be seen as an updating of his Middle Way ideas of the 1920s, suggested by his new theory. Excessive thriftiness could be tackled by redistributing spending power to those with a high propensity to consume (the workers) and by reducing the rewards of thriftiness by fixing a low interest rate. This would remove the scope for savers to live off the scarcity value of capital: 'the euthanasia of the rentier' would be the consequence. Because banking policy was unlikely to be able to maintain an 'optimum rate of interest', Keynes advocated 'a somewhat comprehensive socialisation of investment', an ambiguous phrase which has to be interpreted in the light of his endorsement ten years previously of the growth of the public utility sector of the economy (see above, pp. 273–4). With demand deficiency removed, Fascism and Communism would lose their appeal, and the full benefits and promise of the 'Manchester system' realized: efficiency and freedom and variety of life at home, mutual harmony and peace abroad. In a much-quoted peroration Keynes anticipated his intellectual triumph by writing that 'the power of vested interests is vastly exaggerated compared with the gradual encroachment of ideas.'

III

Keynes did not have to wait long. The intellectual conversion of all the younger British and American economists started soon after *The General Theory* was published; Keynesian fiscal policy began to be used in 1940 in the United States and in 1941 in Britain.

What was accepted was by no means all Keynes had bequeathed. It was the English economist John Hicks, a newcomer to the Keynesian revolution, who in 1937 produced the 'portable' Keynesian model, which has been studied by economics students ever since. In essence, Hicks transforms Keynes's chain logic into a set of simultaneous equations which he depicts diagrammatically by means of his famous IS/ LM curves. This 'generalized' system has room for Keynes's 'special theory'—in which saving is determined by income, investment is relatively interest-inelastic, and liquidity preference rules interest rates—but also for at least some versions of the 'Treasury View' which Keynes wrote *The General Theory* to refute. It all depends on the slopes of the curves. Keynes's theory and the classical theory emerge as 'special cases' of the true 'general theory', with Keynes's special case assumed to be the most useful for policy. Hicks's was an astonishing performance.

Keynes, who, above all, sought to influence policy, did not resist this reconciling way of selling his ideas if it made them more accessible and acceptable to the younger economists. But he took advantage of the controversy which followed *The*

General Theory's publication to restate his theory in 1937 in a way which brought out better than his book had its epistemic assumptions. For the 'fundamentalist' Keynesians this article of 1937 in the *Quarterly Journal of Economics* is the canonical statement of the Master's position.

Keynes's restatement of the 'essence' of *The General Theory* is concerned particularly with the effects of uncertainty on investment and the rate of interest: it draws out from the book, that is, the argument of chapter 12, 'The State of Long-Term Expectations', which emphasizes the volatility of investment demand, and those of chapters 13 and 17, which explain why liquidity, or money, carries a premium. It is, above all, the desire for liquidity which makes a decentralized entrepreneurial economy unstable and ensures that its oscillations normally occur round a subnormal level of activity. Why, Keynes asks, should anyone outside a lunatic asylum wish to use money as a store of wealth? The only intelligible answer is the existence of radical uncertainty—a possibility assumed away by the classical assumption of a 'definite and calculable future'. In the article of 1937 there is no consumption function, no investment multiplier, only vague and uncertain knowledge, fluctuating states of confidence, and courage, fears, and hopes, coped with, as best they can be, by strategies and conventions, themselves liable to be swept away by changes in the 'news'. Uncertainty, Keynes suggests, is the human condition. That is why *The General Theory* retains, in Shackle's words, the 'quality of imperishable relevance to the . . . insoluble problems of time-bound humanity'.

In this final distillation of his thought, money, or what Keynes calls liquidity, emerges, above all, as a strategy for calming the nerves. Technically, he had come a long way since his early days as monetary reformer, but his vision had not changed much. His whole work, like that of his entire generation of economists, revolved round the unruliness of money, its awesome power to disturb the real economy. They all wanted to make the monetary economy behave like a 'real exchange' economy—one in which there was no unemployment. The deepest question posed by Keynes's work is as follows. Is it money which causes the economy to misbehave? Or is it uncertainty which causes money to misbehave? Between these two views the theory of monetary policy is still poised.

5   *Economic statesmanship*

I

Keynes was as creative in administration as he was in theory. For every economic problem which interested him he had ready a 'Keynes Plan', drafted at lightning speed. The common feature of these plans—which go back to his proposal for an Indian Central Bank in 1913, praised by Marshall as a 'prodigy of constructive work'—is that while always ahead of the intellectual orthodoxy of the moment they could be readily fitted to existing administrative arrangements. Keynes could thus present them as evolutionary developments of existing practice. The partial exception is his endorsement of a centrally directed public works programme in 1929, which would have required a revolution in government. But this was a Lloyd George, not a Keynes, plan; Keynes's own preference was to channel increased investment through the public utility corporations. He also favoured indirect (financial) to direct (physical) control over the economy, in order to retain the advantages of decentralized decision-making. This brought him into conflict with socialist methods, if not with some aspects of the socialist ideal.

The outbreak of war with Germany on 3 September 1939 posed the kind of economic challenge he could not shirk; and he responded with two articles, 'Paying for the War', published in *The Times*, on 14 and 15 November, and recast and expanded into a booklet, *How to Pay for the War*, which appeared in February 1940, five months before his return to the Treasury. *How to Pay for the War* has been hailed as the first major application to policy of *The General Theory* model of the economy, and so it was. But it also reflected Keynes's experience as a Treasury official in the First World War.

With full employment assured through the big increase in state orders, the problem Keynes faced in 1939 was to transfer resources to the war effort without undue inflation, disincentive tax levels, or the bureaucratic controls associated with comprehensive physical planning. In the First World War, increased government purchases had caused prices to rise; rising prices had reduced the real incomes of the working class; the 'windfall' profits of entrepreneurs were commandeered by the government in the form of taxes and loans. The results were industrial unrest in the later stages of the war; a high cost of government borrowing, which increased the post-war debt burden; and the ownership by the wealthy of the national debt.

The new Keynes Plan was designed to overcome these problems. Its centre-piece was a scheme for 'deferred earnings'. Excess private purchasing power would be mopped up by a heavily progressive surcharge on all incomes above an exempted minimum, made up of direct taxes and compulsory saving. The latter, credited to individual accounts in the Post Office Saving Bank, would be released after the war in instalments to counteract the expected post-war slump. As Professor Moggridge notes, 'the scheme had the advantage that it could operate through the existing arrangements for national insurance contributions'. Following criticisms of the original plan, Keynes proposed to 'provide for this deferred consumption without increasing the National Debt by a general capital levy after the war'; and to protect the poorest through family allowances—5s. or 25p a week per child—and an 'iron ration' of necessaries to be sold at low fixed prices (*CW* ix. 379–80). In estimating the size of the 'inflationary gap'—the amount by which civilian consumption would need to be reduced to enable output to be transferred to the war effort without prices rising—Keynes, in the absence of official national income statistics, offered estimates, based on the work of Colin Clark, of national output and taxable income, the division of total spending between the government and private sector, and income distribution, all in 1939 prices. It then became relatively easy to calculate how much 'private outlay' had to be reduced to accommodate any desired increase in 'government outlay' at these prices, as well as the sacrifice required from each section of the community.

Keynes's plan had no influence on the budget of July 1940; he was better placed to continue his campaign of persuasion within the Treasury. Kingsley Wood's budget of April 1941 has been hailed as the first 'Keynesian' budget, not because it adopted the specific measures Keynes had proposed (though deferred pay survived in the form of a modest scheme for postwar tax credits), but because it was based, for the first time, on the national accounting framework developed, from Keynes's suggestions, by James Meade and others. Whether it marked general acceptance of the Keynesian Revolution is far more doubtful. The endorsement of the Keynes Plan by prominent anti-Keynesians like Hayek gives the clue to its popularity with economists and Treasury officials: it suggested a method of minimizing wartime inflation. As Jim Tomlinson has remarked: 'Keynesian arithmetic provided a theoretical rationale and quantification for policies which ran with rather than against the grain of the traditional Treasury stance on wartime finance.'

The debate sparked off by *How to Pay for the War* gave Keynes a chance to link his new economics to the political ideas of the Middle Way, ideas which he had espoused since the 1920s. 'Nature's way' (inflation) of first redistributing income from workers to entrepreneurs, and then taxing it, would no longer work, he said, because, in the new conditions of trade-union strength, rising prices would be matched by equivalent wage demands, which would either have to be conceded, defeating the object of reducing civilian consumption, or prohibited, bringing about industrial disruption. Stable prices were the quid pro quo for trade-union collaboration—a thought which goes back to his early days as a monetary reformer. The object of his plan was '*social*: to prevent the social evils of inflation now and later; to do this in a way which satisfies the popular sense of social justice, whilst maintaining adequate incentives to work and economy' (*CW* xxii. 218). The significance of Keynes's proposals was thus twofold: they sought to circumvent the problem of 'cost push' inflation at full employment; and they claimed for the budget a role in social policy which went beyond macroeconomic stabilization.

In another respect, though, they went against the grain of left-wing thinking. For most socialists the war offered an opportunity for physical, rather than financial, planning. State allocation of manpower and supplies in accordance with 'national needs' would replace the 'chaos' of the market. Also, coupon rationing of foodstuffs and clothing had a much more straightforward egalitarian appeal than 'forced saving'. The difference in principle was that Keynes's plan left the disposition of post-tax incomes to individual choice, while rationing required that individuals spent their money on things, and in the amounts, laid down by the state. 'I am seizing an opportunity', Keynes wrote to *The Times* on 18 April 1940 'to introduce a principle of policy which may come to be thought of as marking the line of division between the totalitarian and the free economy' (*CW* xxii. 123). Similarly, the release of deferred pay, 'by allowing individuals to choose for themselves what they want, will save us from having to devise large-scale government plans of expenditure [after the war] which may not correspond so closely to personal need' (*CW* xxii. 122–3). Keynes was once more staking a middle way between the '*invalidism* of the Left which has eaten up the wisdom and inner strength of many good causes' and the 'sclerotic' reaction of the Right to any tampering with the existing system (*CW* xxii. 155). In practice Keynes lost the argument to the central planners, and regulation of aggregate spending took second place to manpower planning, physical allocation of inputs, and rationing of consumer goods.

Keynes was far less involved with the famous 'Keynesian' White Paper on Employment Policy, published on 26 May 1944 (Cmd. 6527). Its first sentence—which Keynes thought 'is more valuable than the rest'—committed the government to the 'maintenance of a high and stable level of employment after the war'. But the text of the White Paper was a compromise between the Keynesians of the Economic Section of the Cabinet and the traditional sceptics of the Treasury, who felt that concessions had to be made to political pressures. Much of its analysis of the prospective unemployment problem was un-Keynesian, reflecting the view of Hubert Henderson that the problems of the British economy were on the supply rather than the demand side. Little thought was given about how to satisfy two of the conditions laid down in the White Paper for sustainable 'high employment': moderation in wage policy (the responsibility of employers and organized labour) and adequate labour mobility.

II

The international economy was the subject of the next Keynes Plan. The inherited gold standard/free-trade system had seemingly been damaged beyond repair by the First World War, the Great Depression, and the nationalist economics of the interwar years. The question was: could British full employment best be secured by a continuation of the Imperial Preference/ Sterling Area arrangements built up in the 1930s, or did the war offer the chance of a 'single act of creation', impossible in peacetime, to restore a liberal system free of the deflationary bias which had wrecked the old one? This question engaged most of Keynes's attention and dwindling energy between 1941 and 1944. Its answer lay in the United States, because American policy would determine the shape of the post-war order.

Keynes's involvement with the United States provides an important context for understanding his economics. Those who take their Keynes solely from the 'closed economy' model of *The General Theory* forget that the problem which exercised him for most of his professional life arose from the effects of the unbalanced creditor position of the United States on the British economy. Most of his economic plans were concerned with ways of overcoming or offsetting this imbalance. They culminate in the establishment of the Bretton Woods system in 1944, and the negotiation of the American loan in 1945, as a result of which Britain tacitly accepted a junior role in an American-managed international economic order. But there was nothing inevitable about this culmination, and for much of his life Keynes actively explored alternatives.

In the 1920s, as we have seen, Keynes wanted to decouple the British (and, more generally, the European) financial system from that of the United States. But even in his *Tract* period he was not a currency floater. He wanted a 'managed' exchange-rate system—something consistent with stability of exchange rates for long periods. More often he hankered for a fixed exchange-rate system, with discretion and devices to give it flexibility. In both the early 1920s and the 1930s, when currencies floated against each other, he had proposed returning to a modified gold standard based at various times on wide bands, crawling pegs, automatic creditor adjustment, or supplementary reserve assets. He was convinced that any fixed exchange-rate system would break down if it was used as an instrument of deflation. Such a system worked best when supported by policies to maintain full employment over time. Stable exchange rates would, in turn, help keep the world growing in step and act as anti-inflationary discipline.

As Kingsley Martin records, Keynes's immediate response to the disintegration of the gold standard in 1931 was characteristic: 'At one stroke Britain has resumed the financial hegemony of the world,' he announced, 'chuckling like a boy who has just exploded a firework under some one he doesn't like.' The spontaneous emergence of a sterling bloc suggested to him a 'reputable sterling system for the Empire ... managed by the Bank of England and pivoted on London' (*CW* xxi. 17). He applauded the Bank of England's nationalistic policy of sterilizing gold inflows to keep the pound undervalued against the dollar and franc, which remained on the gold standard—just as he had praised the same policy pursued by the Federal Reserve Board in the 1920s.

This euphoria did not last. Roosevelt's devaluation of the dollar in terms of gold on 19 April 1933 eliminated Britain's short-lived competitive advantage. Keynes now suggested that Britain and the United States might link their currencies together in a modified gold standard so long as they pursued reflationary policies in tandem. Nevertheless, on 4 July 1933 he proclaimed, 'President Roosevelt is Magnificently Right,' when Roosevelt scuppered the London World Economic Conference by denouncing all plans to stabilize currencies as 'the fetishes of so-called international bankers'. Keynes echoed: 'Let finance be primarily national' (*CW* xxi. 236).

The way to make sense of these twists and turns is to remember that Keynes was offering advice he thought suited Britain best. The pound and dollar, he thought, might be safely linked provided certain conditions were met. He summed up his position in a letter to a German correspondent on 13 October 1936:

1. In general I remain in favour of independent national systems with fluctuating exchange rates.
2. Unless, however, a long period is considered, there need be no reason why the exchange rate should in practice be constantly fluctuating.
3. Since there are certain advantages in stability . . . I am entirely in favour of practical measures towards de facto stability so long as there are no fundamental grounds for a different policy.
4. I would even go so far . . . as to give some additional assurance as to the magnitude of the fluctuation which would be normally allowed . . . Provided there was no actual pledge, I think that in most ordinary circumstances a margin of 10 per cent should prove sufficient.
5. I would emphasise that the practicability of stability would depend (i) upon measures to control capital movements, and (ii) the existence of a tendency for broad wage movements to be similar in the different countries concerned.   (KP, L/36)

Keynes's attitude to the United States softened in the 1930s. He visited it twice, in 1931 and 1934. On the second, and much more important visit, he went to study the New Deal, saw Roosevelt, and explained his new theory of effective demand in Washington and New York. Keynes was greatly impressed. 'Here, not in Moscow is the economic laboratory of the world,' he wrote to Felix Frankfurter on 30 May 1934. 'The young men who are running it are splendid. I am astonished at the competence, intelligence and wisdom. One meets a classical economist here and there who ought to have been thrown out of [the] window—but they mostly have been.' The commitment of the Administration, and of the younger section of the economics profession, to a policy of economic expansion was to be crucial in winning Keynes over to the idea that an American-led world economic system might not be as damaging to Britain's interests as he had feared.

There is a certain paradox, here, for Hitler's New Deal was much more coherent than Roosevelt's and much more successful in getting rid of unemployment. But except for a guarded reference to the advantages of totalitarianism in planning output as a whole, in the German preface to his *General Theory*, Keynes made no public comment on the Nazi economic system, either laudatory or critical. However, he freely condemned Nazism as a barbaric political system, and took to calling Germany and Italy 'brigand powers'. The main reason for Keynes's lack of approbation of Nazi economics was his detestation of the regime. But a subsidiary factor was that, unlike in the United States, there was no body of professional economists, in Germany or anywhere else in Europe outside Sweden, with whom he could seriously engage. The contribution of the Stockholm school apart, the technical discussion following the publication of Keynes's *General Theory of Employment, Interest, and Money* in 1936 was an Anglo-American affair. This is a neglected source of Keynes's simultaneous pull to America, and repulsion from Europe, which followed the breakdown of the supposedly self-regulating international economy in the 1930s.

On the other hand, although Hitler's Germany was in no sense a fit partner for Britain, Keynes at no time urged a preventive war to stop Germany. He approved of the Munich settlement, though not of Hitler's methods in extracting it, thought that whether Hitler seized Danzig or not did not matter in the least, and would have been content to let him take over the Ukraine if he could. As Professor Carr has shown, there were complicated reasons for all these attitudes, but avoidance of another Western European war, and giving Germany its outlet in the east, as part of the rebalancing of Europe he had advocated in 1919 and 1921, were the most important. The United States barely featured in his plans to contain the 'brigand powers'.

The United States was not at first involved in the European and Asian wars, and *all* the belligerents' plans for a post-war economic order left out the United States. Initially, these were based on the reasoning of the 1930s, when Britain, Germany, and Japan had tried to form economic blocs which discriminated against the United States, since none of them felt they could live with America's unbalanced competitive power. The United States, by contrast, had become increasingly internationalist, with Roosevelt's Secretary of State, Cordell Hull, vociferous in support of free trade. Once involved in the war, its major war aim was to dismantle the neo-mercantilist blocs established by the other belligerents. (These hopes extended, more vaguely, to the even more autarkic system established by the USSR.) The defeat of Germany and Japan would automatically eliminate their systems; but the United States could also exert powerful pressure on its dependent ally, Britain.

The first post-war plan was produced by Germany. Dr Walther Funk, Hitler's Economics Minister, proclaimed a European 'New Order' in Paris on 25 July 1940. This called for a European economic bloc with fixed exchange rates and a central clearing union in Berlin. Relations with the United States would be on a barter basis. The purpose of the plan was to restore within Europe what Funk called 'an intelligent division of labour', while shielding Europe as a whole from the deflationary consequences of an international gold standard.

Keynes at the British Treasury saw much virtue in the Funk proposals. He wrote to Harold Nicolson on 20 November 1940: 'If Funk's plan is taken at its face value, it is excellent and just what we ourselves ought to be doing. If it is to be attacked, the way to do it would be to cast doubt and suspicion on its *bona fides*' (*CW* xxv. 2). Even more striking was Keynes's formal response to the German plan on 1 December:

It is not our purpose to reverse the roles proposed by Germany for herself and for her neighbours. . . . Germany must be expected and allowed to assume the measure of economic leadership which flows naturally from her own qualifications and her geographical position. Germany is the worst master the world has yet known. But, on terms of equality, she can be an efficient colleague.   (*CW* xxv. 15)

On 25 April 1941, Keynes envisaged a sterling system including some European countries, free to discriminate against American goods if the United States 'persisted in maintaining an unbalanced creditor position' (*CW* xxv. 17).

He received a rude jolt when he visited Washington from 7 May to 29 July 1941. As in 1915, Britain depended on purchases in neutral United States for which it could not pay. In December 1940 Roosevelt had announced 'Lend-Lease'—a scheme to provide Britain with supplies, not in exchange for borrowed money, as in the First World War, but for an undisclosed post-war 'consideration'. Keynes came as the emissary of a 'great & independent nation', inclined 'to ask as of right what they are only prepared to give us as a favour'. On 28 July, the day before he left, he was handed a State Department draft of the Lend-Lease agreement which, in Article VII, spelt out the 'consideration': a pledge by Britain to avoid 'discrimination against the importation' of American goods—in essence, a demand that Britain trade Imperial Preference for Lend-Lease. Keynes himself may have precipitated the American *démarche* by telling the State Department, on 25 June, that Britain might be forced to resort to discriminatory trade policies to balance her exports and imports after the war. When he saw Article VII, he exploded. His denunciations of 'Mr. Hull's lunatic proposals' went round Washington. All this seemed a rerun of the sour atmosphere of the First World War. But Keynes was now older, and wiser. Besides, in 1941 Britain had no realistic option but to meet American wishes, as, unlike in 1916, there was no hope of a negotiated peace. So Keynes retired to his country house, Tilton, in August to draft a new Keynes Plan. This was his famous proposal for a 'Clearing Union', which now included the United States, initialled on 8 September 1941.

The essential feature of the plan was that creditor countries would not be allowed to 'hoard' their surpluses, or charge punitive rates of interest for lending them out; rather they would be automatically available as cheap overdraft facilities to debtors through the mechanism of an international clearing bank whose depositors were the central banks of the union. However, he was still prepared to fall back on the alternative of a British-led currency bloc, maintained by 'Schachtian devices' if the United States refused to play (*CW* xxv. 21–40). (Dr Schacht, Hitler's economics minister in the 1930s, had developed a successful system of bilateral trade agreements to balance Germany's external accounts.) A second draft, which Keynes initialled on 18 November 1941, added the 'highly substantive proposal' that membership of the Currency Union might be grouped by 'political and geographic units' such as the sterling area (*CW* xxv. 55–7). These suggestions retain their interest as a possible model for a gradual return to a global fixed exchange-rate system today.

American requirements were spelt out explicitly once the United States entered the war in December 1941. The United States insisted that, in return for aid, Britain should pledge itself, after the war, to abandon trade discrimination. This pledge was incorporated into Article VII of the Lend-Lease Agreement signed on 23 February 1942, five days after the fall of Singapore to the Japanese. Keynes now realized that the economic bloc alternative was a non-starter. America would not finance the British war effort to allow Britain to emerge as head of a 'Schachtian' system which discriminated against American exports. Keynes had to apply himself to the intellectual problem of how to fit the British demand for freedom to pursue full employment policies into an American free-trade framework. He was forced to accept that the post-war world would be shaped by American power, as modified by American idealism and British brains. He would also have been less than Keynes, and less of an economist and liberal, had he not been seized by the possibility of using a unique historical moment to recreate an improved version of the liberal economic order which had collapsed in the First World War. Keynes also understood a moral and geopolitical fact. Assuming the defeat of Germany, the choice after the war would be between what he called 'the American and Russian bias'—that is, between world capitalism and autarkic socialism, with not much in between. 'Is there not much to be said', he wrote, 'for having a good try with the American bias first?' (*CW* xxv. 156).

Independently, the Americans had also been thinking about the post-war economic order. Harry Dexter White, a US Treasury official, produced a plan in March 1942. This was for a modified gold standard, to which was attached a modest adjustment facility in the shape of a Stabilization Fund on which subscribing members could draw up to the amount of their subscriptions; a scheme which, by strictly limiting American liability, upheld, in effect, the orthodox doctrine of debtor adjustment. White's total adjustment facility (originally $5bn. later $8bn.) was much smaller than the total overdraft facility ($26bn.) envisaged in the Keynes Plan; and strict conditions were attached to the drawing of quotas. Neither Keynes nor White saw each other's plans till the summer of 1942. Both were adopted as bargaining positions by their respective governments.

The Bretton Woods Agreement, signed on 22 July 1944, after two difficult negotiating sessions in Washington, reflected American rather than British views. British and American conflicts on such matters as exchange-rate management, access to reserves, tariff policy, and responsibility for adjustment reflected national interests, as filtered through the experiences of the inter-war years and expectations of the future. Britain's negotiating achievements were limited to obtaining safeguards, postponements, and derogations within the framework of the

American plan. The chief British success was to secure a 'scarce currency' clause which allowed debtor countries to discriminate against creditor countries under specified conditions.

According to James Meade and Lionel Robbins, members of the British negotiating teams who kept diaries, Keynes's performances at the two Washington conferences of September–October 1943 and July–August 1944 were mixtures of extraordinary eloquence, verbal as well as intellectual, and extraordinary rudeness to and about the Americans. After one negotiating session, Harry Dexter White told Robbins, 'Your Baron Keynes sure pees perfume.' Robbins wrote, after another, how 'The Americans sat entranced as the God-like visitor sang and the golden light played around'. On the other hand, Meade reported Carl Bernstein of the US Treasury 'smarting from Keynes's ill-manners'. (Keynes had said of one of his drafts: 'This is intolerable. It is yet another Talmud.') Keynes's bad manners as a negotiator no doubt reflected exhaustion and failing health, but also his frustration at Britain's impotence. This mingled sense of idealism and consciousness that America ultimately called the tune was true of all the British negotiators. 'In the world of the future we shall have to live more by our wits,' noted Lionel Robbins. The trouble was that wits, too, had to be muted, in deference to the American fear of being made suckers 'especially by the diabolically clever Lord Keynes'.

In the House of Lords on 23 May 1944, Keynes commended the agreed Anglo-American plan in terms both of idealism and necessity. 'What alternative is open to us . . . ?' Unlike in the First World War, he now took pride in the fact that 'in thus waging the war without counting the ultimate cost we—and we alone of the United Nations—have burdened ourselves with a weight of deferred indebtedness to other countries beneath which we shall stagger'. Specifically, without the new framework afforded by the Anglo-American agreement,

London must necessarily lose its international position, and the arrangements . . . of the sterling area would fall to pieces. To suppose that a system of bilateral and barter agreements, with no one who owns sterling knowing just what he can do with it . . . is the best way of encouraging the Dominions to centre their financial systems on London, seems to me pretty near frenzy.

The 'technique of little Englandism' was incompatible with England's imperial heritage. 'With our own resources so greatly impaired and encumbered, it is only if sterling is firmly placed in an international setting that the necessary confidence in it can be sustained' (*CW* xxvi. 9–21). To place American power and money, on terms, behind Britain's 'impaired and encumbered' system of earning its living was thus the ultimate object of the 'special relationship' which the war had made necessary.

III

The defeat of Keynes's Clearing Union plan had highlighted the problem of financing Britain's prospective current account deficit after the war. Keynes eventually estimated this at between $6bn. and $7bn. over a three-year 'transitional' period. On 17 August 1945, three days after the Japanese surrender, the United States abruptly cancelled Lend-Lease. From now on Britain would have to pay for all supplies, including those already ordered. The Clearing Union proposal had been explicitly designed to make balance of payments assistance from America after the war unnecessary (*CW* xxv. 69–70). 'Overdrafts' from the clearing bank would have been automatically available to plug Britain's post-war 'dollar gap'. Britain's quota from the IMF was far too small for this, and, in any event, only a country with a convertible currency could exercise its 'drawing rights'. Sterling devaluation was ruled out, partly because Britain's import surplus was too large, partly because 'repudiation' of Britain's sterling debts (totalling $14bn.) would have killed off the sterling area. Isolationists of Right and Left favoured strict trade controls, but, Keynes asked Beaverbrook on 27 April 1945:

Do you really favour a barter system of trade which would mean, in practice, something very near a state monopoly of imports and exports a la Russe? Do you welcome an indefinite continuance of strict controls and (probably) severer rationing? Do you look forward to our stepping down, for the time being, to the position of a second-class power . . . ?   (*CW* xxiv. 330)

So American help was all that was left.

Keynes hoped that assistance from the United States would take the form of a grant, or at least an interest-free loan. Hugh Dalton, Labour's Chancellor of the Exchequer, recorded that 'Keynes in his talks with Ministers just before leaving for Washington, was almost starry-eyed. He was very confident that . . . he could get six billion dollars as a free gift . . . Nor did he . . . say much to us about the "strings".' The banker Robert Brand said: 'When I listen to Lord Keynes talking, I seem to hear those coins jingling in my pocket.' Soon after Keynes arrived in Washington on 5 September as joint head of the British delegation, he realized the mood had changed. Over incredibly sticky negotiations which lasted three months the six billion dollar 'free gift' was whittled down to a loan of $3.75bn. at 2 per cent interest, with the 'string' that sterling be made convertible a year after the agreement was ratified. This forfeited Britain's transitional protection under the Bretton Woods Agreement. Having been over-optimistic at the start, Keynes drove a bewildered and angry Labour government, step by step, to accept progressively less favourable terms. His health and temper collapsed. In the end he was replaced as joint head of the British delegation by Sir Edward Bridges, who agreed the final settlement.

Keynes's eloquent defence of his handiwork in the House of Lords on 18 December, twelve days after the loan agreement was signed, put the negotiations in the context of events as they had unfolded since the First World War. There was first the argument from necessity. The alternative to the loan agreement, he said, 'is to build up a separate economic bloc which excludes Canada and consists of countries to which we already owe more than we can pay, on the basis of their agreeing to lend us money they have not got and buy only from us and one another goods we are unable to supply'. Secondly, there was the appeal of a shared, reconstituted liberalism:

The separate economic blocs and all the friction and loss of friendship they must bring with them are expedients to which one may be driven in a hostile world. . . . But it is surely crazy to prefer that. Above all, this determination to make trade truly international and to avoid the establishment of economic blocs which limit and restrict commercial intercourse outside them, is plainly an essential condition of the world's best hope, an Anglo-American understanding . . . Some of us, in the tasks of war and more lately in those of peace, have learnt by experience that our two countries can work together. Yet it would be only too easy for us to walk apart. I beg those who look askance at these plans to ponder deeply and responsibly where it is they think they want to go.   (*CW* xxiv. 620, 624)

IV

The familiar context of Keynesian economics is the Great Depression of the 1930s—the collapse of the world economy. But a more persistent context was the unbalanced creditor position of the United States. For the first ten years after the First World War, the United States boomed, while Britain slumped. Keynes saw British unemployment as a problem of sterling's over-valuation against the dollar. From this point of view, his *General Theory* is an addendum to rather than the culmination of his line of thought—the theory of a deep world slump when no amount of monetary manipulation can restore full employment.

Following the collapse of the gold standard in 1931, the world economy broke up into trading blocs based on 'key' currencies. It was as manager of an imperial payments system known as the Sterling Area that Britain went to war with Germany in 1939.

It took the Second World War to put paid to Keynes's hope of a British-controlled payments system as the monetary framework for the British economy. Much shared idealism and responsibility went into the making of the Bretton Woods system. Nevertheless it was the end of British monetary independence. The sterling system could not survive unless it was bolstered by the dollar. Keynes's lifetime spans the passage from control to dependence.

6 Keynes's legacy

I

Any assessment of the work of a past master is bound to reflect the state of mind of its time. At present (July 1995) Keynes's reputation is precariously poised. Ten years ago, one might have said that the Keynesian era was dead and buried. Nigel Lawson, then Britain's Chancellor of the Exchequer, did say so. 'The conquest of inflation', he declared in his Mais Lecture of 1984, 'should ... be the objective of macroeconomic policy. And ... the creation of conditions conducive to growth and employment ... should be ... the objective of microeconomic policy.' There was no commitment to full employment. Rather, the idea was to free up markets as much as possible and accept whatever level of activity they produced. Today, there is some reaction back to Keynes, partly because the deflationary policies pursued over the last fifteen years have left high and persisting unemployment in their wake—as, indeed, Keynes predicted such policies would. Unemployment in the European Union has been rising since the 1970s, stands at 10 per cent of the work-force today and has not fallen by much during the recovery from the recession of 1991-2. It is as if the combined population of Denmark, Ireland, and Switzerland was producing nothing at all—hardly a triumph for market forces.

Although monetarism failed to deliver stable prices and tolerable employment, Keynesian policy as we knew it is not restored. Most governments believe that Keynesian remedies for unemployment will be either ineffective or mischievous, much as they did when Keynes first started advocating them. This partly reflects the view that most unemployment today is 'structural' not Keynesian; that is, it reflects not a shortage of demand but the wrong structure of capital and relative wages. Furthermore, it is widely believed that structural maladjustment came about (or was allowed to continue for as long as it did) as a consequence of the 'Keynesian' policy of creating or maintaining employment in unproductive or loss-making occupations. Even if some part, at least, of current unemployment is conceded to have its origins in a deficiency of aggregate demand, it is believed that expanding demand would cancel the gains on the inflation front, achieved at such cost, since 1979.

In short, Keynesian policies come to us today wrapped up in a history of rising inflation, unsound public finance, expanding statism, collapsing corporatism, and general ungovernability, all of which have seemed inseparable from the Keynesian cure for the afflictions of industrial society. We do not want to traverse that path again. By the 1980s, Keynes, who was praised for having saved the world from Marxism, had joined Marx as the God that failed.

The question of how the Keynesian age came to generate expectations which undermined the Keynesian revolution calls for both a theoretical and a historical explanation. Perhaps a historian is as well placed as anybody to offer one. Both sides of the explanation will be personal to the writer, since there is little agreement on 'what went wrong'. But anyone who wants to keep the spirit of Keynes alive has to face the failures of Keynesianism honestly, without always trying to shield the Master from the mistakes of the disciples. In essence, the Keynesian revolution was ruined by over-ambition—*hubris* might be a better word—driven by impatience and backed by unwarranted claims to both theoretical and practical knowledge. The monetarist counter-revolution was a plea for more modesty, and greater trust in the spontaneous forces of the market.

It is hard to fit Keynes himself into the Keynesian versus Monetarist debate, because his *General Theory* was built to understand the world of the 1930s, not the world of the 1960s or 1970s. It is perfectly possible to get (qualified) monetarist conclusions out of *The General Theory* on certain assumptions about expectations, but these were not the purposes for which the book was written. To understand much of what Keynes had to say about money and credit and exchange rates, the banking system and financial markets, the reader needs to turn to the *Tract on Monetary Reform* and the *Treatise on Money*. For those who seek contemporary inspiration in Keynes, three other facts are worth remembering. First, although he was intellectually over-confident—a trait inherited by his followers—he was notably modest about what policy could achieve in a free society—something which his followers tended to ignore. Secondly, his social aims were, as he put it, 'moderately conservative'. There is nothing in Keynes's social philosophy, or the Liberalism of his day, which would have supported the seemingly relentless expansion of the welfare activities of the state which contributed so heavily to the fiscal crises of the 1970s. Finally, he was an apostle of growth not for its own sake, but only as a means to leisure and civilized living. In fact he argued in the late 1920s that 'technological' unemployment was a sign that the economic problem was being solved. 'The full employment policy by means of investment is only one particular application of an intellectual theorem,' he wrote to T. S. Eliot in 1945. 'You can produce the result just as well by consuming more or working less . . . Less work is the ultimate solution [to the unemployment problem]' (*CW* xxvii. 384).

II

For twenty-five years after Keynes's death, his revolution prospered. Most economists accepted 'the new economics' (even Milton Friedman said in 1966, 'We are all Keynesians now,' a phrase repeated by Richard Nixon in 1972); most governments committed themselves to maintain full employment. To be sure, not all who called themselves 'Keynesians' accepted *The General Theory* as gospel. Indeed, there was a retreat from Keynes's own theory. As a result of Patinkin's work (1956), classical theory was partly rehabilitated, in that the downward rigidity of money-wages was seen as the *essential* obstacle to full employment, as Arthur Pigou had always claimed. In Leijonhufvud's reinterpretation (1968) Keynes's 'unemployment equilibrium' was to be understood as a rhetorical device; his was a disequilibrium theory emphasizing co-ordination failures—an approach which stressed the continuity of *The General Theory* with the *Treatise on Money*, thus narrowing its distance from the monetary disequilibrium theorists of the 1930s. However, a world with downwardly rigid money-wages and the ever-present possibility of a collapse in private investment is still a world which leaves a necessary role for government *policy* to maintain continuous full employment.

Apart from this, three aspects of Keynes's legacy seemed secure. First, practically all economists accepted Keynes's macroeconomic framework. Keynes had invented a new branch of economics, macroeconomics, the study of the behaviour of the economic system as a whole, rather than the study of the behaviour of individuals, firms, or industries. 'Students in the 1960s were taught that we could model the economy, diagnose the state of effective demand and devise appropriate fiscal interventions.' Secondly, *The General Theory* had provided the conceptual breakthrough for constructing national accounts. The consequent mushrooming of economic statistics was hugely influential in the development of econometrics, which, in turn (it might then have been said), provided a secure forecasting basis for macroeconomic policy. Finally, Keynes had restored faith in the capitalist system. Keynesian economics had helped write Fascism, Communism, and some kinds of socialism out of the history of the developed world.

Keynesian theory had also contributed to the emergence of development economics—the study of economic growth in poor countries. Roy Harrod, in particular, extended the Keynesian explanation of short-run unemployment into a model of self-sustaining growth, emphasizing the central role of physical investment. The mid-1960s saw an upsurge of faith in the power of macroeconomic policy to deliver not just full employment, but high rates of growth, and many other desirable social objectives.

Ten years later the counter-revolution against Keynes was in full swing. Milton Friedman's restatement of the quantity theory of money in 1956 was followed, in 1968, by the most influential macroeconomic paper of the post-war years. In this Friedman claimed that attempts by governments to reduce unemployment below the 'natural rate' set by market institutions led only to accelerating inflation. In 1976 the Keynesian revolution in policy was officially declared dead in its birthplace, when Britain's Labour prime minister, James Callaghan, announced that the option of 'spending our way out of recession no longer existed' and in the past had worked only by 'injecting bigger and bigger doses of inflation into the economy'. Throughout the world, price stability rather than full employment became the stated goal of macroeconomic policy.

The monetarist counter-revolution called into question the most fundamental aspects of Keynes's legacy. If nominal changes (changes in money) affect prices, not output, in the long run, as Friedman claimed, we do not need macroeconomics, only an updated quantity theory of money. If, as Friedman claimed, the economy is 'inherently more cyclically stable' than Keynes supposed, while macroeconomic interventions are subject to 'long and variable lags', not only do we not need counter-cyclical policy, it will be destabilizing. If we do not need counter-cyclical policy, we do not need large macroeconomic forecasting models. Finally, Keynesian macroeconomic policy did not preserve capitalism from socialism, but led towards it by the need for increasing political intervention in the microeconomy to make macroeconomic policy work. Instead of trying to stimulate the economy through mixtures of public spending and planning, governments should concentrate on controlling inflation and improving the working of the market system.

Rightly or wrongly, the fate of the Keynesian revolution has been determined by events. The depression of the 1930s gave rise to it; the 1950s and 1960s seemed to vindicate it; the 'slumpflation' of the 1970s (the combination of high unemployment and high inflation) ended it. The legacy of the 1980s is ambiguous, and should betoken a modest revival.

The 1950s and most of the 1960s were a capitalist golden age. By historical standards, unemployment was exceptionally low, growth in real incomes exceptionally fast, economies exceptionally stable; all achieved at a very modest cost in inflation. These successes were widely attributed to Keynesian policies, inspired by Keynesian theory.

Then prosperity started to unravel. From the late 1960s inflation *and* unemployment began to edge up, growth to slow down. In the OECD countries, consumer prices, which had risen by 3.1 per cent a year on average in 1960–8, rose by 10.5 per cent a year in 1973–9. Unemployment, 3.1 per cent a year on average in the first period, was 5.1 per cent in the second. The growth of real GDP per capita slowed down from 3.9 per cent in 1960–8 to 1.9 per cent in 1973–9. In 1971 growing macroeconomic (including external payments) imbalances brought down the system of fixed, but adjustable, exchange rates established at Bretton Woods in 1944, even before the first oil-price shock of 1973–4.

Having been credited with success, Keynesian policy was blamed for subsequent failure. Both conclusions are questionable. Did economic ideas, Keynesian or otherwise, have much influence on what governments did? Did the policies of governments make much difference to what happened? The answer to both questions is almost certainly yes, but the interactions between the three realms of ideas, policies, and events are so complicated that no account of their relationship is likely to command general assent. We can at least try to distinguish between the rhetorical and technical uses of economic ideas, and avoid calling Keynesian the general expansion of state activity after the war, and attributing to Keynesian policy all the consequences, good and bad, which followed from this expansion. As Christopher Allsopp has written, 'The development of Welfare States, industrial intervention, and public expenditure programmes . . . has little to do with . . . the economics of Keynes . . . It is necessary . . . not to lose sight of the fundamental point that the original message was minimalist in spirit.' Beyond this, it is rhetorically useful to be reminded that Keynes was against inflation, nationalization, planning, equalization of incomes, etc., if only because many who have advocated these things have done so in his name.

III

In trying to assess the influence of Keynesian policy on post-war events, an initial problem is to understand what is meant by Keynesian policy. In France and Italy, for example, what would now be called active supply-side policies were routinely mislabelled 'Keynesian'. A more relevant test is the commitment to maintain full employment. But only in Britain and the United States was such a commitment given, and even then ambiguously. The British Employment White Paper of 1944 pledged the government to maintain a 'high and stable' level of employment. What was high? What was stable?

Jim Tomlinson has suggested a more stringent test. The Keynesian revolution, he says, 'should be defined in terms of an attempt to legitimize [budget] deficits as a device for use when the level of aggregate demand required stimulation'. Keynesian policy may then be said to be in operation when budget deficits are deliberately incurred to raise the level of output. On this test there was no Keynesian policy during the height of the 'golden age' because, as R. C. O. Matthews pointed out in 1968, 'the [British] Government, so far from injecting demand into the system, has persistently had a large current account surplus'. The same was true for the United States until 1964. Similarly, there was no active demand management policy in the most successful 'golden age' economies, Germany and Japan. The implication is that the post-war world did not need, and did not get, a Keynesian revolution in policy.

In *The General Theory* Keynes had talked of a happy nineteenth-century 'conjuncture' which allowed employment to be reasonably full without government intervention (*CW* vii. 307).

It may be that the 'golden age' should be seen as resulting from a similar conjuncture. As Crafts and Woodward point out, across the developed world there were 'widespread opportunities to imitate American technology, to contract low productivity agriculture, and to exploit cheap energy'. The opportunities for technological catch-up gave capital a high marginal productivity, leading to high private investment demand. A high rate of productivity growth allowed a sufficient rise in real incomes to satisfy workers' aspirations while keeping unit costs fairly stable. Governments also consumed a much higher proportion of the national income than they had before the war. As John Hicks put it in 1977: 'The combination of more rapid technical progress (surely a fact) with the socialist tendencies which increased demand for collective goods (surely also a fact) could have produced such a boom without the added stimulus of Keynesian policies.'

In this happy conjuncture a key role was played by the United States. In practice, only the United States enjoyed the luxury of an 'autonomous' macroeconomic policy. Under the gold-exchange-rate system established at Bretton Woods only the United States was on the gold standard; other countries held most of their reserves in dollars. Monetary conditions for the system as a whole were set by American financial policy, with other countries' macroeconomic policy being limited to maintaining their currencies' chosen exchange rate with the dollar. Under Truman and Eisenhower, American budgetary policy was conservative, interest rates were low, the balance of trade in surplus. Till the mid-1960s, the United States provided most countries with a reasonably secure anti-inflationary anchor, while supplying them with enough liquidity to prevent the deflationary contractions associated with a pure gold standard. The stability of the monetary regime allowed a progressive liberalization of the payments and trading system which, as Adam Smith would have predicted, was highly favourable to the growth of real incomes. Finally, there were *ad hoc* injections of demand from the United States—notably through Marshall Aid and the Korean war—which had the same stimulating effects as the Californian gold discoveries and the 'small wars' of the mid-nineteenth century. In short, it was the Pax Americana which secured a rough and ready macro-economic balance across the 'free world' during the golden age, much as the Pax Britannica had done in the nineteenth century. The existence of a buoyant international economy (unlike in the 1930s) made national economic problems much more tractable.

However, if purposeful Keynesian policy cannot explain the golden age, the explicit or implicit commitment to avoid a collapse in demand—and just as important, the belief that Keynesian policy would work if required—may well have secured the expectations ('state of confidence') necessary to sustain the private investment boom for so long. In particular, in the 1950s Keynesianism seemed to have erected a decisive barrier to the advance of socialism, whether in the form of public ownership or national planning. The subsequent identification of Keynesianism with a disproportionate growth of the public sector accompanied by growing labour militancy was crucial in destroying the psychological or *expectational* function of the Keynesian revolution—the belief that it would make the world safe for capitalism and capitalists.

It is worth pursuing the nineteenth-century parallel a little further. The boom of the 1850s and 1860s was followed by the depression of the 1870s through to the 1890s, which, as has often been pointed out, was not a slump in the 1930s sense, but a mixed period of prosperity and depression, with enormous technological restructuring accompanied by a shift of competitive dynamism from Britain to Germany and the United States. This is not totally dissimilar to what happened from the 1970s onwards, with competitive advantage shifting this time to the Pacific rim. What was missing from the earlier period was the phenomenon of 'stagflation'. There was heavy unemployment for much of the 1880s, but prices fell. In contrast, was the boom of the 1950s and 1960s 'artificially' prolonged by Keynesian policy?

According to the standard Keynesian story, the long boom was ended by the oil-price shock of 1973–4, though it was acknowledged that the path to this débâcle was strewn with policy mistakes and unexplained 'sociological' happenings like the wages explosion in 1968. But the deterioration of macroeconomic performance had been evident from at least the mid-1960s. It coincided with the switch to active Keynesian policies.

In the 1960s Keynesianism was universalized, 'came into its own', in a double sense: the use of fiscal policy to balance economies was extended to France, Italy, Germany, and to a lesser extent Japan; and fiscal policy became more active and ambitious as fears of recession revived. Broadly speaking, while early Keynesian interest concentrated on securing the full use of existing resources, the Keynesianism of the 1960s tried to secure the full use of potential resources—i.e. growth in the productive capacity of the economy with the object of restraining cost-push inflation and meet the increasing 'social demands' being placed on the economy. What David Marquand (1988) has called the social democratic phase of Keynesianism is associated with a move to the Left in politics, and the serious use, for the first time, of budgetary policy to shift demand from the private to the public sector. The budget simultaneously became the agent of demand management, growth, and welfare. From the 1960s the share of public spending in GDP everywhere started to rise. The most significant macroeconomic episode, from the global point of view, was the Kennedy–Johnson tax cut and 'great society' spending programmes of 1964–6. In retrospect, though it was not evident at the time, this, together with the inflationary financing of the Vietnam war, ended the United States' role as the world's anti-inflationary anchor.

We can identify several plausible reasons for the shift from full employment to growth. In the United States, the observed tendency for unemployment to be a little higher at the peak of each cycle in the 1950s (though the average for the 1950s, at just over 5 per cent, was close enough to the target rate of 4 per cent) revived the old Keynesian fear of the 'secular stagnation' of mature economies. It suggested a growing output gap—the gap between the actual annual rate growth of output and its

potential growth rate. Rejecting the idea that higher unemployment might be caused by technological factors like automation,
the President's Council of Economic Advisers suggested that
demand expansion could lower unemployment to 4 per cent
without 'unacceptable' price inflation, James Tobin arguing
that the evils of 'small increases in prices' had been 'greatly
exaggerated'. The Keynesian promise that demand expansion
could achieve faster growth fed the politicians' desire to boost
the American growth rate to avoid losing the ideological war (as
well as the arms race) against the Soviet Union, which in the
1950s was trumpeting prodigious growth rates and dramatic
technological achievements like Sputnik.

In Europe resort to deficit finance stemmed from a fear that
labour shortages would slow down growth (the erection of the
Berlin Wall in 1961 stemmed the flow of cheap labour from East
to West Germany); from the fear that the opening-up of domestic economies to free trade and capital flows, both globally and
as a result of the formation of the European Economic Community in 1958, would make them more vulnerable to external
shocks; and from the re-equipment of left-wing parties, long out
of power, with up-to-date (that is, non-Marxist) ideologies.
Keynesian growth policy seemed to be what was left when
plentiful supply, protectionism, and obsolete ideologies were
removed from the picture. In slow-growing Britain, growth
policy was adopted to enable it to 'catch up' with industrial
rivals like Germany and France. Japan resorted to deficit
financing in 1965 when it started to lose key post-war instruments like tariffs and control over capital movements. Common to all countries was the belief that fast or faster growth
was needed to raise the feasible real wage, and win trade-union
support for wage restraint by making possible the expansion of
welfare programmes.

In the 1960s, developing countries, some recently decolon-
ized, embarked on state-led industrialization designed to enable
them to catch up with rich ones. Growth would be accelerated
by redirecting underemployed rural labour to heavy industry.
The Keynesian-trained Argentinian economist Raoul Prebisch

developed a 'terms of trade' argument for public investment in import-substituting manufactures. The result was a series of public investment booms within a framework of state owner-ship and indicative planning, largely financed by foreign borrowing.

Expectation that the rate of capital accumulation would fall was not unreasonable after post-war reconstruction and 'catch-up' had run their course. Much more questionable was the extension of Keynesian thinking from the short-run problem of securing full employment of existing resources to the problem of increasing the growth of these resources. For 'growth' Keynesians, active demand management (including fiscal defi-cits) was required not just to prevent or offset recessions but to realize the economy's long-run growth *potential*, an altogether more elusive idea. Keynes himself would have said—in fact he did say—that at full employment any exogenous injection of demand leads to inflation (see, for example, *CW* ix. 350). This is the 'special case' to which classical economics applied, when faster growth of output can come about only through increased productivity and improved technique—matters on which Keynes had nothing distinctive to say. The growth Keynesians argued, *au contraire*, that productivity growth was endogenous to the growth process. The rate of output growth depended on the rate of growth of investment; the faster investment could be induced to grow, the larger would be the productivity gains, owing to the effect of dynamic economies of scale, leading to a 'virtuous circle' of rising productivity, greater competitiveness, and higher growth. Given sufficient total demand, output could always be induced to rise more than proportionately to the input of labour. Thus high employment was no barrier to demand-led expansion: growth, in the jargon, was demand-, not supply-constrained.

Demand expansion went hand in hand with indicative plan-ning. In the British National Plan of 1965 indicated growth rates were worked out for each sector over a five-year period to raise the expectations of businessmen. But the key indicator was the projected growth of public spending. This would tell industrial sectors how much they needed to expand capacity, and at the same time guarantee that the increased output would be bought. Thus public spending emerged as the real engine of growth—a fateful conjuncture in Keynesian political economy. Governments also encouraged company mergers to realize minimum efficient scale. Devaluation was added as an instrument to help lift economies onto higher growth paths, rather than simply to overcome disequilibria in the balance of payments as envisaged at Bretton Woods.

In retrospect, all the presuppositions underpinning the dash for growth, in developed and developing countries alike, turned out to be intellectually and politically insecure. No one in fact knew how to make an economy grow faster over time than it was actually growing. Did the causation run from productivity growth to output growth or from output growth to productivity growth? Economists disagreed. Again, the Keynesians were remarkably sanguine about the effects of the growth of the public sector on productivity growth, wage behaviour, and business expectations. They thought that a little inflation (how much?) was stimulating, and had no inkling of inflationary expectations. Finally, they greatly exaggerated the extent of 'disguised' rural unemployment in developing countries, and hence the benefits to growth to be obtained by transferring these supposedly costless resources into industrial production. If there is a common theme linking these presuppositions, it was that the state is wise and the market is stupid.

Even Keynesians would now concede that the economic and social goals of the 1960s were over-ambitious. The record is clear: by the decade's end the OECD inflation rate had doubled from 3 per cent to 6 per cent, without any improvement in real variables. The rising inflation which was the real legacy of the growth of Keynesianism of the 1960s set Keynesian macroeconomic policy an impossible task in the 1970s. Once inflation had been let loose, government interventions were bound to be seriously destabilizing, involving either acceptance of higher unemployment to check the rise in prices, or acceptance of higher inflation to check the rise in unemployment. The oscillation of policy between these choices produced a rising 'misery index' (inflation plus unemployment) for most of the 1970s. Monetarism gained respectability by being able to explain worsening stagflation in terms of the interaction between 'stop-go' Keynesian macroeconomic policy, and wage behaviour which adapted ever more quickly to inflationary expectations.

In the most general sense, excessive pressure of demand led to what a classical economist would have predicted: a worldwide explosion in costs due to supply shortages. The wages explosion in the West, starting in 1968, had its counterpart in the rise in raw material and energy prices, starting in 1972 and culminating in the fourfold increase in oil prices in 1973–4, which reduced the real wage warranted at full employment for industrial countries. Direct controls over wages ('incomes policies') broke down as the decade progressed, producing a squeeze on profits, which could be offset only by pumping more money into the public sector. Western countries became, in the phrase of the day, 'ungovernable'.

Eventually governments had had enough. In face of the second oil price rise of 1979–80, Western governments tightened fiscal and monetary policy, bringing about the most severe slump since the 1930s. Developing countries, which had maintained their public investment booms throughout the 1970s by borrowing recycled petrodollars at negative real interest rates, found themselves faced with crippling foreign debt burdens as export earnings collapsed, real interest rates rose to punitive levels, and foreign investment dried up. In return for rescheduling and new loans, the IMF imposed tough stabilization packages. World-wide, state-led growth policies had precisely the opposite effect to those intended: they had raised, not lowered, the cost of producing goods and services, and they had lowered, not raised, the capacity of economies to produce marketable output. The Keynesian age was over.

IV

Even at this distance, it is hard to disentangle the specific Keynesian responsibility for these disasters from the more general climate of opinion and economic and social pressures causing governments and economies to behave in the way they did. The overestimate of the power of macroeconomic instruments was certainly important; but just as significant was a fatalistic acceptance, by both Left and Right, of a collectivist and corporatist future, made inevitable, so it seemed, by the increasing scale of business organization, the growth of encompassing pressure groups, and the demand for an increasing range of social and economic entitlements. After 1974–5, when governments had truly lost power to 'manage' their economies, the worst that can be said about Keynesianism was that it presented a barrier to new ideas and the development of alternative political strategies. For by this point in time the Keynesian revolution could not renew itself. It had spawned pathologies inhospitable to its remedies, and it had no intellectual or political resources left to understand them, or deal with them. Keynes cannot be blamed for this exhaustion. Nevertheless, certain aspects of his legacy proved troubling, in so far as they appeared to paralyse criticism from within the Keynesian camp of extensions and applications of his theory to problems and situations for which it was not intended.

First, two incautious phrases in *The General Theory* gave a rhetorical warrant for the belief that public spending is better than private spending. Keynes conceived that the maintenance of full employment might require a 'somewhat comprehensive socialisation of investment' (*CW* vii. 378); he also said that if the Treasury paid people to dig holes and fill them up unemployment would fall 'and the real income of the community, and its capital wealth also, would probably become a good deal greater than it actually is' (*CW* vii. 129). However, Keynes was always alert to the effect of policy on business psychology. He understood that excessive state spending would undermine confidence in the direction of policy and raise funding problems for the government, which would jeopardize the aim of maintaining a low long-term real rate of interest. No one has more eloquently or succinctly summarized the mechanism of the 'inflation tax' than Keynes in 1923: 'A government can live by this means when it can live by no other. It is the form of taxation which the public finds hardest to evade and even the weakest government can enforce, when it can enforce nothing else' (*CW* iv. 37). He understood that if public finance is judged unsound it will not be able to fulfil its genuine Keynesian purpose, as forward-looking agents take steps to protect themselves from the risk of repudiation or monetization of government debt. Yet he never explicitly discussed how much of the community's spending could be safely or efficiently left to the state in a free society.

Secondly, there was no clear guidance in *The General Theory* as to what Keynes meant by full employment, either conceptually or statistically. A 'general theory' of employment which nourishes the belief that the level of employment is entirely determined in the goods market, and not at all in the labour market, is seriously misnamed. To be sure, in one passage Keynes distinguished between voluntary and involuntary unemployment (*CW* vii. 6), or as it was later put between 'classical' and 'Keynesian' unemployment, but his rhetorical purpose was to deny classical explanations of unemployment, and these were also ignored by his followers. Richard Kahn has testified to the fact that 'the concept of "voluntary unemployment" left me very cold' and that the distinction between the two types of unemployment 'has not proved to have any practical significance'. The reason is that *The General Theory* can be read as saying that if the state controls the wages fund and allocates labour, voluntary unemployment can always be converted into involuntary employment, and the rate of unemployment reduced to zero—as indeed it was in the Soviet Union. Keynes did not think like this, but his more collectivist followers, influenced by wartime planning, did, and there is nothing in *The General Theory* which explicitly says that voluntary unemployment is a choice which, in a free society, can or should be dealt with only by changing labour market incentives.

One has to go outside *The General Theory* to discover what Keynes habitually thought about the nature of unemployment. In *The General Theory* he adapted, and clothed in new terms, a much older distinction between 'normal' unemployment, related to slowly changing labour market institutions, and 'abnormal' unemployment resulting from a cyclical downturn. He thought that the order of magnitude of 'normal' unemployment in Britain was about 5 per cent—the pre-1914 average, leaving 5 per cent in the 1920s, and nearer 10 per cent in the 1930s, 'abnormal'. Thus as late as 16 December 1944 he wrote to Beveridge, 'No harm in aiming at 3 per cent unemployment, but I shall be surprised if we succeed' (CW xxvii. 3). Keynes also seems to have thought of 'normal' unemployment as that level of unemployment at which money-wages (and prices) are stable. When unemployment is above normal, money-wages fall, when it is below normal, they rise. This is close to the neo-Keynesian idea of the Non-Accelerating Inflation Rate of Unemployment (NAIRU)—the level of unemployment required to contain inflation. But it was left to non-Keynesians to draw the conclusion that the only feasible way of lowering the level of 'normal' unemployment (or the NAIRU) in a free society was through labour-market reforms. The Keynesian obsession with incomes policies left the defence of contractual freedom to the monetarists.

Thirdly, Keynes bequeathed no adequate theory of prices. Keynes himself cannot be accused of being soft on inflation. Not only had he graphically analysed the rotting effect of inflation on the social system of capitalism (CW ii. 235–6) but in 1920, with British consumer prices rising by 20 per cent a year (the same as in 1975), he had urged a severe dose of 'dear money' and savage public expenditure cuts as the only alternative to state socialism: 'I would do this because I put very high the danger of going on with our present diseases without a drastic and unpleasant cure. And I would do it though I knew I risked a depression and possibly a crisis.' And he wrote in 1940: 'With all unorthodox [i.e. socialist] methods of control . . . excluded, I feel myself that I should give today exactly the same advice that I gave then' (CW xvii. 184–5). Delay in imposing and sticking to a 'dear money' policy in the mid-1970s made the subsequent situation much worse than it need have been.

This point can be generalized. In the pre-Keynesian era, the price level fell in a depression, rose in a boom, and on average stayed the same. It was thus easy for Keynes to be both an expansionist *and* a price stabilizer: in fact it could be shown that stability of the price level *required* that spending be increased when prices were falling. In the Keynesian era prices went on rising during both upturn and downturn, though at different rates. The achievement of Keynesian policy in the 1970s was to change the popular perception that unemployment was an unacceptable cost of *laissez-faire* into the perception that it was an acceptable price for reducing inflation. Nor was this just ideological prejudice. Keynesian policy to expand employment is *unusable* until inflationary expectations have disappeared from the system, since if inflation is expected to rise workers will simply demand higher wages.

How did this perverse situation come about? Despite Keynes's own anti-inflationary credentials, the models derived from *The General Theory* were constant price models: they focused, that is, on inadequate, not excess demand. But a 'general theory' of money must include both possibilities and intermediate positions, and it is quite true that *The General Theory* accepted the quantity theory of money as valid at full employment: 'So long as there is unemployment, *employment* will change in the same proportion as the quantity of money; and when there is full employment, *prices* will change in the same proportion as the quantity of money' (*CW* vii. 296). More realistically, Keynes acknowledged that inflation could start before full employment was reached—he referred to 'positions of semi-inflation' when output still rises but prices rise more (*CW* vii. 302)—owing to structural rigidities (skills and geographical mismatches) and trade unions' ability, as the labour market tightened, to push up wages ahead of productivity. In such a situation is aggregate demand still to be considered deficient? Keynes did not say. Should demand management aim to maintain what Abba Lerner called 'low full employment' and price stability, or 'high full employment' with controls on wages? Keynes did not say. He confined himself to the observation that the task of restraining wage push was 'a political rather than an economic problem' (*CW* xxvi. 38); he was 'inclined to turn a blind eye to the wages problem in a full employment economy' (*CW* xxvii. 385).

In place of a theory of inflation, there was an empirical observation dating from 1958, the Phillips Curve, showing a stable relationship over time between the level of unemployment and the rate of change of money-wages and, by later inference, prices. Keynes's grey area of 'semi-inflation' became the 'safe zone' of the Phillips Curve, within which governments were said to have a 'menu of choice' between degrees of inflation and of unemployment. Conservative-minded Keynesians wanted to run the economy at a slightly higher 'margin of unused capacity' in order to lower inflation. This was a possible policy deduction from *The General Theory* model. But it was condemned as immoral by the growth Keynesians, who wanted to expand demand till the last person seeking work at any single moment was employed, using incomes policy to control costs, either with the agreement of the trade unions, or by legislation. But, as Alan Coddington observed, the Keynesian habit of treating the centralization of power as a residual from the solution to problems of economic management ignored the question of how much power the government actually had, or should have in a free society. The failure of Keynesians to take supply constraints seriously, the product of the depression perspective of *The General Theory*, destroyed not only the intellectual balance which Keynes himself tried to hold, but also the political balance of the Keynesian revolution. By the late 1970s lovers of liberty and those who valued efficiency started to desert the Keynesian camp in droves.

Keynes was less guilty of political naïvety than some of his detractors believe—he once remarked memorably that politicians have only ears not eyes—but he paid little attention to the political process by which policy is made, and therefore often gave the impression that, provided the state apparatus was equipped with the right theories and run by benevolent Old Etonians, it could be safely entrusted with much more discretionary power over economic policy than the Victorians would have considered prudent or desirable. It is easy to believe that he himself would have been more sensible and cautious in policy advice or conduct than later Keynesian economists and politicians; but it is difficult to find, either in *The General Theory*, or in other of his writings, any explicit discussion of the necessary limits which should be placed on discretionary economic action, either because the Prince was inherently corrupt as the Victorians believed, or for the sake of the credibility of the policies being pursued or commitments entered into. Keynesians like Christopher Dow noticed that the 'fine tuning' interventions of British governments in the 1950s tended to be destabilizing, but attributed this to incompetence, even though it was apparent to more independent-minded observers like Terence Hutchison that governments were trying (with some success) to manipulate the economy to win elections. More importantly, Keynesians did not suspect that inflation might be endogenous to the political process, characteristically attributing the increasingly malign outcomes of the 1970s to random shocks, avoidable errors, or the stupidity or selfishness of trade-union leaders, etc. It was left to the anti-Keynesian public choice school of economists to argue rigorously that politicians were in the business of maximizing a political utility function rather than a social welfare function, and to erect on this insight proposals for subjecting economic decision-making to constitutional or other rules. Whether the public choice theorists are right or wrong in the motives they ascribe to politicians and bureaucrats, the credibility issue has to be faced in an era of global capital markets. Unfortunately experience of Keynesian management in the 1970s has led the markets to mistrust any government which does not bind itself with hoops of steel to maintain a low rate of inflation.

The fundamental criticism of Keynes is not that his theory of output as a whole was so 'general' that it could be applied in any type of society ranging from conservative-liberal to totalitarian—something he explicitly acknowledged in the German preface to *The General Theory* (*CW* vii, p. xxvi)—but that he

362   *Keynes*

never specified what types of application were appropriate to a free society and what were not. It is difficult to know from his writings, economic and political, where he would have drawn the line. He probably did not think it was necessary to do so, relying, in a very English way, on the automatic restraints of a community which 'thinks and feels rightly' to stop rulers doing dreadful things in his name (*CW* xxvii. 387–8).

In the light of this background, all too briefly sketched in, one can see why Keynesian policy has been in abeyance since the end of the 1970s, despite the heavy and persisting unemployment. There has been a general loss of confidence in the managerial, administrative, and spending activities of the state. The Keynesian revolution has been engulfed in a 'rhetoric of reaction', promiscuously directed at all forms of collectivism. The main political project over the more recent period has been to disinflate economies, restore public finances, de-corporatize and deregulate industrial relations, roll back (if possible) public spending, and privatize state industries. Unemployment has been viewed by the governments in power either as the necessary cost of accomplishing these reforms, or as something to be tackled after they have been accomplished. Such policies reflect the expectations formed by the Keynesian experience.

There remain fascinating questions. Could a more modest version of Keynesian policy in the 1960s have prevented the formation of expectations which made it unusable? Would Keynes himself have tried the incomes-policy route? There is no way of knowing. But it is worth remembering that Keynes was never someone to go down with a sinking ship, even one sailing under his flag. He would have tried to preserve the baby—his baby—while throwing out the bathwater.

V

Today, Keynesian policy cannot be openly avowed, though political pressure can still cause it to be pursued by stealth. Macroeconomic policy is increasingly pragmatic and a-theoretical. How it will evolve is uncertain. But two observations seem reasonably secure. With the globalization of markets, especially capital markets, the era of national economic management, which opened in 1914, is over. Keynesian policies, if pursued at all, will need to be on a global, or at the very least, regional basis. The era of discretionary demand management is also over. Whatever the eventual form of the policy framework it will be much more rule-bound than it was in the 1960s or 1970s. The Keynesian view of governments as benign social welfare maximizers is discredited beyond present repair. However, money supply or balanced budget rules will not be credible if the markets expect that political pressure will force them to be broken.

The question of how much Keynesianism will be needed to keep the world economy stable and prosperous in the years ahead is much harder to answer. It will partly depend on the outcome of the transition from Communism to capitalism in the former Soviet Empire and China. Will the transition usher in an era of very turbulent politics or will it reopen frontiers long closed to trade and commerce, and restore that confidence in progress and prosperity shattered by the 1914–18 war? The nature of the conjuncture will determine the governing ideas which capitalist economies will need; but the ideas will also determine the nature of the conjuncture. One cannot get away from this mutual dependence in social life. It should come as no surprise to learn that the ever-fertile mind of Keynes is a rich source of ideas directly relevant to the problems of the transition economies (*CW* xviii. 394).

How much is left of Keynes? Keynes always insisted that economic models must be 'relevant to the contemporary world' (*CW* xiv. 296), and said of his remedies that they are 'on a different plane from my diagnosis . . . not meant to be definitive, [but] subject to all sorts of special assumptions and are necessarily related to the particular conditions of the time' (*CW* xiv. 122).

Today there is no generally accepted model either of the macroeconomy or of the microeconomy, or of the relationship between the two. On the one side, we have the anti-Keynesian monetarism of Milton Friedman, and the 'new classical' macroeconomics, associated with Robert Lucas and Thomas Sargent—the 'radical wing of monetarism'—which deny validity to Keynesian models and power (except possibly a perverse power) to Keynesian policies. The 'new classical' macroeconomists agree with the monetarists that macroeconomic policies affect nominal, but not real, variables, and that unemployment will always gravitate to its 'natural rate'. With the monetarists they believe that the 'natural rate' of unemployment can be lowered by supply-side policies designed to improve business incentives, deregulate goods and labour markets, and privatize state-owned industries. The main analytic contribution of the new classical macroeconomists is the rational expectations hypothesis. Rational agents utilize all available relevant information in making their decisions. They make correct forecasts of the effects of announced government macroeconomic policies, the forecasts (in most rational expectations models) being based on the quantity theory of money. Expansionary (or contractionary) macroeconomic policy has no real effects even in the short run (the Phillips Curve is always vertical), since prices are immediately adjusted to the anticipated monetary conditions. The paradoxical conclusion is that Keynesian measures to lower unemployment below its 'natural rate' can achieve their promised results only by surprise, hardly a basis for usable policy. This reinforces the monetarist contention that macroeconomic policy should follow fixed rules to minimize expectational errors.

On the other side, Keynesians believe that demand matters, and that there remains a significant role for purposeful government policy in reducing unemployment. European experience of the 1980s and early 1990s bears out Keynes's contention that shocks to demand, whether coming from the private sector or the government, can lead to persisting unemployment. Why this should be so is not clearly understood. If individuals are rational optimizers, how is it that unwanted unemployment can persist when opportunities exist for mutually beneficial trade? The puzzle has belatedly given rise to a lively Keynesian research programme. The 'new Keynesians' have tried to understand the causes of rigid wages and prices, simply assumed as facts of life by the Keynesians of the 1950s. They have developed models to explain imperfect adjustment to shocks based on information costs, co-ordination failures, menu costs, efficiency wage hypotheses, sunspot equilibria, hysteresis, and so on. These models are designed to show that, even with rational expectation, labour markets may not clear. The Post-Keynesian school has continued to emphasize Keynes's stress on the importance of time and uncertainty, the use of money as a store of value, and the 'animal spirits' theory of investment. Conventional behaviour by capitalists or workers which produces perverse results for the economy as a whole is seen as a sensible response to uncertainty, or in the Sraffian and Kaleckian versions of Post-Keynesianism, to the class struggle.

Despite their disagreements on the role of macroeconomic policy, there is a growing agreement between all the schools, Keynesian and anti-Keynesian, that supply-side measures can lower present unemployment, either by sweeping away obstacles to market transactions or by rebuilding damaged capacity, or by a mixture of both.

The question of what, and how much, governments should *continually* do to stabilize economic activity at a high level will not disappear. The answer one gives will depend partly on what one thinks the economy is like, partly on what one thinks governments are like. If an unmanaged economy is 'inherently more cyclically stable' than Keynes thought, the answer is: not very much. The very least government should do is not make things worse. Friedman believes that most traumatic shocks are political. Governments are irretrievably tempted to manipulate the monetary parameters in order to secure helpful short-run results. Therefore their discretionary activity should be strictly circumscribed by rules. Keynes believed that unmanaged economies are inherently volatile, with a tendency to subnormal activity, so that policy can play a large part in both stabilizing and raising their performance. He thought governments could be sufficiently trusted to carry out contra-cyclical policy with competence and probity.

It is difficult to resolve this question empirically. It can certainly be argued that Keynesian policy (with all its impure political admixtures) made matters worse than they would have been from the mid-1960s onwards. But history shows that private-sector activity can be very volatile. Moreover, monetarism failed to predict the high persisting levels of European unemployment which followed the disinflationary policies of the early 1980s, and it has failed to produce a viable financial rule.

This leads to the conclusion that economics has consistently oversold itself as a 'guide to action', as opposed to an organized method of thinking about states of affairs and about the design of institutions capable of sustaining well-being beyond the actions of a particular government in a particular place at a particular time. Economists have not, in Keynes's phrase, become as useful as dentists. One cannot help reflecting that it was in the 1960s, when theoretically based macroeconomic policy was most actively used, that it started to go seriously wrong, and that it was those very prejudices and institutions which constrained the discretionary use of Keynesian tools in the 1950s which kept economic policy relatively circumspect. Eisenhower Keynesianism did more good than Kennedy Keynesianism.

If we are to draw a lesson from post-war historical experience it is that Keynesianism works best as a discretionary resource in a rule-based framework which places strong constraints on the actions of governments and which promotes the well-being of peoples through the widest possible measures of free trade. Those who look for inspiration to Keynes today are more likely to be impressed by the care and thought which he gave to the design of the Bretton Woods system than with Keynesian prescriptions for the parochial diseases of individual economies. Consciously or unconsciously we are trying to recreate the happy conjuncture which produced the 'golden age', much chastened by the experience of the intervening years. Whether we succeed will depend, in part, on the quality of statesmanship.

References

Numbers refer to the pages on which the references occur

225 *The Diary of Beatrice Webb*, ed. N. and J. McKenzie, iv (1985), 19 June 1936, 371.

Russell Leffingwell: Lamont Papers, Harvard University, File 103–15, Russell Leffingwell to Thomas Lamont, 29 Aug. 1931.

226 J. Meade: in D. Worswick and J. Trevithick (eds.), *Keynes and the Modern World* (1983), 266.

D. Bensusan-Butt, *On Economic Knowledge* (1980), 35.

L. Tarshis, 'The Keynesian Revolution: What it Meant in the 1930s', unpublished.

O. T. Falk, 'The Tuesday Club', 23 May 1950, unpublished.

227 *The Diary of Virginia Woolf*, ed. A. O. Bell, iv (1982), 19 Apr. 1934, 208.

228 B. Russell, *Autobiography* (1967), i. 72.

K. Clark, *The Other Half: A Self-Portrait* (1977), 27.

K. Martin in *New Statesman and Nation* (28 Oct. 1933).

K. Singer, 'Recollections of Keynes', *Australian Quarterly* (June 1949), 50–1.

230 *Diary of Virginia Woolf*, ed. Bell, iv, 12 Aug. 1934, 236–7; iii, 21 Apr. 1928, 181.

232 Walter Stewart: Clay Papers, Nuffield College, Oxford, Box 62, W. Stewart to J. Marshall, 16 May 1949.

H. Stein, *The Fiscal Revolution in America* (1969), 147–8.

233 Singer, 'Recollections of Keynes', 50.

235 N. Davenport, *Memoirs of a City Radical* (1974), 50.

236 Pigou and Schumpeter: see J. Cunningham Wood (ed.), *John Maynard Keynes: Critical Assessments*, ii (1983), 22, 125, respectively.

A. Marshall, *Principles of Economics* (8th edn. 1920), 85.

Singer, 'Recollections of Keynes', 55–6.

254 Ibid. 52.

H. M. Robertson, 'J. M. Keynes and Cambridge in the 1920s', *South African Journal of Economics* (Sept. 1983), 407.

F. A. Hayek, 'A Rejoinder', *Economica* (Nov. 1931), 401.

256 Letter from A. C. Gilpin to author, 22 May 1993.

262 G. E. Moore, *Principia Ethica* (1903; paperback edn. 1959), 188.

Ibid. 189.

265 Keynes's paper read to the Apostles, 23 Jan. 1904: date supplied from the record of meetings of the Apostles by Geoffrey Lloyd, then Fellow and Tutor of King's College, Cambridge; subsequently confirmed by Dr Roderick O'Donnell.

267 See R. M. O'Donnell, *Keynes: Philosophy, Economics, and Politics* (1989); A. M. Carabelli, *On Keynes's Method* (1988).

268 A. Fitzgibbons, *Keynes's Vision* (1988).

273 P. Clarke, 'The Politics of Keynesian Economics 1924–1931' in M. Bentley and J. Stevenson (eds.), *High and Low Politics in Modern Britain* (1983), 177–9.

M. Freeden, *Liberalism Divided* (1986), 166–71.

275 Keynes on Baldwin: *The Diary of Beatrice Webb*, ed. N. and J. McKenzie (1985), 19 June 1936, 370–1; see also A. L. Rowse, *Mr Keynes and the Labour Movement* (1936).

283 Cannan Papers, London School of Economics, Box 20c.

300 Bank of England spokesman: Macmillan Committee on Finance and Industry, Minutes of Evidence, Cmd. 2897, vol. 2, Qs. 7690–7847.

Ibid. Qs. 5565, 5650, 5654, 5684–6, 6500–24.

303 Hawtrey Papers, Churchill College, Cambridge, 11/3, para. 22.

D. H. Robertson, *Economic Journal* (Sept. 1931), 407.

308 Jens Warming: N. Cain, 'Cambridge and its Revolution', *Economic Record* (1979), 113.

317 D. Champernowne in R. Lekachman (ed.), *Keynes's General Theory: A Report of Three Decades* (1964), 55–60.

319 D. H. Robertson, 'Some Notes on Mr. Keynes' General Theory of Employment', *Quarterly Journal of Economics* (Nov. 1936); repr. in J. Cunningham Wood (ed.), *John Maynard Keynes: Critical Assessments* (1983), 99–111.

322 J. R. Hicks, 'Mr. Keynes and the 'Classics': A Suggested Interpretation', *Econometrica* (Apr. 1937); repr. in Cunningham Wood (ed.), *Keynes: Critical Assessments*, 162–72.

326 D. Moggridge, *Maynard Keynes: An Economist's Biography* (1992), 631.

327 J. Tomlinson, *Employment Policy: The Crucial Years 1939–1955* (1987), 24.

331 C. H. Rolph, *Kingsley: The Life, Letters, and Diaries of Kingsley Martin* (1973), 203.

332 Frankfurter Papers, Library of Congress, Reel 66.

333 W. Carr, 'Keynes and the Treaty of Versailles' in A. P. Thirlwall (ed.), *Keynes as a Policy Adviser* (1982), 103–6.
For details of Walther Funk, see A. van Dormael, *Bretton Woods: The Birth of a Monetary System* (1978), 6–7.

334 Keynes's visit to USA: see E. Playfair to S. G. Waley, 16 May 1941, in Moggridge, *Keynes*, 657.

337 James Meade: S. Howson and D. Moggridge (eds.), *The Wartime Diaries of Lionel Robbins and James Meade 1943–1945* (1990), 106, 159, 133.

339 H. Dalton, *High Tide and After* (1960), 73–4.

345 'Students in the 1960s'; D. Worswick and J. Trevithick (eds.), *Keynes and the Modern World* (1983), 127.

346 Callaghan at the Labour Party Conference: see W. Grant and S. Nath, *The Politics of Economic Policy Making* (1984), 144.

347 Christopher Allsopp: in D. Helm (ed.), *The Economic Borders of the State* (1989), 182.

348 Tomlinson, *Employment Policy*, 108.
R. C. O. Matthews, 'Why has Britain had Full Employment since the War', *Economic Journal* (Sept. 1968); repr. in Charles Feinstein (ed.), *The Managed Economy* (1983), 119.

349 N. F. R. Crafts and N. Woodward (eds.), *The British Economy since 1945* (1991), 7–8.
J. R. Hicks, *The Crisis in Keynesian Economics* (1974), 3.

352 J. Tobin, 'The Intellectual Revolution in US Economic Policy-Making', University of Essex Noel Buxton Lecture (1966).

357 Richard Kahn: in D. Worswick (ed.), *The Concept and Measurement of Involuntary Unemployment* (1976), 23, 27.

360 A. Coddington, *Keynesian Economics: The Search for First Principles* (1983), 42.

361 J. C. R. Dow, *The Management of the British Economy 1945–1960* (1970), 384.
T. Hutchison, *Economics and Economics Policy in Britain 1946–1966* (1968), 121–2.

Further Reading

Biography

There have been four biographies of Keynes: Roy Harrod, *The Life of John Maynard Keynes* (1951); Charles Hession, *John Maynard Keynes* (1984); D. Moggridge, *Maynard Keynes: An Economist's Biography* (1992); and R. Skidelsky, *John Maynard Keynes: Hopes Betrayed 1883–1920* (1983), and *John Maynard Keynes: The Economist as Saviour 1920–1937* (1992). A concluding volume will complete this biography.

Theory

Only a tiny sample of a vast secondary literature can be given here. Michael Stewart, *Keynes and After* (3rd edn. 1986), is the most accessible introductory text. E. Eshag, *From Marshall to Keynes: An Essay on the Monetary Theory of the Cambridge School* (1963), the classic account, needs to be supplemented by R. J. Bigg, *Cambridge and the Monetary Theory of Production* (1990). D. Patinkin, *Keynes's Monetary Thought: A Study of its Development* (1977), as well as his essay on Keynes in the *New Palgrave Dictionary of Economics*, ed. J. Eatwell, M. Milgate, and P. Newman (1987), are standard technical accounts. J. R. Hicks's *Critical Essays in Monetary Theory* (1967) has an illuminating 'Note on the Treatise [on Money]'. Richard Kahn, *The Making of Keynes's General Theory* (1984), is important first-hand testimony; G. L. S. Shackle, *The Years of High Theory: Invention and Tradition in Economic Thought 1926–39* (1967), is an excellent account of the 'double revolution' in Cambridge. Three stimulating interpretations of *The General Theory* are M. Milgate, *Capital and Employment: A Study of Keynes's Economics* (1982), E. J. Amadeo, *Keynes's Principle of Effective Demand* (1989), and A. H. Meltzer, *Keynes's Monetary Theory: A Different Interpretation* (1988). P. Clarke, *The Keynesian Revolution in the Making 1924–1936* (1988), is essential reading; R. W. Dimand, *The Origins of the Keynesian Revolution* (1988), covers some of the same ground from a technical standpoint. P. V. Mini, *Keynes, Bloomsbury and The General Theory*

(1991), is a stimulating, off-beat, essay. John Williamson's essay, 'Keynes and the International Economic Order' in D. Worswick and J. Trevithik (eds.), *Keynes and the Modern World* (1983), is exemplary.

Legacy

D. Patinkin, *Money, Interest and Prices: An Integration of Monetary and Value Theory* (1956), and the Hicks-Patinkin exchange which followed it in the *Economic Journal* (June 1957 and September 1959), were key to establishing the 'synthesis' between the neoclassical theorists and the policy Keynesians; an accommodation challenged by A. Leijonhufvud, *On Keynesian Economics and the Economics of Keynes* (1966). (See also Leijonhufvud's essay, *Keynes and the Classics* (Institute of Economic Affairs, 1969.) David Marquand, *The Unprincipled Society* (1988), offers a lively interpretation of 'Keynesian social democracy' in Britain; for the impact of Keynesian ideas in the United States, H. Stein, *The Fiscal Revolution in America* (1969), is the key text; for Keynes's influence on other countries, see Peter A. Hall (ed.), *The Political Power of Economics Ideas: Keynesianism across Nations* (1989). Eric Roll, *The World after Keynes: An Examination of the Economic Order* (1968), is a standard offering from the 'golden age'. The crucial monetarist text is Milton Friedman's Presidential address to the American Economic Association, 29 December 1967, on 'The Role of Monetary Policy', published in the *American Economic Review* (Mar. 1968), 1–17. The main text of 'new Keynesianism' is N. G. Mankiw and D. Romer (eds.), *New Keynesian Economics* (1991). Paul Davidson's *Money and the Real World* (2nd edn. 1978) is the statement of one of the leading 'Post-Keynesians'. Henry Hazlitt (ed.), *The Critics of Keynesian Economics* (1960, 1977), is a collection of anti-Keynesian and sceptical essays.

Index

OXFORD

MORE OXFORD PAPERBACKS

This book is just one of nearly 1000 Oxford Paperbacks currently in print. If you would like details of other Oxford Paperbacks, including titles in the World's Classics, Oxford Reference, Oxford Books, OPUS, Past Masters, Oxford Authors, and Oxford Shakespeare series, please write to:

UK and Europe: Oxford Paperbacks Publicity Manager, Arts and Reference Publicity Department, Oxford University Press, Walton Street, Oxford OX2 6DP.

Customers in UK and Europe will find Oxford Paperbacks available in all good bookshops. But in case of difficulty please send orders to the Cash-with-Order Department, Oxford University Press Distribution Services, Saxon Way West, Corby, Northants NN18 9ES. Tel: 01536 741519; Fax: 01536 746337. Please send a cheque for the total cost of the books, plus £1.75 postage and packing for orders under £20; £2.75 for orders over £20. Customers outside the UK should add 10% of the cost of the books for postage and packing.

USA: Oxford Paperbacks Marketing Manager, Oxford University Press, Inc., 200 Madison Avenue, New York, N.Y. 10016.

Canada: Trade Department, Oxford University Press, 70 Wynford Drive, Don Mills, Ontario M3C 1J9.

Australia: Trade Marketing Manager, Oxford University Press, G.P.O. Box 2784Y, Melbourne 3001, Victoria.

South Africa: Oxford University Press, P.O. Box 1141, Cape Town 8000.

PAST
MASTERS

RUSSELL

A. C. Grayling

Bertrand Russell (1872–1970) is one of the most famous and important philosophers of the twentieth century. In this account of his life and work A. C. Grayling introduces both his technical contributions to logic and philosophy, and his wide-ranging views on education, politics, war, and sexual morality. Russell is credited with being one of the prime movers of Analytic Philosophy, and with having played a part in the revolution in social attitudes witnessed throughout the twentieth-century world. This introduction gives a clear survey of Russell's achievements across their whole range.

PAST MASTERS

General Editor: Keith Thomas

KIERKEGAARD

Patrick Gardiner

Søren Kierkegaard (1813–55), one of the most original thinkers of the nineteenth century, wrote widely on religious, philosophical, and literary themes. But his idiosyncratic manner of presenting some of his leading ideas initially obscured their fundamental import.

This book shows how Kierkegaard developed his views in emphatic opposition to prevailing opinions, including certain metaphysical claims about the relation of thought to existence. It describes his reaction to the ethical and religious theories of Kant and Hegel, and it also contrasts his position with doctrines currently being advanced by men like Feuerbach and Marx. Kierkegaard's seminal diagnosis of the human condition, which emphasizes the significance of individual choice, has arguably been his most striking philosophical legacy, particularly for the growth of existentialism. Both that and his arresting but paradoxical conception of religious belief are critically discussed, Patrick Gardiner concluding this lucid introduction by indicating salient ways in which they have impinged on contemporary thought.

PAST MASTERS
General Editor: Keith Thomas

FREUD
Anthony Storr

Sigmund Freud (1865–1939) revolutionized the way in which we think about ourselves. From its beginnings as a theory of neurosis, Freud developed psycho-analysis into a general psychology which became widely accepted as the predominant mode of discussing personality and interpersonal relationships.

From its inception, the psycho-analytic movement has always aroused controversy. Some have accepted Freud's views uncritically: others have dismissed psycho-analysis as unscientific without appreciating its positive contributions. Fifty years have passed since Freud's death, so it is now possible to assess his ideas objectively. Anthony Storr, psychotherapist and writer, takes a new, critical look at Freud's major theories and at Freud himself in a book which both specialists and newcomers to Freud's work will find refreshing.

PAST MASTERS

General Editor: Keith Thomas

HOBBES

Richard Tuck

Thomas Hobbes (1588–1679) was the first great English political philosopher, and his book *Leviathan* was one of the first truly modern works of philosophy. He has long had the reputation of being a pessimistic atheist, who saw human nature as inevitably evil, and who proposed a totalitarian state to subdue human failings. In this new study, Richard Tuck shows that while Hobbes may indeed have been an atheist, he was far from pessimistic about human nature, nor did he advocate totalitarianism. By locating him against the context of his age, Dr Tuck reveals Hobbes to have been passionately concerned with the refutation of scepticism in both science and ethics, and to have developed a theory of knowledge which rivalled that of Descartes in its importance for the formation of modern philosophy.

PHILOSOPHY IN OXFORD PAPERBACKS
THE GREAT PHILOSOPHERS
Bryan Magee

Beginning with the death of Socrates in 399, and following the story through the centuries to recent figures such as Bertrand Russell and Wittgenstein, Bryan Magee and fifteen contemporary writers and philosophers provide an accessible and exciting introduction to Western philosophy and its greatest thinkers.

Bryan Magee in conversation with:

A. J. Ayer	John Passmore
Michael Ayers	Anthony Quinton
Miles Burnyeat	John Searle
Frederick Copleston	Peter Singer
Hubert Dreyfus	J. P. Stern
Anthony Kenny	Geoffrey Warnock
Sidney Morgenbesser	Bernard Williams
Martha Nussbaum	

'Magee is to be congratulated . . . anyone who sees the programmes or reads the book will be left in no danger of believing philosophical thinking is unpractical and uninteresting.' Ronald Hayman, *Times Educational Supplement*

'one of the liveliest, fast-paced introductions to philosophy, ancient and modern that one could wish for' *Universe*

Oxford
Paperback
Reference

THE OXFORD DICTIONARY OF PHILOSOPHY

Edited by Simon Blackburn

* 2,500 entries covering the entire span of the subject including the most recent terms and concepts

* Biographical entries for nearly 500 philosophers

* Chronology of philosophical events

From Aristotle to Zen, this is the most comprehensive, authoritative, and up to date dictionary of philosophy available. Ideal for students or a general readership, it provides lively and accessible coverage of not only the Western philosophical tradition but also important themes from Chinese, Indian, Islamic, and Jewish philosophy. The paperback includes a new Chronology.

'an excellent source book and can be strongly recommended . . . there are generous and informative entries on the great philosophers . . . Overall the entries are written in an informed and judicious manner.'
Times Higher Education Supplement